Communicating for Change

Communication, Media, and Politics

Series Editor
Robert E. Denton Jr., Virginia Tech

This series features a broad range of work dealing with the role and function of communication in the realm of politics, broadly defined. Including general academic books, monographs, and texts for use in graduate and advanced undergraduate courses, the series will encompass humanistic, critical, historical, and empirical studies in political communication in the United States. Primary subject areas include campaigns and elections, media, and political institutions. Communication, Media, and Politics books will be of interest to students, teachers, and scholars of political communication from the disciplines of communication, rhetorical studies, political science, journalism, and political sociology.

Titles in the Series

Forthcoming

Communicating for Change

Strategies of Social and Political Advocates

John P. McHale

/*//*

HN
18
M3835
2004

ROWMAN & LITTLEFIELD PUBLISHERS, INC.
Lanham • Boulder • New York • Toronto • Oxford

ROWMAN & LITTLEFIELD PUBLISHERS, INC.

Published in the United States of America
by Rowman & Littlefield Publishers, Inc.
A wholly owned subsidiary of The Rowman & Littlefield Publishing Group, Inc.
4501 Forbes Boulevard, Suite 200, Lanham, MD 20706
www.rowmanlittlefield.com

P.O. Box 317, Oxford OX2 9RU, UK

British Library Cataloguing in Publication Information Available

Library of Congress Cataloging-in-Publication Data Available

ISBN 0-7425-2972-X (cloth : alk. paper)
ISBN 0-7425-2973-8 (pbk. : alk. paper)

Printed in the United States of America

∞ ™ The paper used in this publication meets the minimum requirements of American
National Standard for Information Sciences—Permanence of Paper for Printed Library
Materials, ANSI/NISO Z39.48-1992.

Contents

Acknowledgments

This work is the result of several years of work with political activists and input from several scholars. I must thank Dr. Pam Benoit, who educated me on the meaning of rigor and gave more of her time and effort than any protégé could ask. She is an inspiration to me in my future diligence in providing advice to other authors. I thank Dr. Kimberley McHale, my life helpmate, for supporting me through this creative process and continually providing feedback on my work. Dr. William Benoit has also been a valuable example of a rigorous scholar and provided valuable input in the preparation of this manuscript. I thank Michael Kramer, Michael Porter, and Mary Joe Neitz for their positive feedback and their time and energy. I also thank the advocates who participated in this study and let me into their confidences. This is their story. In addition, I thank Robert E. Denton Jr., Brenda Hadenfeldt, Mary Bearden, and Kärstin Painter for their encouragement and revision ideas. Without the help of all of these good people, this book would not have been possible.

Foreword

The worth of a book is to be measured by what you can carry away from it,"
according to James Bryce, the English diplomat and author. *Communicating for
Change* measures up to this standard because there is a great deal that can be
carried away from this book by scholars and activists. It provides a detailed
examination of the media's use of three local social advocacy groups. John
McHale chose to study communities that supported environmental protection,
promoted universal health care, and opposed the death penalty. These particular communities were selected because the literature on the communication
activities of these groups was virtually nonexistent, and his own prior advocacy
activities had earned him a level of access to key leaders in each of these groups,
which is often difficult or impossible for outsiders.

Although there have been studies of social movement rhetoric (Bowers, Ochs,
and Jensen, 1993; Nathanson, 1999; Stewart, 1980), these studies have not
focused on the use of media by social advocacy groups. Scholars will find that
McHale's extension of media-richness theory and contributions to the bona fide
groups' perspective offer provocative insights. The media-richness literature
(Daft, Lengle, and Trevino, 1987; Rice and Shook, 1990; Sitkin, Sutcliffe, and
Barrios-Choplin, 1992) suggests that the media varied in richness, or social presence, and that the media would be used differently in corporate organizations.
By extension, the media used by advocates also varied in richness and would be
used differently by social advocacy groups. First, McHale's analysis expands this
theory by adding media characteristics (e.g., permanence, distance) that reflect
the unique concerns of social advocates. Second, the bona fide group perspective
(Gouran, 1999; Putnam, 1994; Putnam and Stohl, 1990) provides a useful
description of the fluidity of group boundaries. McHale found that there were
many overlapping boundaries between these groups that were the result of shared

memberships. He was also able to articulate the positive effects of this cooperative networking between the groups. Communication scholars can carry away a richer understanding of media functions and forms and the influence of contextual factors on communicative choices.

Although there are important theoretical contributions, this book has very practical advice to offer activists that is based on interviews and observations of the media activities in the three social advocacy groups. I know these issues were always at the forefront in McHale's thinking as he was writing because he was always looking for ways to improve the impact of the messages of the groups he was working with in his own advocacy activities. In *Communicating for Change*, he describes the media choices that are available, the audience that social advocacy groups may want to reach through their communications, the functions of the messages from these groups, and assessment of how each medium can accomplish the functions required for social advocacy. This prompts suggestions like: Advocates should fax the media to get the attention of their personnel rather than using traditional press releases. Advocacy groups who establish connections with other groups will build more people power and be able to generate more attendance for events. Advocates who use multiple forms of media for accomplishing a single function (e.g., lobbying, fund raising) will be more successful than those who rely exclusively on a single medium. As these examples begin to illustrate, this study provides a handbook for social activists who want to improve their communication. In reading this book, activists can carry away useful information that will make their messages more targeted and effective.

John McHale has become an expert in the communication of social activism. As part of this project, he was involved in anti–death penalty rallies and helped to organize rallies for Joe Amrine. This led him to produce a documentary, *Unreasonable Doubt: The Joe Amrine Story*, to raise public awareness about the death penalty and this particular case. Amrine was serving a short sentence when he was accused of murdering an inmate. His accusers were three fellow prisoners, but he was found guilty and given the death penalty. Now, all three of the prosecution's witnesses have recanted their earlier testimonies. In 2002, federal courts refused to hear the case during the appeals process, but the Missouri Supreme Court decided to reexamine the case. They ruled 4–3 in a decision overturning Amrine's murder conviction. (The Cole County prosecutor has two months to press charges for a retrial.) Sean O'Brien, Amrine's attorney, said that a major factor that brought attention to the case was McHale's documentary: "Historically, miscarriages of justice are not prevented or corrected by the criminal justice system, but by forces outside the criminal justice system" (Shiloh, 2003).

—Pamela J. Benoit
University of Missouri, Columbia

1

Introduction: The Importance of Activist Media Use

The state of Missouri was scheduled to execute Joe Amrine, against whom there were no witnesses and was no evidence. Opponents of the death penalty and supporters of Joe used a variety of means to spread the word about the case in an effort to convince the public and state officials that the execution must not go forward. Joe was a topic of interpersonal communication between advocates and other people. Joe's situation was discussed in advocacy group meetings and explained in anti–death penalty newsletters. Joe's lawyer met with filmmakers to convince them to begin a project about Joe's case. The filmmakers used telephones, e-mail, and interpersonal communication to gather more facts about the case, collected relevant film and video footage, arranged for more shooting for a documentary about the case, worked through the preparation, production, and editing, arranged an exhibition, and promoted the film (and the case) through mass media outlets. The documentary was placed on the Web so more people could view the audio-visual presentation. Members of the public made attempts to save Joe's life by sending e-mail and making telephone calls to elected officials. Joe wrote letters to supporters and communicated to the general public through the documentary, hoping to provide information that might be used for his defense. Those opposed to Joe's scheduled execution protested on the steps of the state capitol and presented a copy of the documentary to the governor's office. The video was handed to the legal council for the governor, who would later sit on the state Supreme Court, which would eventually free Joe Amrine, and interpersonal communication was extended to him in a plea for Joe's life.

This advocacy campaign reveals the web of communicative activities that comprise such efforts. This book analytically deconstructs these types of communicative action in an effort to construct a theory of advocate media uses.

Through a qualitative approach, this book explores the uses of communicative media by local advocates of social and political change on multiple issues, including the death penalty, universal health care coverage, and environmental protection. This work identifies media forms that are used by social and political movement advocates, the functions advocates perceive those uses perform, and the factors that influence uses of communication media in local social and political advocacy campaigns by those active in these efforts, particularly leaders of local efforts. While many aspects of social and political movement communication have been studied, there has been insufficient study of media use by local advocates.

These ideas are valuable in a variety of academic contexts. Sociological study of social movements can be sharpened through application of this study of the functions and factors that influence communicative means used by advocates. Political science scholars can use the resulting theory to further theoretically clarify how successful advocates communicate in order to test predictive power of the theoretical explanations. This book was also influenced by anthropological emphasis of the lived experiences of advocates.

This work possesses heuristic potential in several areas of communication study. Organization communication scholars may advance the theoretical implications raised here in other organizational contexts, such as in corporate settings. There is an overall emphasis on applied communication. The findings could also be valuable in the study of public relations and campaigns. Individual chapters are also useful for the study of the use of particular types of communication, such as group, mass media, interpersonal, and computer communication.

This book is also useful for the activist community. While the wide range of activist communication is explained, categorized, and synthesized into localized theory, it also presents a number of communicative task checklists for advocates. An application of this knowledge in a work geared toward practitioners could be humorously titled "How to Save the World in Twelve Easy Communicative Steps." Activists can use this book as a source of ideas about what they *could* be doing. Whether protecting a park, opposing book banning in schools, fighting for the rights of the least protected, or protesting in opposition to unregulated world trade, it is our democratic duty to speak out when we see injustice. Silence communicates consent. This book identifies valuable strategies that can help amplify our voices and convince others to join us.

This chapter defines activist communication and explores the benefits of studying social movements in general as well as examines the use of communication media by social and political movement advocates in particular.

Throughout this book, we will increase our knowledge about media uses of social advocates and apply communication theory in a new context.

Activists, Advocates, and Organizers

The terms social movement activists, advocates, or organizers used in this book refer to those involved in efforts to influence public opinion and public policy direction, often as part of the endorsement of a framework for the evaluation of social or political conditions. Social movement organizations cannot be artificially separated from interest group activity or issue promotion within political parties (Burstein, 1999). Activist or advocate communication refers to messages sent through the media that promote shifts in the social and political construction of legitimate limits of social, political, or economic activity. The term *social movement activist* refers to those at the vanguard of efforts to shift the public framework used to evaluate social, political, or economic conditions. The traditional distinctions between those within the system and those outside of political power have some value, although boundaries are often unclear. These vanguard elements can also be political party activists. They are also found in lobbyists' offices, an important tactical arena for contemporary social activists. Social movement activists appear in front of congressional hearings and city council sessions. They can be found in films, television, music, and other forms of mass media.

There is some slippage between the concepts of social and political movements and the groups that operate under the auspices of the environmental, anti–death penalty, and health care movements. Social movements are global phenomena, but bounded organizations work for movement goals. The discourse of the larger movement is not the focus of this work. While clear distinctions between the larger movement and the particular groups working toward movement are illusory (tools for scholars), here we look at the media uses of groups that are part of larger social and political movements. This is somewhat problematic, but the groups discussed in this book are part of social and political movement organizations. In his discussion of the evolution of the study of social movements by communication scholars, Griffin (1980) discouraged protracted debate over the limits of which social phenomena could be considered movements. Scholars should utilize an inclusive definition in efforts to study a wide range of situational activism under the rubric of social movement theory and methods. Thus, we treat local advocacy communication as a subset of social movement communication, which includes efforts of advocates to communicate through publications, mailings, mass media, the Internet, interpersonal contact, meetings, phone calls, demonstrations (including speeches, testimony, banners, disruptive tactics, and slogans at demonstrations), and other media that became evident in the early stages of this study. *Tactics* refer to specific uses of these media. *Strategies* are wider plans about the use of tactics.

Media

This book refers to media as forms of communication. Simply, *Webster's New Universal Unabridged Dictionary* defines media as the plural of medium. Medium is derived from the Latin *medius*, or middle. The third definition offered by the dictionary is useful in establishing our use of the term: "Any means, agency, or instrumentality; as radio is a medium of communication" (p. 1118). The fifth definition is simply "environment" (p. 1118). Thus, the operationalized definition includes mediating technology such as radio, telephones, films, and television, but also includes a variety of contexts, including face-to-face communication, communication in small groups, and communication at advocacy events.

The Impact of Social and Political Movements

Social movements have instigated profound change. A wide range of areas of human progress supported through social movement activity was outlined by Stewart, Smith, and Denton (1984):

> In just one century in our country alone, social movements have contributed to the freeing of the slaves, the end of child labor, the suffrage of blacks, women, and 18–20 year olds, the eight-hour workday and the forty-hour week, direct election of U.S. Senators, the graduated income tax, social security, collective bargaining, prohibition, the end of prohibition, and desegregation of public facilities and schools. (p. ix)

Social movements have been powerful forces in modern history and have influenced public opinion, public policy, and increases in citizen access and social consciousness. These impacts of advocacy movements justify inquiry into the uses of communication media by advocates.

Influencing Public Opinion

Social and political movement advocates can persuade people to consolidate or change their opinions on public questions. Much of the impact of social advocacy has been due to an influence on public opinion (Burstein, 1999). Burstein argued that social movements must be understood in the complex interaction between public opinion, nontraditional social movement tactics, issue promotion in the political parties, and organized interest groups. Public opinion is the most important factor in legislative decisions, according to Burstein, but in the ways cited above, social movements may indirectly influence policy direction in a number of ways. Burstein argues that electoral dimensions and issue salience are important in evaluating the impact of social movements on public policy:

> Elected officials . . . respond primarily to the wishes of the majority, especially when the majority feels strongly about an issue. SMOs [social movement organizations] therefore cannot directly influence policy when they disagree with the majority on issues it cares about. SMOs can influence policy directly, however, on the issues the public cares little about; and they can influence policy indirectly by changing the public's policy preferences and its intensity of concern about particular issues. (p. 4)

Thus, social movement advocates can persuade the public to support specific issue positions. A link between social movement activists and policymakers can become stronger if social movement communication is capable of increasing the salience of an issue in the view of the public, policymakers, or both, and influencing legislative action.

Other scholars concur that social movement activity can influence public opinion. The collective power and the effective use of nonconventional as well as conventional techniques by environmentalists, civil rights advocates, peace activists, feminists, or other groups has had some impact upon public opinion in Western democracies since the 1960s (Dalton, 1993). Gamson (1990) explored the success of tactics such as protests, court action, and political lobbying used by fifty-three social movements between 1800 and 1945, and focused on the specific aspects of the organization of each group to identify how organizational characteristics influenced levels of success. Gamson found that many of these social movements had had an impact on public opinion, but success depended upon the political context and the tactics used.

Social movements have influenced opinion on labor policies (Goldfield, 1989; Skocpol and Finegold, 1990) and women's issues. Costain and Majstorovic (1994) studied the dynamic interactions between the women's movement, congressional action, and public opinion. Their content analysis of the *New York Times* coverage of women's issues, data on public opinion, and information on congressional action on female issues revealed "that there is a delicate balancing act between Congress and social movements, with public opinion the lure that attracts both sides" (p. 131). While Costain and Majstorovic conclude there was a relationship, because of the complexity of this relationship, they were unable to quantify the impact of social movements in this environment.

Support from voters, contributors, and lobbyists is important to elected officials. If public opinion shifts, politicians eventually react. Social movement communication can facilitate reconceptualization of evaluative frameworks used to judge issue positions or salience, as we will see later. Thus, advocacy movements have had an indirect impact on political life through influencing public opinion. Social movement communication can also more directly impact policy, as addressed in the next section.

Influencing Public Policy

Obviously, if social movements influence public consideration of an issue, they can also influence public policy. But social movement advocates can also communicate directly with elected officials in efforts to promote change through public policy. They can exert influence in policy formulation, policy implementation, or the policy positions of political parties.

Policy Formulation

Social advocates can influence the adoption of policy positions by government. Social movement communication can impact policy, given appropriate social and political opportunity afforded by context, indirectly, through affecting public opinion or accepted perceptual frameworks around various issues, or more directly, through communication with policymakers. In this second situation, social movement communication can be most effective when it substantively concerns communication about the popularity of a policy option to lawmakers or administrators of preexisting policy. Burstein (1999) posited a "salience hypothesis: The greater the impact of social and political movement organizations on an issue's salience in the minds of the voting public, the greater their (indirect) impact on legislative action, provided that there is a discrepancy between the public's preferences and public policy" (p. 16). Social movement communication can be most effective when it substantively concerns communication about the popularity of a policy option to lawmakers or administrators of preexisting policy.

Policymakers can be convinced that the public supports a policy through social movement communication. Social movements have had an influence on environmental policies, but failed to alter U.S. nuclear weapons policy in the early and mid-1980s (Rochon and Mazmanian, 1993). Rochon and Mazmanian suggested that many social movements fail to achieve their goals, but that potential social movements may affect the political landscape in several ways. The authors argued that the most effective route for a social movement to impact the political landscape is to gain access to the policymaking process. Rochon and Mazmanian conclude that in the instance of environmental groups, key advocates gained access to policymaking bodies and retained their institutional independence, but freeze advocates were marginalized through absorption and cooption. Despite fears of institutional cooption and alienation from the more extreme activists involved with a social movement, access and input into the policymaking process play an important role in the exploration of the political significance of social movement communication.

Policy Implementation

Social and political activists can also substantially impact policy implementation (Burstein, 1999). While at times policy formulation and policy implementation can co-vary, the distinction between formulation and implementation is that of the temporal relationship with the act of making policy decision action. *Formulation* refers to the deliberation preceding a policy decision. *Implementation* refers to the actions of government entities responsible for putting a policy into action. In some instances social movement organizations can influence policy direction when issue salience is low in public opinion, as suggested by Burstein: "The lower the salience of an issue to the public, the greater the impact of interest organizations on the implementation of laws bearing on the issue" (p. 18). There is, however, little research on the impact of movement organizations on policy implementation. Burstein did identify several studies on the impact of movement organizations in precedent-setting cases on implementation early in the process (Blumrosen, 1993; Clark, 1977; Lo, 1990; Zemans, 1983). In implementation, as with policy formulation, social movement elements will fail to influence public policy if their goals are inconsistent with public opinion and if policymakers are aware of that disparity. However, further study of how advocates use various media to communicate to elected officials is warranted.

Policy Positions of Political Parties

Activist communication can also have more indirect effects on governmental institutions and influence on political parties. Social movement communication can influence political parties, both in the United States and in other nations (Hershey, 1993; Rohrschneider, 1993). For example, some politicians who were active in the Green Party in Germany in the early 1980s later joined major parties and exerted a more environmentally radical voice in these major, established political parties. This is another way in which social movements can indirectly influence public policy formulation.

Promoting Opportunities for Citizen Input and Social Consciousness

The ability of some social movement groups to increase opportunities for citizen input into the policy process is politically important. Although such opportunities may be more prevalent in systems that are new or are going through major changes, such as the situation in Eastern Europe in the early 1990s, this has been the case in the United States as well. Berry (1993) suggests:

> Citizen groups have changed the policymaking process in valuable and enduring ways. Most importantly, they have broadened representation in our political system. Many previously unrepresented or underrepresented constituencies now have a powerful voice in Washington politics. (p. 40)

Liberal citizen groups, which arose by the mid–1960s, were catalytic in the proliferation of many other interest groups, most notably business advocacy organizations. Ironically, such an impact creates an opportunity for counter-movement communication. Issue networks also arose as the result of expanding political expression of a plethora of interest groups. In addition, activity by such groups has increased the participatory opportunities for citizen and business groups to contribute to institutional changes in the policy-formulation process. Berry (1993) states that the growth of such groups has possibly increased the quality of policymaking in the United States:

> The increasing number of interest groups coupled with the rise of citizen groups has actually improved the policymaking process in some important ways. More specifically, our policymaking process may be more democratic today because of these developments. Expanded interest group participation has helped to make the policy-making process more open and visible. (p. 41)

Berry concludes that while increased participation has the potential to disrupt the policymaking process, in the case of the United States, that has not occurred. The decision-making process of the national government appears both able to respond to problems that require policy decisions and to allow the input of nongovernmental actors in the formulation of policy that represents the interest of the governed.

Several scholars have studied the impact of social movement communication on increased citizen access to the governmental decision-making process in other nations (Chong, 1993; Hager, 1993). According to Rochon and Maz-

manian (1993), social movements can affect political life by increasing participation opportunities in the policy formulation process.

Social movement communication is sometimes a vital component in challenges to political structures. Kitschelt (1993) explores democratic theory and
the rise of citizen social movements and concludes that new citizen groups
have challenged "competitive elite democracy" (p. 13). Kitschelt outlines a
liberal democratic model, an organized democratic model, and a direct democracy model, and argues that challenges to representative forms of democracy
occur in a historical, cyclical fashion. Many social movements have played a
role in this cycle of legitimation challenges and reaffirmations of structural
legitimacy. Kitschelt also argues that left-leaning social activists could promote
participatory expression by their own members as well as other social movement groups, and even went so far as to argue that social movement activism
can produce an opening of the democratic process and opportunities for citizens to have input into the policymaking process. Kitschelt concludes that contemporary social movements push for systemic openness and increased
communication access and can achieve some level of direct participation,
although the success of such movement is conditional upon the immediate
context within which a social movement group operates. For instance, timing
can be a critical element in the eventual success of social movement communication. The fall of the Soviet government provides a valuable example of how
social movements can promote systemic openness (Duka, 1997; Garcelon,
1997).

Social consciousness has also been influenced by social movement activity.
Waters (1998) examined the development and impact of a new type of social
movement in France since the early 1990s and suggests that while traditional
social movements were focused on particular issues, these emergent movements placed more emphasis on continued civic involvement. Informal links
between members of these movements as well as formal types of member
interaction are important points of activist communication. Waters concludes
that the "new citizenship" endorsed by these movements emphasizes the
importance of civic values and the role of individuals within the political
process.

In sum, social movements are significant democratic forces that can influence public opinion, public policies, citizen access, and social consciousness.
The following section deals with the communication of social movement
activists.

Social and Political Activist Communication

Communication through various media is the primary tool of social movement
advocates. Certainly, there are other ways to influence political outcomes, such

as campaign fund donations, but ultimately these are also communicative gestures. However, the communication of advocates is a necessary element in any
activity:

> One can lack any of the qualities of an organizer—with one exception—and still be
> effective and successful. That exception is the art of communication. It does not mat-
> ter what you know about anything if you cannot communicate to your people. In
> that event you are not even a failure. You're just not there. (Alinsky, 1971, p. 81)

Social and political movement activists use communication to contribute to
the construction of public reality, to mobilize members and establish a collective identity, and to reach multiple audiences. Communication media are necessary tools of effective social advocacy.

Constructing Public Reality

Social movement advocate communication is the key tool for influencing perceptions of the public, a central phenomenon that enables advocates to influence public opinion. Ferree (1992) explored the history of the application of
rational choice theories to the study of social and political movements. Rationality is subjectively constructed. Ferree argues: "The narrow definition of what
is rational excludes the principles, goals, and means of expression that have
been historically favored by subordinated groups" (p. 47). Interests other than
a narrowly defined self-interest can motivate activists in a social movement.
Also of value is Ferree's assumption that what is rational is socially constructed
through discourse. Thus, it is important to study advocate communication
because of the centrality of communication in the constitution of political and
social reality.

Human motivation can be justified by a variety of different logics. All frameworks of rationality are based upon a system of assumptions that are negotiated
in discourse. For instance, the emergence of the rhetoric of Malcolm X made
the programmatic implications of Martin Luther King, Jr., more rational, more
reasonable to the average American. The potential impact of social movement
communication on frameworks of evaluation of issues justifies the study of
media-use choices made by local advocates. Through these uses, advocates can
influence these socially constructed frameworks.

Advocate communication can be influential in the public creation of the
symbolic reality. Morris and Mueller (1992) edited a compilation of essays that
explain the importance of the sociological exploration of social movements
beyond rational choice theory or resource mobilization approaches. Morris and
Mueller sought to contribute to "a more comprehensive social movement the-

ory built around those processes that lead to the social construction of the symbolic world of the individual actor, as well as social movement cultures and collective identities" (p. 21). Communication is implicitly identified throughout the volume as a necessary element in this theoretic approach:

> In contrast with the economistic rational actor of early resource mobilization theory, the new social movement actor both actively constructs and is constrained by a world of complex social meanings rooted in specific historic contexts and based on the experiences and identities of race, gender, class, and nationality. Within these contexts, the new actor identifies and constructs the meanings that designate the relevance for mobilization of grievances, resources, and opportunities. (pp. 21–22)

This collection of essays represents a variety of perspectives and analytic approaches to the study of a "new actor" in social movements. The approach recognizes, at least tacitly, that communication is at the center of social negotiation of appropriate frameworks of evaluation.

Influencing public opinion can be achieved through social movement communication. However, the traditional limited consideration of the impact of advocacy communication on public opinion is inadequate for the discussion of social movement communication and public attitudes. The cumulative effect of the wide range of communicative media utilized by advocates confounds traditional social scientific research design. Noelle-Neumann's (1999) discussion of the impact of mass media examines difficulties similar to those found when studying the impact of advocacy communication:

> The effects are for the most part unconscious, so that direct questions are hardly helpful. Moreover, they generally result from an aggregate of different sources—no medium, newspaper, or program has an isolated effect. Media research in the past decade has shown that the public is influenced in a roundabout or indirect way, rather than directly, since people's social nature and their notions about their social surroundings are shaped by the climate of opinion ("spiral of silence"). (p. 54)

Thus, rather than conceptualizing the possible impact on public views, it is valuable to consider the wider frame in which the public evaluates issues. While this book does not look at rhetoric or the impact on public evaluation of issues, it will examine the media through which attempts can be made to contribute to this "climate of opinion." Negotiation of these frames is an important aspect of social movement communication. Ultimately, such negotiation is communication. As Anderson (1996) contends:

> Whatever the tension between collective meanings and local practices, the construction of reality is essentially a communication enterprise. The peculiar human character appears within this constructed reality through the practices of communication. For

the hermeneuticist, our accomplishments arise out of our collectivity, not out of our individuality. Communication makes possible that collectivity. It is managed through the iconic, discursive, and the performative practices that are the resources of our communicative efforts. In hermeneutic empiricism, a study of human behavior is the study of communication. (p. 135)

Social movement communication can be a present force in the cultural and social negotiation of the appropriate conceptual frameworks within which a policy issue is framed in the minds of the public and policymakers. This process is communicative. According to Rochon and Mazmanian (1993), social movement communication can influence the value structure of a society. The use of communication media is the locus of frame construction and negotiation.

Many scholars have recognized the importance of social communication and the social negotiation of evaluative frameworks. Morris and Mueller's (1992) work contains a valuable explication of the role of communication in the meaning attribution central to social movements. The social construction of consciousness plays a central role in social movement activity, according to the contributors to Morris and Mueller's book. However, their book lacks a systematic exploration of the communicative tactics of social advocates. According to Kriesi and Wisler (1999), social movement communication can be a catalytic factor in an individual's decision to adopt a new worldview. The persuasion that can give rise to such reconsideration of basic assumptions is necessarily a communicative process.

Mobilizing Members and Promoting a Collective Identity

A fundamental aspect of social movements is the construction and maintenance of collective identity (Kriesi and Wisler, 1999). The psychological study of social movements is valuable for realizing the centrality of communication in the establishment of collective identity. Gamson (1992) examined the social–psychological assumptions that have guided psychological motivations of social movement activity. He identified that collective identity, conceptions of solidarity, and meaning construction justify expansion of the traditional resource-mobilization framework. Consciousness must be a central feature of the study of activist motivations. He incorporated Goffman's (1974) discussion of framing in an effort to understand the cultivation of collective identity for those involved in social movements.

Gamson (1992) also states that mass media could be an important element in the battle of meaning over an issue. The contest over the accepted definition of a situation is a central function of social movements. However, the impact of mass media depends upon the nature of the issue. The role of the mass media is also dependent upon face-to-face interaction between individuals and in small groups. The attribution of meaning to mass media messages is socially constructed and is interpreted through the lenses created by interpersonal discourse. Gamson's emphasis on the communication necessary to influence the framing of pertinent issues is particularly valuable. He also outlined the concept of micromobilization, in which "individual and sociocultural levels are linked through mobilizing acts in face-to-face encounters" (p. 74). His point here was merely that interpersonal communication is an important medium for the mobilization and maintenance of movement organization. The concepts of collective identity, solidarity, and micromobilization are rooted deeply in psychological analysis. Gamson, however, failed to identify that research traditions in the study of communication can be valuable for further study of the role of interpersonal communication as the connection between the social (i.e., macro) and individual (i.e., micro) levels of meaning construction in social movements. Gamson did not evaluate how media are used to establish and maintain this collective identity.

Communication is an essential element in the cultivation of the collective identity that is a feature of successful advocacy activity. Klandermans (1997) observes that volunteers in social movements share collective identity, and that such consciousness can unite at an extra-organizational level. Klandermans implies that communication is necessary to forge and maintain such shared beliefs, although competing voices also influence the maintenance of shared beliefs. "The transformation of social issues into collective action frames . . . a process in which social actors, media and members of a society jointly interpret, define and redefine states of affairs" (p. 44). Klandermans, however, did not explicitly recognize the necessary nature of communication in the negotiation over and dissemination of collective action frames, or the rhetorical vision accepted and endorsed by members of a social movement. Klandermans did identify the importance of communication in earlier research on nineteenth-century women's reform in New York. While Klandermans discusses communication networks, he emphasizes resources rather than uses of media to facilitate the resource sharing.

When there is inadequate communication, collective identity may fracture. The lack of collective identity contributed to divisions within right-wing advocates in the late 1980s. Klatch (1988) explored the conflict of female members and factions within the New Right in American politics in the 1980s and found that differences in conceptual frameworks, or *Weltanschauung*, gave rise to differences on policy positions of those within the New Right. However, Klatch did not look at the uses of various communication media used by those in the New Right. What is valuable from these studies is the recognition that communication is a vital component of the establishment and maintenance of collective identity of social movement activists.

Using Communication Media to Reach Multiple Audiences

Social movement advocates must communicate to multiple audiences. In some instances, advocates may only intend to communicate to the most active group members. In other instances, the intended audience may include citizens who occasionally participate in group activities. At other times, social movement advocates wish to reach the public-at-large. Finally, advocates may want to communicate with elected officials. It will be valuable to study how advocacy groups communicate not only with the most active members, but also to the general public and elected officials. The study of advocates' media choices must consider how the composition of the target audience influences media use.

Conclusion

Ultimately, a possible benefit of this work is the development of theoretically grounded criteria that could be used to evaluate the efforts of specific activist communication. In addition, the application of media–richness theory in this new context warrants study. The findings also have practical applied value for activists. The resulting theory can help advocacy activists maximize their communicative effectiveness. This book also suggests valuable avenues for future research on social movement communication.

In summary, social and political movement communication impacts public opinion, public policy formulation, and promotion of increased citizen access and social consciousness. Specifically, the communication of social advocates can influence the construction of public reality, mobilize members, maintain collective identity, and reach multiple audiences. Additional knowledge about advocate media choices will be valuable to scholars and advocates.

The study of the uses of communication media by advocate activists has been neglected. This text focuses on perceptions of social advocates regarding effective communication media use. This qualitative inquiry approach explores how social and political advocates use a number of communication media to formulate a theory of activist media use.

The practices relevant to this study revolve around the advocacy against the death penalty, for universal health insurance coverage, and for an increase in environmental awareness. The three groups studied are of political importance. While neither national candidate in the 2000 presidential campaign opposed the death penalty, the death penalty issue was salient in the presidential race. George W. Bush was repeatedly asked in the 2000 campaign about the possibility of innocent people having been executed in Texas, where Bush was governor. In June 2000, CNN noted that Bush was "enduring a week as the target of anti–death penalty protests." Likewise, the *New York Times* reported "Death penalty protesters dogged Bush during a three-day swing through Washington state and California this week" ("Death Penalty," 2000). According to the same *Times* story, Texas was scheduled to execute one person every week between the middle of June 2000 and the date of the 2000 presidential election. Bush's record was used as ammunition for anti–death penalty activists in Washington and California.

The battle for governmental health care coverage is also an important issue. In 1998, forty million Americans were not covered by health insurance (Ballard and Goddeeris, 1999). A significant number of those without coverage were children. The basic distribution of natural resources reflects income levels of Americans, and those who are not covered are primarily the working poor. This situation concerns many socially progressive activists in the United States, but their efforts have been virtually ignored in the social movement literature. The health care issue was prominent in the 2000 presidential campaign (Benoit, McHale, Hansen, Pier, and McGuire, in press). In addition, according to NBC (2000), 16 percent of Americans stated that health care was an important issue in the 2000 election.

Finally, the issue of environmental protection is an important issue to many people. According to a poll conducted by the Gallup Organization in July 2000, 4 percent of the American public stated that environmental protection was the most important issue influencing their vote for the president. Likewise, environmental protection was a prominent issue in the presidential campaign discourse in the 2000 race (Benoit, McHale, Hansen, Pier, McGuire, in press).

Analysis of data gathered through observation, interviews, and advocacy literature was used to ascertain the meaning of advocacy communication. The sources of my data provided a wide range of perspectives concerning activist communication. Theoretically, the scope of activities provides a rich database. The sources utilized in this study provided the opportunity to triangulate and compare a variety of views. This book traces the development of theoretical propositions that are part of the grounded theory of activist communication (Glaser and Strauss, 1967; Strauss and Corbin, 1998). We will see what forms of communication media are used, what functions advocates perceive that these uses performed, and what factors were perceived to influence uses of various communication media by social and political movement advocates.

2

Face-to-Face Interaction

Personal encounter, however it happens, is what gets us involved in deep issues that change our lives forever. It's always involved, in some way or another, in meeting people. You can only look at movies, and read books, and hear speakers so long, but somewhere in there we have got to get our hands in there, and get directly involved with people, because that is where the passion happens, and that is where the life-changing experiences happen. And with me, it's going to be this man [Patrick Sonjea, a death row inmate].

Sister Helen Prejean, the author of *Dead Man Walking* (1993) and an anti–death penalty advocate, explained in a public address (from which the epigraph to this chapter is taken) how face-to-face communication with Patrick was the source of a quality communicative experience for her, and it contributed to her gumption on the issue, her will to engage in advocacy communicative praxis. Face-to-face, interpersonal communication refers here to dyadic communication exchanges, wherever they occur. Gumption, a word of old Scottish origin, refers to advocates' will to act in advocacy, the enthusiastic initiative in the enactment of advocacy communicative praxis. This communicative contact is perceived by advocates to be a valuable advocacy tactic. Interpersonal communication between advocates and with people outside advocate communities is perceived by advocates to perform a variety of functions.

This chapter explores the uses of interpersonal contact by advocates, the explicate characteristics of this communication, and discusses factors that influence the use of face-to-face communication by advocates. Advocates use interpersonal, one-on-one dyadic communication to reach several audiences, including other advocates, advocates of other issues, and nonadvocates. Advocates' use of these various types of interpersonal communication enables them to perform a variety of functions, including increasing attendance at events, arranging logistical details, building community, educating the general public, lobbying, and facilitating mass media coverage. This intimate communication can be influenced by the characteristics of the communication media, internal group factors, intended audience, and external factors. Personal initiative (i.e., gumption) of advocates is a uniquely necessary element for face-to-face advocacy communication, which highlights the importance of initiative for all advocate communication. Physical presence is an essential feature of face-to-face communication.

Intended Audience

As with all advocate media use, analysis of the dynamics of advocates' use of dyadic, face-to-face communication reveals several intended audiences. Different types of interpersonal communication can be identified through explication of the contexts of these interactions. Knapp and Vangelisti (2000) indicate that different types of relationships arise due to the nature of personal interaction. For instance, advocates may feel more comfortable interacting face-to-face with an individual with whom they have interacted previously. Likewise, previous relationships influence the tone of interpersonal communication. Differences in the relationships between advocates and others provide a conceptual tool for distinguishing types of one-on-one communication used by advocates. A feature of personal advocacy communication that is shared with other media uses is that the interaction may have more impact if there is a history between those interacting. These statements from activists come from individual and focus group interviews. Consistent with my research protocol, I assigned pseudonyms to protect their identity. The inquiry method is described in Appendix B. Lana, an environmental advocate who is also a city employee, said that the relationship between individuals creates the context in which a face-to-face communication exchange is decoded: "If you have a conversation with a stranger, it might not have the same effect. . . . I already had an interest in the action, but the action would be based on the personal bond with another person. That interaction is good." The intended audience influences the use of interpersonal communication because the familiarity with a person influences advocates' willingness to engage in interpersonal communication, as Vincent suggested. Interpersonal advocacy communication can be richer if there is a previous relationship between the communicators, as Jossey suggested: "Personal interaction is so important. Not just the personal interaction, but also the relationship behind the interaction." Her perceptions reveal that, as with all media use, the meaning of a use can only be appreciated within the lived context. The personal character of interpersonal communication can vary based upon the relationship of those communicating.

The first type of interpersonal interaction used by advocates is face-to-face communication with fellow advocates who are or have been involved in common activities. Obviously, as with all types of interpersonal interaction, there is a continuum: In these groups, there are advocates who have worked together. The first type of interpersonal communication used by these advocates was between those in the same groups who work together on advocacy activity. For instance, at Earth Day coalition meetings, there was a general spirit of interpersonal openness because there were established relationships among advocates.

A second type of advocacy interpersonal communication occurs among those who are involved with particular causes, but who share the ideological positions of the activists studied here. Many times, such interpersonal communication can be a conduit for cooperative efforts. For instance, one day while walking downtown I saw Joan. At the time I was trying to fill slots on the stage for Earth Day. She is not really involved with that group, but I knew she was a poet and performed environmentally conscious poetry. In this case, I asked her to perform at the event and she agreed. In such cases, advocates who primarily work for differing but similar issues can solicit attendance at events sponsored by their respective groups.

Another type of interpersonal interaction undertaken by advocates is with nonadvocates, including the public, media personnel, and politicians. In the case of the nonadvocate general public, they may engage in interpersonal conversations about advocacy issues with advocates. For instance, at a party at my home, Tony discussed the anti–death penalty position in numerous interpersonal conversations with people who were not active advocates of the issue. These random recipients of advocate messages can be more or less receptive to the messages of advocates. Often this type of interpersonal communication takes place around advocate events: The events, the activity, can attract the attention of the public, and subsequent interpersonal interaction between advocates and the attentive, attending nonadvocates is used by advocates to further persuade nonadvocates of the validity of their positions. If the random person seems interested, the advocates often attempt to gain contact information through this face-to-face interaction.

On a few occasions, advocates also used interpersonal contact to communicate with mass media personnel. For instance, Vincent, one of the producers of an anti–death penalty documentary, interacted face-to-face with at least six reporters and five photographers from local newspapers in conjunction with the mass media coverage of the release of the production. Newspaper and television news reporters seek face-to-face contact with key figures in their stories. Thus, through facilitation of face-to-face meetings with reporters, advocates were able to use mass media outlets.

Another type of interpersonal communication that advocates use is between advocates and politicians. These political officials, as with other audiences of advocates' face-to-face communication, can be more or less sympathetic to the causes endorsed by the advocate. While these instances were not frequent in this study, they did occur, especially between the most active advocates and state politicians. In sum, advocates use face-to-face dyadic communication to reach several audiences, including other advocates, advocates of other issues, and nonadvocates.

Advocate Use of Face-to-Face Communication

Advocate use of these various types of interpersonal communication enable them to perform a variety of functions, including increasing attendance at events, arranging logistical details, building community, educating the general public, lobbying, and facilitating mass media coverage. Interpersonal communication is perceived to be necessary to accomplish these functions.

Increasing Attendance at Events

Advocates use personal communication to increase attendance at events through mobilizations of advocates. For instance, interpersonal contact is valuable for drawing the attention of advocates to events. In one example, an advocate explained that he heard about an antideath penalty event through word-of-mouth, but did not see other media advertising the event. Lenny, a doctoral student and an important personality in university politics who was involved with several antideath penalty events a year, explained:

> I heard about the [antideath penalty] event through word-of-mouth. And that surprised me, because there were no bulletins, no posters, no signs, going up around the university about this. My adviser in my department is a leading advocate. So I am generally informed if an execution is coming up. I usually find out when an execution is coming just through personal conversations and I am usually interested.

Personal invitations and shared face-to-face communication can be compelling sources of information about events. Jossey, an occupational therapist, is an environmental and anti–death penalty advocate who provides logistical support to three or four advocacy events a year, such as providing long-distance rides or cooking food for traveling advocates. She learned of one event she attended "not from mass media, but from interpersonal relationships. I heard about the event from friends." After-dinner conversation had drawn her into this anti–death penalty event. Jossey got involved in local activities of the Journey of Hope, an international group of people who have lost family members to murder, but who actively oppose the death penalty. In another instance, one very active environmental advocate (ten hours of involvement a month), who was also a municipal official, perceived that advocate use of interpersonal communication was valuable to communicate to the advocate community: "Word-of-mouth. Letting people know about an event." This advocate believed that a variety of means could be used to get people to talk about the event, but ultimately, personal, face-to-face communication was a valuable source of publicity.

Incidental mention of advocacy activity and issues in conversations primarily about other subjects can be a viable means for advocacy mobilization communication. Interpersonal communication can be used to raise advocacy issues in everyday, friendly conversations. Flanders, occasionally active (attending two or three advocacy events a year), noted that this face-to-face communication can come up like any other area of neighborly conversation: "If I just had a conversation about the event with my neighbor in the yard, it could just be another topic for conversation." Another advocate, a high school teacher who is involved with five or six events a year, reported being most affected by informal conversations with a group of friends who are advocates: "On the health care issue, when there's been conversation . . . there's no solicitation, just 'This is what we're doing.'" This sometimes-advocate was most compelled to become involved when she started spending interpersonal time with advocates who were more involved. For this advocate, as with others identified here, incidental, personal communication is perceived to perform a mobilizing function.

Redundancy of interpersonal contact can perform a mobilizing function according to advocates, making this interpersonal contact, according to advocates such as Lenny, more effective. Lenny suggested that most of his advocacy communication is shared face-to-face: "It is usually never telephone, but rather interpersonal, face-to-face [communication that gets me involved]. I think I heard about [a civil action] from three different sources." These multiple personal contacts are mutually supportive. Testimony from these advocates reveal that face-to-face communication can be valuable for mobilizing advocates, as in the case of Jossey, and can increase attendance at events.

Arranging Logistical Details

Mobilizing advocates involves getting them to attend advocacy events, but arranging logistical details must take place to plan and commit to the work necessary to sponsor and execute an event. As with advocates' use of other media, face-to-face communication can perform logistical functions, including arranging expenditure of advocate time and energy. Jossey believed that interpersonal communication could also provide an opportunity to make advocacy-task commitments: "I communicate about my volunteering through social interaction. Friends were saying that they were involved, and in interpersonal conversation, I became involved as well." This involvement aided in providing logistical support. In the context of this face-to-face interaction, Jossey then made an offer to provide logistical support for an anti–death penalty event. As a result of interpersonal conversation with another advocate, Jossey eventually took off a day of work to cook meals for members of an international anti–death penalty group traveling through the region, and she toured a portion of the state with another advocate who was on a national tour. She provided his ride in the region. In this case, face-to-face communication with other advocates was a catalyst for her extensive involvement. Dates were discussed and arrangements were tentatively agreed upon at a casual dinner party.

Interpersonal contact is important for the fulfillment of communicative tasks. One advocate, Ed, explained that the commitment involved with one-on-one communication with physical presence encouraged advocates to be more effective in planning efforts. Ed was discussing details of Earth Day plans through face-to-face communication with one other member of the planning committee:

> The work gets done interpersonally, more than with the phone. When we work, we tend to work together in person. Could we work together on the phone? We could, but we don't. We work more when we work together [in a dyad].

In this instance, Ed perceived that mutual presence could be an incentive for accomplishing advocacy tasks.

Building Community

Face-to-face communication between advocates can be a way to share information and build camaraderie. For instance, the time spent traveling to events or working on newsletters provides many opportunities for advocates to develop interpersonal relationships. These relationships are the emotional glue that holds prolonged advocacy communication efforts together. Face-to-face communication performs the important function of community building.

Advocates perceive that face-to-face communication performs a community-building function. Abby, the key leader in the environmental- and peace-related advocacy activity in the community, contended that interpersonal connection was a necessary condition for a strong advocacy community:

> You want to build strong social connections, you have to bring people together physically in the same place at least some of the time, and have them sharing a sense of

being part of the group, social relationships that go beyond just talking to each other on the phone and e-mail.

Abby perceived that while e-mail and telephone communication can be sufficient for logistical communication, face-to-face communication between advocates was necessary for building social networks, upon which advocacy activity is based. In all of the groups studied, face-to-face communication performed a valuable community-building function. Interpersonal advocacy has an intimate character that is perceived as helpful for nurturing community. Joan, the internationally active, hard-core activist on a variety of social justice issues (a self-labeled "rad"), suggested that this intimacy translated into a stronger subsequent relationship between those in such conversations: "Personal contact brings up the level of the personal. The interpersonal communication brings [us] closer together." The timing of universal health care advocacy events also revealed the importance of face-to-face communication for community building. At all of these events, the actual programs started a half hour after the advertised start time. The first half hour was spent mingling. The leading advocate in the community, Nancy, contended that this provided an important opportunity for advocates in attendance to interpersonally connect as a way to strengthen the universal health care advocate community. This personal contact strengthens communal bonds.

Educating the General Public

Face-to-face communication can be used to educate others about advocacy issues and activities. I use the term educating rather than persuading or spreading propaganda because that is the term used by the advocates. Advocates believe they are spreading truth and that by merely sharing the perceived "facts" to others, they will increase support for their advocacy positions. Educating is *in vivo* code for spreading advocate ideas or facts that support those ideas—and this is an assumption I adopt throughout this book. Face-to-face interaction can educate the public about advocacy issues. Face-to-face advocacy communication allows personal interaction with the uniqueness of each human being. According to Nancy, a leading state advocate on the universal health care issue, the purpose of a number of the universal heath care events, at which a national leader on the issue met with various people, was to offer opportunity for face-to-face communication. This was also the goal of some anti–death penalty efforts. Tony suggested this recognition could help change the minds of the general public: "Interpersonal communication is important. You must engage them with recognition of where they sit. This kind of good communication is critical to get more folks to reevaluate mandated murder by the state." Examples of this can be found throughout Tony's advocacy. A number of times, when curious people passed by a civil action event and made a comment, in support or opposition, Tony would separate from the group of protesters and attempt to engage the individual in interpersonal conversation; he would solicit those individuals' opinions and attempt to respond to them. Advocates such as Tony can attempt to convince people outside of advocate communities that an advocacy's position merits consideration and subsequent action.

In another instance, Brenda, an active advocate (seven to eight events a year), explained that advocacy issues arose in discussions with coworkers: "I've been involved in interpersonal communication about universal health care efforts, with people who are at work with me."

Advocates perceive that face-to-face communication with the public performs a persuasive function. Matt, a leading anti–death penalty advocate in the community for over forty years, commented: "Talking to people, individuals like that, was what our efforts are all about." Interpersonal contact can be a valuable tool for the advocate communicator . . . one changed mind is a positive step." Matt said this after advocates engaged in face-to-face communication with some uncommitted citizens after an anti–death penalty civil action (a midnight vigil at the governor's mansion in protest against an execution). In an interview, Joan suggested that she believed face-to-face, communication was the most important tool for convincing the public that a particular advocacy position is correct: "I think that person-to-person contact is what will let us make people change their minds. I think that face-to-face, human-to-human contact, not machine to machine, . . . is the most important thing for a change in public opinion." Joan suggested that human interaction is more persuasive than communication that is mediated through technology.

Lobbying

Another avenue for advocacy communication is face-to-face communication with elected officials. Advocates attempt to engage politicians by visiting the offices of their elected officials personally. Advocates believe that face-to-face communication with elected officials can further advocacy causes.

Advocates use face-to-face communication for persuading elected officials to adopt an advocacy position. Matt suggested that interpersonal contact with politicians is "one of the most powerful tools we have." Advocates such as Matt believe interpersonal communication with elected officials can be useful for trying to get these politicians to support advocate positions.

Personal contact with elected officials can occur by coincidence. In one instance, Tony, a leading state advocate of abolition of the death penalty, ran into several elected officials at a restaurant. One of them was the newly elected governor. Tony described these face-to-face encounters:

> I was at a restaurant, and I ran into this representative, who has gone on record against the death penalty. He was a cosponsor of moratorium legislation last year. He is a good man. I like him. But, anyway, there are random encounters, like at [this restaurant].

Tony explained that it took some personal initiative to talk to the state representative:

> I saw Rep. McKenna walking, and I said to myself "I have got to say hi to him." I don't see this guy very often, I've dropped in his office a couple times during the legislative session, and I haven't seen him. So it was like representative McKenna is a . . . nice man, a good guy, you know. I just wanted to say hi to him, and here, see what he was up to and we chatted for a few minutes . . . maybe a minute and a half.

As Tony finished the personal conversation with the representative, he saw the governor: "Then I noticed that he was sitting next to the governor. I introduced myself, said 'hi.' I don't think I mentioned my name! But that's okay. Personally, he remembered me as a human being [from a previous encounter]." While this was face time, Tony spent that time advocating an antideath penalty position. Tony recognized the importance of the human element of face-to-face communication and enacted personal initiative for the interpersonal communication. The governor recognized him from a meeting the two had had before the candidate was elected governor:

> So I said "we've visited with you in April about the death penalty, a . . . [g]roup of five of us." I said, "The guy is scheduled to be executed in about a week, about two weeks, who is mentally retarded, and sixteen years old at the time of the crime. You are going to be dealing with this guy, whose execution order is to come across your desk in the next week or so. It's a clemency application for this fellow that's about to be executed."

This interaction required Tony to possess some knowledge about the case:

> It was nice. It was a nice conversation. I started by saying congratulations on the election, you know, I'm glad you got voted in. I started off with that. I guess I was brown-nosing up to him. I did vote for him.

Access to the previous governor was difficult to obtain. "We never got to visit with the previous governor, but I've met with this governor twice. Once before he was elected, and once tonight, after he was elected." Such encounters are rare, according to Tony.

Tony recognized that in such exchanges, too much communication could be disadvantageous: "But I didn't want to bug the governor too much. I wanted him to enjoy his evening. I'm sure he came in [the restaurant] to see [a basketball game at a local university], have a good time, and watch the game. That's what he was in town for." Tony recognized that it is wise for advocates to end a communicative encounter after they perceive that their point has been made.

The embodied presence of advocates like Tony denotes commitment. Tony believed that this display of commitment is very important: "The personal contact is so critical, really. [The governor] will never see this fellow who's expected to be executed. Still never know him as a human being." Thus, Tony felt that personal contact between an elected official and an anti–death penalty advocate can help humanize those on death row.

This encounter between Tony and the governor occurred by chance. However, advocates can also lobby at the offices of elected officials. Tony suggested that advocates visit these offices: "Also going to the offices and asking to try to meet with them, and if not meeting with them then relating to them in their comment books. [One politician] would always have comment books available in his offices." These comment books are similar to a guest book; visitors to the politicians' offices can record that they visited the office and the nature or the intent of the visit. Tony suggested that it was important for advocates to devise a goal for such visits:

> It depends on what you want to do with their office. You have to figure out what your target is. Years ago I had a big target of having a meeting with an ex-governor, who was the governor at the time. And that was our goal, to have a meeting with him. It was so we can have that personal contact.

Tony suggested that advocates could communicate even if they do not get a chance to meet with an elected official in their office: "But it depends what your goal is. You can go there just to have a presence. You can go in with twenty to thirty people and be there. You can present petitions signed by several hundred people." While the petitions are beyond the purview of interpersonal communication, the physical presence of advocates during visits to the offices of politicians communicates. This interpersonal presence may also increase considerations of petitions in an instance like this.

Tony works with other organizers to have at least one lobbying day a year during which anti–death penalty advocates spend the day visiting the offices of representatives, senators, and the governor at the state capitol. Activists use events during the day to gather and rally with chants and speakers. However, the Lobbying Day also facilitates face-to-face interaction with representatives or the staff of representatives. Individuals or small groups meet with these officials, with the intention of engaging them in face-to-face communication. One female advocate, a college professor, who helped organize several environmental events a year, explained that she had used interpersonal communication with her elected officials: "One time I did go to the office of an elected official and lobby." In that case, she had visited an office of a legislator in Washington, D.C. Advocates can also visit the local offices of elected officials. Thus, various other communication tactics can be used in conjunction with personally visiting the offices of elected officials. These advocates obviously perceived interpersonal contact with elected officials to be a useful advocacy tactic.

Facilitating Mass Media Coverage

The advocates studied here used interpersonal communication to facilitate coverage on mass media outlets. As an antideath penalty advocate, I personally delivered a press release about an antideath penalty event to a number of print and television reporters. In at least eight cases, I used interpersonal communication with mass media personnel in an effort to facilitate mass media coverage of antideath penalty events. Tony used interpersonal interaction with a television reporter who was covering an antideath penalty event in order to arrange specific times for interviews that would be featured in a live feed on the 5:00 PM news. In these instances, advocates used interpersonal communication to facilitate mass media coverage of their activities.

Advocates use face-to-face communication to perform a variety of functions, most importantly for arranging logistical details and building community, but also for increasing attendance at events, persuading the general public, lobbying, and facilitating mass media coverage.

Influences on Advocate Face-to-Face Communication

Face-to-face communication can be influenced by the characteristics of the communication media, internal group factors, intended audience, and external factors. However, as we will see in the consideration of the labor and financial cost, the unmediated nature of face-to-face communication accentuates the importance of personal initiative.

Characteristics of Interpersonal Advocacy Communication

Feedback, multiple cues, language variety, and a personal character are part of face-to-face, interpersonal advocacy communication. These characteristics of interpersonal communication influence advocate use. Physical presence is an important element of interpersonal advocacy communication that is not treated as a characteristic in my scheme per se, but rather as a condition that influences resulting characteristics. Earlier in this chapter, physical presence was identified as an essential feature of face-to-face communication. The physical presence of communicators is a precondition for a number of these characteristics. Thus, I do not treat the physical presence of the interpersonal communicators as an explicit category, but as a condition from which characteristics arise, specifically the characteristics of feedback, multiple cues, language variety, personal character, and symbolic personal commitment.

Feedback

The instantaneous nature of dyadic communication allows opportunity for much feedback in face-to-face advocacy exchanges. There is more potential for feedback between interpersonal communicators than communication through any other media. There is more physical interactivity in face-to-face advocacy communication than in telephone communication: Physical presence of the communicators allows feedback opportunity. Advocates perceive that face-to-face interaction is synchronous and instantaneous, as opposed to other media forms.

Multiple Cues

Interpersonal communication also contains nonverbal elements. Thus, face-to-face communication offers more nonverbal cues than telephone communication. Lenny suggested:

> Oh, because you have all the body language and the stuff that's going on that you can't read in a phone. And I think that people pay more attention, you know, you are getting more information when you are directly with the person. Phone [communication] is limited . . . you are not seeing the person; you are not seeing their expression when they are saying something.

Another sometimes-active advocate suggested that a difference between talking to a person about an event and reading about an event involved nonverbal communicative elements: "When you talk to an individual it's very personal and there is the eye contact. He can't put it in the recycling bin. It's very personal and real." Thus, this advocate perceives that interpersonal advocacy communication entails more types of cues than printed communication.

Language Variety

Adapting to one's audience is possible in face-to-face interaction, as with some other communicative forms. There is opportunity to use a variety of language in face-to-face interaction. The most significant example of this occurs when advocates communicate with fellow advocates with less formal language than if they were talking to elected officials or to individuals with whom they are not familiar. Context influences the formality of the language used in advocacy communication. As Teresa, a very active advocate, suggested: "If I am talking to a *compadre*, my language is more chilled, relaxed . . . our discussions are more informal, because we know each other. Talking to a stranger on the street about advocacy issues or events, I am more careful with my language, the way I am talking." As with the use of other media, the relationship of the individuals communicating influences the tone, an additional feature of language variety, of face-to-face advocacy interaction.

Personal

A characteristic of interpersonal advocacy communication is that it is a more personal connection between human beings than advocacy communication through other means. The personal nature of face-to-face communication is intensified by the characteristics explicated above. Face-to-face communication is very personal because there are high levels of feedback, the presence of multiple cues, and language variety. The commitment entailed in face-to-face communication is compelling. Jossey suggested: "It's typically when you're with the person, in the same room; you've made the time to be with that person. So you can be open to more. Typically, whatever they have to say, you would be more likely to consider." The physical presence that contributes to feedback, multiple cues, and language variety also contributes to the personal character of advocate interpersonal communication.

Printed communication is less personal than telephone communication, so this difference is even more accentuated between face-to-face communication and printed communication. Advocates suggest that face-to-face communication is viewed as more personal than posted announcements. Ed suggested that this personal element was more compelling than just seeing a paper announcement for an advocacy event: "Interpersonal contact is like getting a personal invitation to an event. If you know the person, if you trust them, it could mean a whole lot more than to see some flyer." Again, the personal commitment of the inviter is perceived to increase the effectiveness of the communication.

Face-to-face communication with elected officials is also perceived as more personal than writing a politician a letter. When Tony was asked if a meeting with an elected official was different from sending him or her a letter, he responded, "It is immeasurably different." Tony implied that the physical presence entailed in interpersonal advocacy communication with elected officials is different from attempting to contact them by mail because it can force the candidate to consider the issue more than if an elected official was sent a letter. Tony suggested that officials like the governor would rarely get to see a personal letter sent to them on an issue: "If I had sent him a letter, he would never have seen it. He would never have read it. That personal contact is so important." Tony suggested that letters to elected officials would not have the interaction that is present in face-to-face encounters: "Meeting face-to-face, there's a chance you might get a dialogue, which you can't get in a letter." A letter is easier to ignore than physical presence: "You send a letter to one of these officials, there's no guarantee that they'll get to look at it, or even that it will elicit a single thought. It is a whole lot harder for them to turn away a human being." There is more presence in face-to-face interaction. The present human being demands attention more than a piece of mail and makes the communicative action more noticeable to an elected official.

The personal character of interpersonal communication influences the use of interpersonal communication by advocates. The Journey of Hope advocates traveled the nation in order to have that interpersonal contact. As the president of the organization stated: "I cannot overemphasize the power of the personal contact." Thus, this advocate commits the time and resources necessary to procure financial support and people power in local areas to enable thousands of personal contacts.

The "human contact" cited as important by an anti–death penalty advocate is an experiential, symbolic culmination of factors and commitment to the advocacy communicative exchange. This internationally active advocate, who had a high national press profile at the time of Timothy McVeigh's execution, addressed this symbolic union. This advocate, Charles, lost a loved one in the Oklahoma City bombing yet opposed the death penalty in general and in the case of McVeigh in particular:

> For me personally, I really go for face-to-face communication if not voice-to-voice communication. For me e-mail is one of the least favorite ways. I like that *human contact*. And I think when we have that *human contact* we can more easily relate to the subject. [Emphasis added]

Thus, face-to-face communication entails "human contact" and symbolic value that is greater than the sum of its particular characteristics. The president of an international anti–death penalty organization, Dave, also thought that people felt more invited when they were contacted by human beings rather than by postcards:

Yeah, I think [interpersonal invitations] got their attention better. So many people get so much mail. And so many e-mails . . . it is really easy. I send a thing out that asks people to do something, but the problem is that it's in a pile. We really have an info glut in our culture. People are really inundated continuously.

Advocacy communication through other media, such as computers or mass media, lacks the symbolic union present in face-to-face advocacy communication. Abby discussed characteristics of face-to-face interaction that accentuated the symbolic union that is characteristic of interpersonal advocacy interaction:

Visiting with someone is a much more intimate, connected kind of experience. You get to see the person's body language, you get to interact with them, and you merge fields if you will. You're sharing space; you're sharing the experience much more than if you're just a voice on a phone.

There is a symbolic joining in the act of interpersonal advocacy communication. This characteristic is closely related to the community-building function performed by interpersonal communication between advocates. The particular characteristics of advocate media uses make particular media more or less appropriate for performance of particular functions. Interpersonal communication is valuable for building community because of the characteristic of this symbolic connection.

There is personal commitment implied in interpersonal advocacy communication. Flanders explained: "My neighbor was obviously involved and seemed to have a personal stake in the event, and the issue seemed very near to their [*sic*] heart. And that made me . . . more likely to attend." Again, the personal connection was compelling for this advocate. Lenny also explained that he felt more comfortable talking about advocacy efforts in person rather than on the telephone:

I think there's always kind of . . . you want to get off the phone. You know, it is not as comfortable. I never feel as comfortable talking on the phone, or picking up the phone and calling somebody, as I do running into him or her, or seeing him or her at a meeting. And I don't know, I think a lot of people have that. It is not a phone phobia or anything; it is just a little hesitation.

There are symbolic differences between getting an invitation from a friend to go to an event and getting a postcard about an event in the mail. The perceived personal investment and implied commitment to attend by the solicitor is a symbolic feature that increases the effectiveness of communication about advocacy events. Linda, a universal health care organizer and a longtime activist in welfare issues, suggested that if a friend personally invites her to an event, there is an assumption that Linda would be spending social time with that person at an advocacy event. This assumption is not present in a nonpersonalized postcard:

> The difference for me, between getting an invitation to an event from a friend, versus getting a postcard in the mail, is when I hear about an event from a friend, I think that the friend is probably going to go to that event. And that means a lot to me . . . it's almost a social thing for me, you know. I hang out with like-minded people, I believe in the issue; these are the people that I like to hang out with for a social event. I'm a busy person. I know this event can happen, I know my friends are [going] to be there, so I go.

This advocate did not perceive that the symbol of commitment in face-to-face communication was present in paper communication. This symbolic personal investment perceptually implied by personal contact is perceived by other advocates to be better than paper-communication forms. Jossey suggested that the symbolic personal commitment made through interpersonal advocacy communication is emotionally powerful:

> The one that's more powerful is the personal contact. There is a relationship there. I'm all about relationships. That's even been more of the reason that I go. If a friend of mine said hey I'm going and would love to have you there. And I might feel [a] little guilty if I didn't go. If it's a nameless piece of paper, I don't have to attend to it.

Interpersonal personal advocacy contact can be emotionally powerful, according to Lenny: "Well, it is good that it is real interaction between people. And . . . it is also creating, you also define yourself by . . . when you think about it, and you form an informed opinion." Interpersonal interaction can unite advocates in a personal way because it entails the characteristic of symbolic union between communicators.

This analysis reveals that the most salient characteristic of face-to-face communication is that the physical presence allows much opportunity for feedback, nonverbal cues, and language variety, which contribute to emotionally engaging personal quality.

Internal Group Factors

Internal group factors, including people power, financial resources, and group history support the use of face-to-face communication. The resource requirements that influence face-to-face communication include people power and finances. While the cost of interpersonal contact is low, advocates must exert some labor to conduct advocacy work through interpersonal communication. The most influential internal group factor is personal initiative, a part of people power.

People Power

As discussed earlier, people power and resources can influence advocates' use of face-to-face communication. People power is synonymous for numbers of volunteers, the time they can give, and the personal initiative of the advocates involved. For instance, advocates may have to travel in order to have interpersonal contact with more people. The national advocate from the Oklahoma City bombing antideath cause obviously perceived personal contact to be valuable in advocacy efforts. His commitment to this contact was evident in the familiar hardships imposed by his travel responsibilities. He lamented that it seemed as if he spent more time away from his wife than with her. His time and energy are taxed much by his desire to personally connect with other advocates and the general public on the death penalty issue. The perceived labor required for face-to-face advocacy communication influences the use of interpersonal contact by advocates. The one-on-one encounter takes time, according to advocates, and that labor is clearly a cost of this form of communication.

The importance of personal initiative is evident in the case of face-to-face advocacy communication. Gumption separates the advocates who use these opportunities to engage in face-to-face communication from those who do not. Advocates may need to muster the courage to take advantage of serendipitous situations. Personal initiative can be required in situations like the one in which Tony found himself at the restaurant with the governor or in a happenstance conversation with a coworker; face-to-face advocacy communication may require the activist to be bold. This is accentuated in the case of face-to-face communication in which no mediating technology is required. Personal initiative is necessary for all media use, but advocates' use of interpersonal communication, their gumption, is marked by making a choice to talk about advocacy activity and issues.

The cost of interpersonal advocacy communication is two-sided. On the one hand, it costs nothing to talk to people about advocacy events or issues. On the other hand, gaining physical contact can be difficult and costly to arrange, as was the case with the Journey of Hope anti–death penalty advocates who traveled throughout the world to disseminate their advocacy message.

Financial Resources

Some face-to-face communication requires financial expenditures, as in the cost of transportation. In another example, Tony traveled to cities throughout the state with the wife of a death-row inmate in order to visit people and to engage in face-to-face communication about the issue. The wife who traveled with Tony personally advocated a stay for her husband at various events. Tony said that he and the wife of the accused had spent the previous day at various events in Kansas City in an effort to communicate to as many people as possible the doubt that exists in her husband's case. The trip required gas money and access to dependable transportation.

Thus, face-to-face advocacy communication is moderately efficient because it is labor intensive but can require financial expenditure. Abby suggested that interpersonal communication could be more efficient in some instances than the use of other communication media: "The efficiency of communication is much more, is much greater in terms of speed of sharing just pure information with e-mail or a phone call [than with face-to-face communication]. But you have to get together." The mutual presence necessitated in personal communication symbolizes commitment. Ed suggested that the act of meeting is investment in the communicative encounter: "Because you were committed enough to drive somewhere, or get somewhere. You've made the appointment. Your physical presence is already an investment." This advocate believed that physically working together increased the efficiency of advocacy communication tasks. However, the excerpt also reveals that individual, face-to-face communication is labor intensive and requires much effort. Traveling in order to communicate face-to-face requires people power: time, numbers, and personal initiative. Face-to-face communication is more demanding than use of other media. This characteristic limits the ability of advocates to interact face-to-face with intended audiences. Interpersonal communication is perceived to entail a higher personal investment than advocacy communication through other media.

Efficiency refers to the potential in quantity of audience members reached and the effectiveness of the communicative experience as opposed and weighted against the people power and financial expenditures required to complete an act of communicative praxis. The Latin root of the word is *efficere*, which means accomplish. Gaining a desired end with a minimum of resource expenditures is a key feature of the concept of efficiency. In this ethnographic study, evaluation of efficiency is based on the perceptions held by advocates, their understanding of characteristics that arise in their life-world.

Logistical Resources

Few financial resources are necessary for other instances of face-to-face communication that don't require travel. Tony and the woman needed money for gas and a dependable automobile. In the case of an international, active anti–death penalty advocate group, the Journey of Hope organization had a bus that allowed members to travel in order to communicate face-to-face with as many people as possible. The bus was an essential resource. Access to technology, which is usually related to financial resources, is less important due to the nonmediated nature of face-to-face communication.

External Factors

In the example of Tony and an anti–death penalty group meeting with a gubernatorial candidate before an election, the political context influenced the ability of advocates to gain the ear of the governor after the election. This important external factor, an electoral outcome, influenced the disposition of the candidate who was ultimately elected to engage in face-to-face communication with Tony. In this case, the governor had some affinity for some anti–death penalty decisions. The electoral outcome of the gubernatorial election influenced the use of face-to-face communication in two ways. First, because Tony had met with the candidate/governor before the candidate's electoral success, Tony's reluctance to engage the governor in interpersonal communication was decreased. In addition, the success of the candidate influenced the person who was now the governor to be more receptive to the interpersonal conversation with Tony at the restaurant. Simply, if the candidate had not won the election, Tony would have just been talking to a former gubernatorial candidate. In this case, the previous relationship between Tony and the governor accentuated the influence of the external factor of the electoral outcome on the interpersonal exchange. Tony was happy to report that the governor subsequently signed legislation that prohibited a death sentence for mentally retarded people found guilty of murder. Tony was invited by the governor's office to attend the event, at which he stood in line next to the governor as the governor signed the bill.

Conclusion

This chapter, because of the tight focus on one medium, underemphasizes the multiplicity of media used in concert to promote events or issue positions. Advocates usually employ multiple media in concert with one another, as one advocate explained: "At . . . getting a postcard, I still always read them, and, when I get [a] postcard, I put it on the refrigerator, and then I can be reminded about the dates, and then I might also be reminded by the personal contacts." Advocates perceive multiple forms of mobilization solicitation as useful.

Overall, face-to-face communication is viewed by activists to be a useful element in advocacy campaigns. Advocates perceive that face-to-face communication can evoke effective communicative experiences. These activists use

face-to-face communication to reach several audiences including fellow advocates, the public, politicians, and media personnel. This face-to-face communication performs a variety of functions, including increasing attendance at
events, arranging logistical details, building community, persuading the public,
lobbying, and facilitating mass media coverage. Factors that influence advocate
use of face-to-face communication include characteristics of the form, internal
group factors, and external factors. This analysis reveals that face-to-face, interpersonal advocacy communication is characterized by feedback, multiple cues,
language variety, and personal character. Internal group factors, including people power, financial resources, and group history, influence advocates' use of
face-to-face communication. Personal initiative is a necessary element in advocate uses' of face-to-face communication.

3

Talking on the Telephone

The phone call is more personal [than paper communication], if it's from somebody I know. It's more direct, and it's more specific. It's more a call to specific activity. . . . Some logistics can be taken care of with the phone, and some of it is." Ed, an advocate that lends logistical support to several environmental and anti–death penalty events a year, explained one way that telephones could be useful for advocacy. According to the U.S. Census Bureau, by the year 2000, over 94.1 percent (110 million) of American homes had telephone service, and Americans made over 500 billion calls a year (U.S. Census Bureau, 2000). This chapter explores advocates' use of telephone technology. First, I identify advocates' uses of the telephone. I then identify the intended audiences of these uses. Third, I explicate the functions that advocates perceive the uses perform. Finally, I explore the factors that influence advocate telephone use. Consistent with the theory of advocate media use offered in this book, they are influenced by media characteristics, internal group factors, and external factors.

Forms of Telephone Media

Several telephone communication technologies are used by advocates, including telephones, answering machines, and cellular telephones. According to Hopper (1992), the sale of answering machines rose from fewer than one million in 1982 to over thirteen million in 1989. Almost 70 percent of American households owned telephone answering machines by 1998 (Branscum, 1998). As public access to telephone devices has increased, so has advocates' access to these devices.

Traditionally telephone signals traveled through wires, but the rise of cellular technology has freed communicating advocates from the limitations of physically fixed telephones. The spread of cellular technology has made radio transmission of telephone signals available to advocates. In 1996, there were 44 million cellular telephone subscribers in the United States; by 2001, there were 109.5 million cellular telephone users (Kirchofer, 2001). The General Accounting Office has reported that over 110 million Americans currently use cellular telephones (Chidi, 2001). These general technological trends likely influence advocates' access to telephone technology.

Intended Audience

The intended audiences of telephone communication influence advocate uses. Three major target audiences of advocacy communication were found to be important when considering the intended function of telephone communication: fellow advocates, politicians, and media personnel. Of these, telephones were used most to communicate with other advocates. Often, contact with only one person was necessary for logistical communication. As addressed in the section on functions of advocates' telephone use, lobbying communication is directed at politicians. Advocates also use the telephone to communicate to media personnel in order to publicize events. As could be expected, telephone communication is not frequently used to communicate to the general public.

There is a difference between a friend talking to another friend about advocacy issues on the telephone and talking about these issues on the telephone to a stranger. Diane, a university student and a nationally active advocate against the death penalty explained:

> There is a difference between getting a call from the phone tree [an arrangement in which one advocate calls a number of other advocates, who each, in turn call a number of advocates], and getting a call and talking about an event with a friend. Often I'm talking on the phone to really good friends. When I'm talking to a person like that on the phone, it's just like talking in person.

As with other forms of communication, the relationship between advocates on the telephone can make these conversations feel like face-to-face conversations. In sum, the target audiences for advocates' uses of telephones include other activists, elected officials, and journalists.

Activists' Use of Telephone Technology

Telephones, answering machines, and cellular telephones enable advocates to perform a number of functions. (Fax messages are also transmitted through telephone lines, although since fax messages are now more often transmitted between computers, I discuss fax technology in chapter 8.) These include increasing attendance at events, arranging logistical details, building community, raising funds, lobbying, and facilitating mass-media coverage.

Increasing Attendance at Events

Advocates use telephone communication to mobilize other advocates and increase attendance at events. The advocates' comments included in this book indicated that the telephone was used to personally inform members of upcoming events advocating universal health care, abolition of the death penalty, and environmental protection. Advocates engage in mobilization communication with telephones by spreading the word about an event. Before each of numerous universal health care events, I received a telephone call from the universal health care advocate, Nancy. One advocate who has attended between six and eight antideath penalty events a year explained that the telephone was useful for drawing his attention to an event:

> I think the antideath penalty event was mentioned to me on the telephone. I was told that there was going to be this lecture. But I think a follow-up call was made, and specific arrangements were made. I think over the phone, I would know that it is definitely a serious invite. If you call me specifically it might generate my interest on the subject.

Thus, this advocate felt that the telephone calls piqued an interest in a particular event for members of the group. Some advocates use a phone-tree technique to spread the word about advocate events.

In one instance, in conjunction with the Journey of Hope tour, Tony called me to activate the phone tree. He gave me a rough script over the phone. I called twenty-three advocates and got fifteen answering machines. Answering machines are easier on the caller because relevant information can be left on the machine. The telephone scripts gave some information about the particular cases of condemned inmates, and then requested that advocates attend civil actions in protest. Such anti–death penalty telephone-tree scripts identified locations of upcoming events such as the local courthouse, the governor's mansion, or a penitentiary where an execution would take place. Anti–death penalty advocates used a phone tree to draw the attention of the advocate community toward specific events and to provide information that enabled advocacy action.

Telephone banks can also be used to mobilize advocates for events by gathering a number of people at a central location with a number of telephones to conduct a mass calling. One of the leading environmental and social justice groups in the community used telephone banks for mobilizing advocates for an annual dinner (for which fund raising was not the purpose). A telephone bank differs from a telephone tree in that those participating in the telephone-bank technique gather at a central calling location.

Advocates use telephones to contact media personnel and elected officials to increase publicity for advocacy events. Advocates also use the telephone to contact mass media outlets in hopes of gaining media attention for their causes. As addressed in chapter 7 on mass media, advocates seek the attention of media personnel, particularly for advocate events. Telephone calls are used to follow up on press releases faxed through computer technology to media outlets. Calls are made to news directors, or specific reporters, if advocates know agreeable and receptive news personnel. In one instance, the cellular telephone was also used to arrange for an activist to personally contact regional media personnel.

Arranging Logistical Details

Advocates use all of the types of telephone media discussed here (telephones, telephone answering machines, and cellular telephones) to make arrangements for advocacy activity. Mobilization communication may get advocates to attend an event, but organizers use telephone technology to engage in logistical communication to make arrangements, plans, and complete the tasks necessary for an event to occur. As with mobilization, the primary audience for such communication is other advocates. But the target audience is wider for mobilization than for logistical communication; mobilization communication functions to convince advocates to attend events, while logistical communication concerns arrangement of details and solicitation of the effort and investment of resources from the members of an advocate community. The latter would be directed toward only the most committed members of the group. For instance, the locations of universal health care events were usually arranged through telephone conversations between advocates and administrators of locations such as city facilities or church meeting rooms. In another instance, telephone communication was valuable in organizing logistical arrangements for the Earth Day efforts. The immediacy of telephone communication allowed the committee to make and finalize decisions in a short period of time. This was also the case with the abolitionists: One anti–death penalty meeting was halted several times because members of the group had difficulty locating the telephone numbers of potential musicians for an upcoming event.

Advocates also used answering machines and voicemail for logistical communication, which was often successfully delivered and confirmed through answering machine messages. For example, telephone tag, in which callers respond to each other's answering machines without ever actually talking to a person, was a valuable endeavor when both parties shared accurate information. It was also frustrating at times, but if advocates left complete information with the message, the messages could complete necessary communicative functions. In a specific example, the Earth Day committee used a number of answering machine messages to successfully procure a stage for an event. One very involved environmental advocate and community activist was also a municipal officer and, thus, was a conduit between the environmental coalition and the city. Lana said that telephone tag could be sufficient to successfully communicate with other advocates on logistical matters:

> I like answering machines for that reason too. Sometimes you can conduct business without . . . ever really talking directly to the person. You can leave your spiel, and they can call back and talk to your machine and give their spiel, and sometimes you don't need to really connect to get stuff done.

This excerpt accentuates another difference between mobilization communication and logistical communication; the latter is primarily two-way, while the former is primarily one-way. Logistical communication usually requires discussion of details and statements of responsibility for duties; mobilization communication requires no response from the recipient.

Cellular phones were used to reach particular advocates whose skills were needed to fulfill logistical requirements at a moment's notice. This technology allows for instantaneous communication. Advocates also used cellular telephones to engage in logistical communication while mobile. For instance, massive activities of the international antideath penalty organization discussed in this study were largely coordinated through cell phone communication. Revised schedules were negotiated and checked with cell phones. Rides were arranged, confirmed, and revised with cell phones. Cellular technology can also be useful for logistical coordination in other contexts, such as allocating advocate volunteers during an event. The Earth Day coalition discussed using cellular technology in 2002 to better coordinate the use of volunteers during the event. There were concerns aired that in some areas there were too many volunteers with nothing to do, while in other areas there were not enough volunteers. Someone suggested that if the organizers could be in contact through the use of cellular phones, then advocates could react to some of these problems by appropriately allocating people-power resources as needs arose.

Building Community

Advocates use telephone technology to build a sense of community. Advocates, on the telephone, use conventional, interpersonal communication such as small talk, friendly conversation, and personal inquiry to develop friendships and build community. For instance, some advocates made thank-you calls for those involved in the organization and execution of advocacy. In one case, three days after an anti–death penalty advocacy event, I received a call from the local organizer thanking me for my participation. He also expressed regret that he had not communicated with me before he left with the marching group. He expressed gratitude for my contribution in the event. I communicated in return a desire to be included in other such events. As an activist who has access to resources (such as a public address system) and who can be counted on to fulfill commitments, he indicated he would contact me in the future. Thus, thank-you calls are an example of community building and can be a way to ensure access to resources for future communicative activity.

Telephone calls can also contribute to a communal sense when they are used for other functions simultaneously. When I reached an actual person on the phone, I talked about the issue and tactics, but sometimes interpersonal relations began to be discussed if the caller was an acquaintance, which was not uncommon. But time is a valuable commodity, and I would feel the need to move on. This is a recurring tension in advocacy media use: Personal contact is emotionally compelling and contributes to a sense of community, but it is not as efficient as more impersonal media uses.

Raising Funds

Advocates also use telephone technology to solicit financial support from members of advocate communities. It is possible to solicit funds from audiences other than advocates. However, the advocates in this study made these calls only to people who have a record of supporting or inquiring about advocacy activity. For instance, local environmental advocates used a telephone-bank technique to solicit membership renewals and/or donations through a mass calling. In cases such as this, advocates used interpersonal contact through telephones to reach out to the advocate community for financial support.

Lobbying

Advocates use telephones to contact elected officials in order to lobby for specific actions, or arrange encounters for lobbying efforts. Phone trees can also be used to activate advocate calls to elected officials in order to request specific actions. One anti–death penalty organization activated a phone tree before most executions in order to encourage advocates to call the governor's office to halt the killing. Advocates in this study were seldom able to talk to their elected officials, but were able to talk with the office personnel for these officials. These staff members record the number of calls that the politician receives and differentiate the positions advocated by callers. Advocates sometimes refer to this as "logging numbers." However, advocates such as Tony perceive such calls as just a drop in the proverbial bucket:

> With the telephone we try and add some numbers to the tally. Years ago we found out that what they did was, the office of constituent services, they had like a blackboard, or a wipe-off board, on which they would record the pros and cons. That way they can just go to the governor and say we got fifty calls today, thirty-eight of them opposed to the execution, twelve for it. Just so they can offer some kind of information, some semblance of representation, democracy.

While the communication indirectly gets to the elected official, advocates perceived a representation of their voice reached politicians.

Advocates can also use the telephone to arrange meetings with elected officials for the purpose of lobbying; they sometimes call elected officials as a precursor to such persuasive efforts. Tony reported using this approach in several instances with elected officials, although most of this communication was indirect.

Advocates also called the offices of elected officials to inform or remind the officials about advocacy events, particularly those held at the state capitol. In one instance, in conjunction with a lobbying event at the capitol, Nancy called the offices of selected representatives in order to draw attention to the events.

Facilitating Mass Media Coverage

Advocates used the telephone to publicize events to media personnel. In many instances, field notes revealed that advocates often communicated to newspaper, radio, and television personnel through telephone communication. While promoting a documentary that protested the execution of a Missouri man, I would remain by the telephone before and after advocacy events involving the film in order to be accessible to questions and confirmations with local media. Following the presentation of the documentary to the governor's office in conjunction with civil action, I received at least six telephone calls from mass media personnel. Cellular telephones can also be valuable tools for the coordination of people power to create additional uses of other media. In one instance, the international anti–death penalty organization, Journey of Hope, used cellular technology to contact a member with the resources necessary to fax a news release to media personnel.

In summary, advocates use telephone technology for increasing attendance at events, arranging logistical details, building community, raising funds, lobbying, and facilitating mass media coverage. Telephones, answering machines, and cellular telephones were types of telephone technologies represented in examples of these functions throughout this section. Advocates used these devices to communicate with a number of audiences, including other advocates, politicians, and media personnel.

Factors That Influence Advocates' Use of Telephones

As with other media, factors that influence advocates' use of telephone-communication technology include media characteristics, internal group factors, and external factors. In this section, advocates describe how these factors led them to choose telephone technology to accomplish their advocacy of social causes.

Characteristics of Advocate Telephone Use

Telephone advocacy communication has a variety of characteristics that enable advocates to use it for the advocacy functions identified above. Through constant comparison, a typology of the prominent characteristics of advocate telephone use has been created. These characteristics influence the use of telephone technologies by advocates. This explication of characteristics of telephone use is informed by previous research of telephone conversation and media richness. Hopper (1992) used conversation analysis methods to study features of telephone conversation. Media-richness theorists have also explored characteristics of telephone communication and compared telephone use to other media (Daft and Lengel, 1986; Daft, Lengel, and Trevino, 1987; Rice and Shook, 1990; Sitkin, Sutcliffe, and Barrios-Choplin, 1992). These scholars have posited four criteria of media richness: feedback, multiple cues, language variety, and personal focus. These works contribute a theoretical perspective that aids my explication of characteristics of advocate telephone use, a rich medium because of its instant feedback, verbal cues, and personalized character, but not as rich as some communication-media forms because of its lack of visual cues.

Advocates use telephone technology to perform the above-mentioned functions because of the characteristics of telephone uses, such as instantaneous feedback, lack of visual cues, language variety, a quasi-personal character, intrusiveness, and distance.

Instantaneous Feedback

The immediate feedback available in advocate telephone uses contributes to interactive potential of telephone uses. Daft, Lengel, and Trevino (1987) suggest, "Instant feedback allows questions to be asked and corrections to be made" (p. 358). This is evident in advocates' use of telephone communication. One less active advocate, Jossey, suggested: "Typically on the telephone, it's one-on-one. And it seems like its more confirming things like 'Yes I will, they cannot bring that,' trying to organize things." Thus, the ability of advocates to check details and confirm in an interactive way is possible because of the interactive nature of advocacy telephone communication: The interactivity of advocate telephone uses, arising from the potential for immediate feedback, allows users to decrease uncertainty quickly. The interactivity made possible by the immediate feedback of telephone conversations makes advocates likely to use the media when time is limited, and when an advocate needs to communicate only with one person. For instance, when Nancy needed a ride for a health care speaker at the last minute, she used the telephone, not a letter or e-mail. When Tony sensed that the media was not receiving sufficient notification of anti–death penalty events, and that more attention needed to be focused on events taking place that night, he called someone to send out additional faxes. A phone conversation was most appropriate to contact an advocate to do this task because Tony felt that the situation demanded immediate attention.

If time were not a factor, advocates may perceive telephone answering machine messages as sufficient for some tasks. For instance, if advocates have the time to wait for a call to be returned, telephone answering machines could be sufficient to deliver a message. If not, advocates would try to call again at a later time. Phone tag may allow advocates to exchange necessary information in the most convenient and nonintrusive manner. Communicating advocates have a choice: If a person is not reached, callers must decide whether to leave a message and/or to call back at another time.

Lack of Visual Cues

Comparison of telephone uses to the uses of other media reveals that the telephone lacks the visual elements present in face-to-face communication in the form of nonverbal cues and the graphic forms present in paper communication and visual mass media. Telephone, although it lacks visual cues, may possess verbal cues such as tone, rate, or pitch that are not present in print media. In addition, when advocates are working on extensive organizational details, information that is visually presented on paper may help with logistical communication. Ed, an advocate most involved with logistics of environmental events, suggested that logistical communication could be more difficult when planners are not physically together and cannot look at the same visual representation of complex arrangements:

The phone calls tend to be more about setting up. Not going into the details. It's hard to keep track of eight bands and twelve time slots. The logistics are tough, without seeing it on paper. If we are both looking at the paper, then we can talk about it using the piece of paper as a reference. If we were doing that on the phone, if we both had a list, it might work. But we don't, so it's hard to do that on the phone. There's a visual element to looking at the schedules together.

While this excerpt does not suggest that logistical communication is impossible with telephone communication, it does reveal that this advocate believes that some logistical discussion is easier when advocates are physically together. Thus, the lack of visual cues in advocacy telephone communication makes it inappropriate for highly complex logistical planning.

Language Variety

Telephone communication can also involve different types of language. Language variety, as employed by media richness scholars, refers to the availability of different language forms. Telephone communication, like all other advocate communicative forms, possesses some potential for language variety. For instance, communicators can employ informal or formal language on the telephone. The use of informal language between advocates who have a previous relationship is appropriate for logistical communication. On the other hand, calls made by advocates who do not personally know the recipient tend to be more formal. This is consistent with Hopper's (1992) findings: In openings of telephone conversations, informal greetings are more frequent when the communication is between those who know each other than between strangers. Thus, advocates who call strangers for a telephone tree or bank used a more formal opening than those used between advocates who have a relationship. In addition, advocates' use of the telephone allowed natural or technical language; the availability of technical language allowed advocates to successfully communicate numerical information on the telephone. If numbers were required for logistical detail, this numerical data could be shared over the telephone. For instance, in one call, I discussed financial details about a showing of the documentary *Unreasonable Doubt* at a church in a Midwestern city, an example of variety of language. Likewise, friendly, natural language could be used for community building.

Quasi-Personal Character

Another characteristic of telephone communication is that it is perceived to have a more personal character than some other media. Rice and Shook (1990) suggest that higher media richness is associated with "social presence" (p. 200), and advocate telephone calls possess some personal social presence. Joan suggests: "It's very personal to get a phone call. It's like a personal invitation. Please come." Telephone conversations have a quasi-personal human element. Tony explained: "The phone tree puts a very friendly reminder in their ears, a human voice as opposed to electronic beeps . . . or seeing products. With the newsletter the message doesn't necessarily pop out and engage you. E-mail is kind of the same way." Telephone use is perceived to have a more personal character than uses of these other media. However, because the communication is mediated by the technology of the telephone, and because the communicators are physically separated, this is quasi-personal interaction.

On the other hand, one advocate suggested that it is easier to get off the phone than to disengage from a physically present interpersonal communication:

> Phone calls are much easier to disconnect than in person in interpersonal communication. It's easier to shut it down. When someone solicits, if you don't know the person and someone tries to solicit over the phone, it's like you're calling me in my home, I want to disengage, thank you.

Thus, there is less presence in telephone conversation than in face-to-face communication, enabling telephone users to disengage with less feelings of guilt about disengaging.

The personalized nature of telephone calls makes advocates like Tony prefer them to many other communication forms. This quasi-personal characteristic is perceived to be more compelling, more persuasive than nonpersonal messages. Unfortunately, this one-on-one approach to communication through the telephone is time consuming. Some techniques such as a telephone tree or a telephone bank can spread the word, but each telephone call is still only to one person.

Leading advocates (those who repeatedly initiate and execute advocate activity) perceive that telephone calls are effective for mobilization because they perceive a compelling, implied personal invitation in a telephone call. For instance, because Abby perceives that telephone banks are effective for mobilization, he will try to use the technique. Abby, one of the leading environmental, and social, justice advocates in the community for over ten years, suggested that phone banks have made a difference in mobilizing advocates for an annual dinner:

> Like last year in the fall of 1999, we did a phone bank to our members to invite them to our annual dinner and in the fall of 2000 we sent out postcards and then e-mails. But we didn't do the phone banks. There were a lot more people in 1999 than there

were in 2000. I don't think the organization was weaker, but I think people just didn't
feel as invited. So that in 2001, I think we will go back to the phone bank for that.

These advocate experiences are strong evidence for the effectiveness of phone
banks for some forms of advocate mobilization. Abby contended: "It makes a
difference" and perceived this personal element to be effective for mobilizing
advocates, or getting them to attend an event.

Likewise, a regional anti–death penalty organization uses the telephone-tree
technique for mobilization because of the personal character of telephone calls.
Tony, an active, state anti–death penalty organizer, commented: "The thing
that we need to activate better . . . no guarantee that it will ensure a great
turnout, is the phone tree." Joan, an internationally active advocate of social
and environmental justice issues, also perceived the activation of telephone
trees as an effective technique of telephone use for the mobilization of members. In fact, at one point Tony perceived that the success of a particular series
of events was influenced by the ability of the anti–death penalty advocates to
activate their phone tree:

> We probably had more numbers than we usually do because we did a better job of
> outreach to our base. We activated our phone tree. I made maybe twenty-five calls to
> people who then each made between ten and twenty telephone calls. The reality of
> it is . . . that we reached out to the so-called converted, the people who are the com-
> mitted. People who wanted to be on the phone tree, to get information about the
> alerts. And even then we probably reached out to about three hundred people.

But Tony's judgment of the effectiveness of the phone tree shifted in mideval-
uation: "And a sixth of those people showed up? That is sad. For that particular
vigil, I would've liked to see a lot more. But it was more than we have had."
Thus, phone trees are used to activate advocates, but not as successfully as Tony
hoped it could be. In the end, Tony suggested that phone calls are also valuable
for member mobilization: "If you're working to get people mobilized for an
event, I think you have to depend more on personal contact, like phone calls
and activating the phone tree." The personal attention of a telephone call is
more compelling than the impersonal character of some media such as postcards or listserv e-mails. The personal character of advocacy telephone communication leads some advocates to perceive that the use of telephone trees
can be a critical factor in the success of an event.

Telephone communication is perceived as effective because of the human,
personal element involved. Tony referred to the personal character of telephone communication when discussing the effectiveness of telephone use: "I
think that person-to-person contact means a lot to folks, they tend to respond

better. I know I do." Tony suggested that this influenced his use of the telephone: If he had the time, he preferred to use telephone communication rather than other media.

Intrusiveness

Abby also perceived that the intrusive character of telephone banks contributed to their usefulness for environmental advocacy fundraising efforts. Membership renewal, solicited in conjunction with the announcement of the annual organizational dinner, was also an important fundraising vehicle for the local organization. Abby explained that because the calls demanded the attention of the receiver, this contributed to the usefulness of telephone banks for fund raising:

> And people complain about calling them. With the phone bank for fund raising, people say "Why don't you send me something in the mail?" And I said well we would be happy to send you something in the mail again. We did send a mail order out a month ago but no one replied. But we hate to bug you, but we are trying to reach everybody that are our members to see if they want to renew their membership. At that point, they say, "Well, I guess we want to renew."

While the other advocates in this study did not use the telephone bank for fund raising, the empirical evaluation from a leader of one group is strong evidence for the perceived effectiveness of telephone banks for fund raising. As suggested by Hopper (1992), the one who calls (summons) demands the attention of the recipient: In the instance of these membership renewal efforts, callers get the attention of recipients more than with postal-delivered paper communication. These two examples show that telephone technology was perceived as useful for gaining financial resources. Abby was committed to using the technique again because he perceived that this use of telephone technology was effective for event promotion and fundraising, so he attempts to use the technique in his advocacy efforts. The intrusiveness of telephone calls demands attention.

Distance

Telephone enables advocates to communicate across great distance. Hopper (1992) identified this obvious characteristic of telephone communication. Thus, telephone communication has the characteristics of instantaneous feedback, language variety, a quasi-personal element, intrusiveness, and distance. However, telephone conversation lacks visual cues present in communication through some media. These characteristics, as well as other factors, influence advocacy use of telephone technology. Advocate telephone communication is less valuable than face-to-face communication, but more valuable than advocates' use of other media, such as paper communication. Use decisions are influenced by the richness of telephone communication: If advocates need quick feedback, but do not require physical presence, telephone use could be sufficient. If advocates need a richer, more emotionally compelling exchange, or if there is a necessity for a visual component, telephone use may not be sufficient, and richer communication may be required. Functional requirements are critical for the appropriateness of telephone use. For instance, advocate events (a communicative environment) lack the characteristics needed for logistical functions because there is limited two-way intercourse. In whatever case, the consequence of the richness of telephone communication for advocates is that if a task requires quick feedback and personal attention, telephone use is appropriate.

Internal Group Factors

Internal group factors, including resources and group history, also influence advocate telephone uses. Each group has its own particular idiosyncrasies, often based on the personality characteristics of the group members, and these factors influence how groups communicate. Internal group factors that influence advocate use of the telephone include people power, finances, and group history. People power is *in vivo* code for numbers of contributing advocates and the time and effort they contribute to advocacy efforts.

People Power

One of the most important resources is people power. Available people power influenced advocate use of telephone technology for the groups studied. Tony at one point explained that time and effort are required for successful telephone communication. Tony and others in the anti–death penalty community met with a gubernatorial candidate before the candidate was elected into the governor position:

> And we had a great . . . gathering, and this can be a lesson, well, for all of us, because this is probably one of the better things I have worked out. I had to dog this guy; I had to call him like a dozen times. But about a dozen different times I called him and they just kept telling me that somebody was going to call me back, different staff people.

People power can influence the techniques that advocates choose to use. A female environmentalist and a staff member at a business set up and operated under the auspices of a local social and environmental justice organization. Paige suggested that the reason the advocacy group did not use telephone banks was that: "We don't have the personnel." Abby also commented: "We do the phone banks for fund raising and letting people know about events. We don't do phone banks for all events because it's pretty labor-intensive." Ironically, the antideath penalty group that did use telephone trees said that their group did not use telephone banks because it lacked volunteers. Telephone banks are more appropriate for fund raising, while telephone trees are more appropriate for mobilization.

Knowledge possessed by advocates is another resource that influenced media uses. Joan contended that the local support group for Mumia Abu-Jamal, a political activist who was awaiting execution on Pennsylvania's death row, did not use telephone trees because the group did not have a telephone-number list. If someone in the group had taken responsibility to build such a list, there would have been sufficient leadership to begin working on a telephone-tree plan. Unfortunately, such leadership was not present. Joan commented, however, that there was intragroup networking, so word was being spread in other ways. The telephone trees of other organizations could have been activated for media events, but adequate people power was lacking. Telephone-contact information is also a resource. Universal health care advocates likewise valued telephone numbers; phone numbers and names were solicited at each of their public events.

A narrative explanation of one antideath penalty group's cellular telephone experience provides an example of the importance of the number of internal factors that influence telephone use. The newness of this technology makes knowledge about it important for its adoption by advocates. Tony explained that he needed to have a cellular phone to coordinate the numerous events across the state in conjunction with the tour of the Journey of Hope members. First, people power was necessary to investigate and procure a cellular telephone. Tony expended some people power and called around to providers to shop for the best package. Knowledge was also important for the acquisition of a cellular telephone. Tony explained that he knew little about such service and that inexperience slowed his use of a cellular phone.

Unfortunately, Tony's lack of habitual knowledge of cellular telephone use presented a problem when Tony accidentally left the cellular phone on the roof of the van in which he was traveling about halfway through the week of statewide Journey events. The van traveled through a busy intersection before he realized he had left it on top of the vehicle. He and his fellow passengers retraced their path, but the phone was not seen again. Knowledge, in the form of habit, might have influenced this situation. Fortunately, Tony possessed the foresight to buy the insurance he was offered by the cellular dealer and was able to replace the telephone.

Financial Resources

Financial resources influence advocates' use of telephone technology, which is evident when considering long-distance telephone calls or the cost of cellular telephone service. Joan suggested that she hated to see so much of her money go to "Ma Bell" for long-distance calls related to advocacy activities. At several meetings of one anti–death penalty group, some conversation revolved around finding the lowest rate for in-state long-distance telephone calls. When Tony needed a cellular telephone for Journey of Hope coordination, financial resources were provided by a local chapter of a national anti–death penalty organization. He canceled the service after the Journey of Hope tour through the state. The environmental coalition discussed the possibility of using cellular technology for the coordination of volunteers, although the need was not perceived to justify the costs. Telephone costs for the local environmental advocates were small because most of the activity was local and the group used e-mail as their primary logistic media. Universal health care advocates had little need for cellular technology, although at a universal health care rally at the capitol, one organizer lent Nancy her cellular telephone so that Nancy could call the offices of several key legislators to draw their attention to the event. For traditional telephone uses, donations at events and funding provided by the local League of Women Voters covered the telephone costs for universal heath care advocacy.

Group History

The history of a group's previous telephone techniques can influence the use of such communication techniques as telephone trees or telephone banks. One aspect of group history is the institutional knowledge developed over time, but logistical considerations are also relevant; if a group has used a telephone tree in the past, it has developed through its history the people power and resources to use the technique again. When asked why a particular group did not use a telephone tree, one environmental advocate stated: "We just never have." As with all other media uses, if a group has done something before, it likely possesses the organizational resources to use it again.

Some internal group factors did not appear to have much influence on advocate telephone uses. Social advocacy groups did not influence one another in how they used telephone technology. Likewise, overlapping membership was not a salient influence on advocates' telephone uses. While these internal group factors did not appear to have an influence on advocates' use of telephone technology, other group factors such as resources and group history did. Constant, comparative method is not exclusively inductive. Rather, concepts developed inductively can then be deductively explored in further inquiry. As interviews revealed, there were factors that influenced media use, and further questions were developed to explore those factors. In addition, as noted earlier, the writing of this book was a continually recursive process: As theoretical ideas, such as influential factors, arose in later chapters, earlier chapters were honed with these theoretical considerations in mind.

So as we can see, internal factors can enable or prevent telephone uses. Some advocacy groups fail to effectively build the kind of communication network necessary for the use of the telephone-bank or telephone-tree techniques. Ed pointed out: "We didn't build phone trees. We probably should have. We can use the phone a lot to relate information. We couldn't keep in touch with people as much as we should have. We should have built phone trees." Telephone trees offer a way to divide the labor necessary to maintain healthy contact between advocates. Ed suggested: "Phone trees can help people keep in contact with each other, to focus on certain issues. Phone trees are a great division of labor. One person doesn't have to sit down and call twenty-eight people and spend three hours of time that they don't have." This division, however, requires volunteers, time, knowledge, and leadership as well as other resources that some organizations simply do not possess.

External Factors

External factors can also influence media choices. In the case of this medium, these external factors include technological trends and political context.

Technological Trends

Technological trends in society have influenced advocates' use of telephone technology. As noted earlier, cellular telephone use doubled in the past five years in the United States. Certainly the increased use of cellular telephone technology in society, in general, has made it easier and cheaper for advocate groups to use the technology. As cellular telephone use increases in society in general, so will advocates' use of cellular telephones. This assumption, while not evidenced, is intuitively logical. In another, more recent example, answering machine use by advocates has increased as general use in society has increased. This has made it more likely that advocates would use the technol-

ogy, according to Ed: "Answering machines are more common now. Leaving
a message on a machine . . . it's similar to e-mail I guess. It is just part of life."

Political Context

Political context, or the prevailing political mood, is perceived by advocates to
influence their use of telephone technology. One internationally active advocate voiced a fear that her phone may have been bugged by government agencies during republican presidential terms. Whether this was the case or not is
not the issue. If a political environment exists that contributed to her fear, she
relied less on the phone because of this perceived fear. It is valuable to note
that this advocate's perception of the political context, rather than the perceptions of the political context perceived by others, influenced her telephone use
for advocacy efforts.

In one example, the municipal authorities in Washington, D.C., recognized
the utility of cellular technology. An advocate of universal health care stated
that she had seen on the Web that during the 2001 presidential inauguration
celebrations in Washington, D.C., police declared that possession of a cellular
phone by demonstrators would constitute possession of a weapon. According
to charges not evident in searches of coverage of the events in the mainstream
media, the declarations had no legal basis, yet the D.C. police detained any
activist they saw using a cellular telephone. Those arrested were released after
the three most active days of the inauguration events, due to the lack of statutory justification for the arrests. However, the universal health care advocate
suggested the police wanted to squelch the use of cellular telephones by dem-
onstrating advocates, and that was likely the result. In this case, the power of
police to suppress political communication influenced advocates' use of cellular
telephone technology in conjunction with inaugural protests. This example
speaks to the importance of political context because if the city officials and
police administration had been sympathetic to the causes of protesting advocates, the speech may not have been squelched (even if it was just a rumor).
Thus, the political context likely led to more cellular telephone use in the short
run, but the actions of the Washington, D.C., police probably overall
decreased cellular telephone use during the inauguration weekend and beyond.
Technological trends and political context are external factors that are perceived by advocates to influence their use of telephone technology.

Conclusion

I have explicated advocates' use of telephone technologies and identified factors that influenced their use of this medium. As I have argued throughout

this chapter, telephone communication is perceived as valuable for a variety of functions. As with any medium, poor telephone communication can hinder advocacy efforts. When incorrect or unclear information was communicated through telephone technology with these groups, as with all other communication forms, it was disadvantageous to the efforts of advocates.

In this chapter I have explored uses of telephone communication by advocates. There are several telephone-communication technologies that are used by advocates, including telephones, answering machines, and cellular telephones. Advocates used telephones for increasing attendance at events, arranging logistical detail, building community, lobbying, and facilitating mass media coverage. Consistent with the theory of advocate media uses offered in this study, the characteristics of media, the intended audience, internal group factors, and external factors influence advocate use of telephone technology. I identified the characteristics of advocate use of telephones, including instantaneous feedback, lack of visual cues, language variety, a quasi-personal character, intrusiveness, and distance. Internal group factors that influence advocate use of telephone include people power, finances, and group history. Technological trends and political context are external factors that are perceived by advocates to influence advocate use of telephone technology. Consistent with the theory of advocate media use, advocates utilize telephone communication to engage others in quality communicative experiences.

4

Meeting in Small Groups

There is a weakness of a group that's based on one individual. If it's just that one individual, then it's not a group effort. You're kind of defeating the purpose. Groups have a goal of eventually changing public policy. An individual can make a damn good effort, and, [do] ultimately, whatever they can think up to do themselves, in some form or another. But a group can make that effort more effective.

This excerpt from Tony, a leading regional organizer on the anti–death penalty issue, reveals that he perceives that advocate efforts that depend on an individual to accomplish short-term communicative goals of a group may be less enduring than advocate efforts in which a group works together to share the time and energy necessary to plan and execute advocate communicative activity. This chapter identifies advocates' uses of group communication as it outlines the functions these uses perform. This chapter then explicates factors that influence advocates' media use of small-group communication, consistent with the definition of media that include the environment, or setting, in which communication takes place. The result is an analysis that reveals the importance of intergroup communication, initiated and coordinated within small-group settings, and that shows that group communication plays a symbiotic role with uses of other media in the sense that the activities of advocates in group settings are often the locus of origin for many other advocacy group media uses. In this next section, analysis of advocates' use of group forms for different functions reveals the importance and variety of such uses. Much if not most communicative activity is incubated and nurtured to fruition through advocate communication in group settings. While small-group intergroup networking is not the same as small-group meetings, because much of intergroup networking was conducted in small-group settings, it will also be discussed in this chapter.

Audiences of Small-Group Communication

Activities of small groups vary; some are more formal, some less. In some group settings, brainstorming is appropriate; in others, it is not. The advocates studied in both organizational and coalition meetings predominantly employed an open, consensual form (Burgoon, 1971; DeStephen, 1988; Hill, 1976; Kline and Hullinger, 1973; Knutson, 1972; Knutson and Holdridge, 1975; Marr, 1974; Morris and Hopper, 1980; Spillman, Bezdek, and Spillman, 1979). While implied, informal hierarchies did develop, the meetings of these groups were consensually democratic. Advocates used small-group communication to reach two audiences: advocates (in the same group or advocates in different groups) and politicians.

Advocates

Initially, the advocacy groups studied here utilized organizational meetings, to which all group members were invited, but which usually only the most committed attended. The ideological leanings of these groups influenced the character of the meetings: While there were functional leaders, these ad hoc leaders almost always asked if someone else wanted to lead the meetings. In most cases, organizational meetings began with solicitation of pertinent items for the meeting agenda. As illustrated in the next section, advocates performed a variety of functions in these organizational meetings. The target audience for organizational meetings is primarily other advocates in that particular group.

Advocacy groups can network with other groups and ask if they could participate in communication at events. For instance, most of the universal health care events were sponsored by a number of local organizations, from welfare reform organizations to civic groups like the League of Women Voters. In the case of the Mumia event (Mumia is a longtime activist who is currently on death row in Pennsylvania for the murder of a policeman, a crime he may not have committed), many organizations were cosponsors, including black studies organizations, Amnesty International, a peace studies university organization, a Native American support organization, the local National Association for the Advancement of Colored People (NAACP), an affiliation of Artists for Peace, and several other important local organizations that advocated peace. The Mumia event was a fundraising benefit and rally that featured speakers, poetry, and musical performances. Communication with other organizations in order to facilitate multigroup sponsorship for events is also reported in the e-mailed minutes of an anti–death penalty group. In this case, a university-affiliated religious organization was mentioned. The organizations had obviously worked together in the past. Plans were made to initiate communication with the religious organization concerning cosponsorship of an event. The Earth Day coalition, with its representation from many groups, naturally worked with many other community environmental advocacy groups. Intergroup networking was a pervasive communication form in the most active advocacy communities.

Small groups with other primary purposes can also take advocacy positions. For instance, academic-representative organizations such as student-government structures can serve as advocacy mouthpieces. One graduate student association officer who attended a few civil action rallies a year assumed that a democratic organization, student or otherwise, should make statements on larger social issues:

> I think that one of the purposes of democratic organizations is also social awareness. Being aware of how our actions are impacting other people and other human beings. That is a reasonable thing for these kinds of organizations to do.

Student organizations can be used as venues for advocacy communication. This advocate believed that in this way additional communities would consider the topical issue: "I think it is desirable, you know, . . . it is [good] to have a group of graduate students, from different schools, in different professions, or different organizations, from many different perspectives. And I think it is desirable to inform all of them." Advocates can use group settings of other organizations as venues for advocacy, especially, as discussed later in this chapter, when these groups have overlapping membership.

Politicians

Small-group settings can be venues for communicating to politicians. Tony, a leading anti–death penalty advocate in the state, explained how a group of people was able to meet with a politician before the candidate was elected governor. The meeting was not a public event, but rather a private meeting between the politician and the leaders of several anti–death penalty groups. Environmental advocates also used a group venue for advocacy: Abby reported that he and other advocates from the community met with a politician on the nuclear issue.

Functions of Advocate Use of Small-Group Communication

Small-group communication can have a variety of functions, including increasing attendance at events, arranging logistical details, building community, lobbying, and educating the public. Exploration of these functions reveals that small-group settings are particularly important for coordination of advocate communicative activities: The most important target audience of the group format is fellow advocates.

Increasing Attendance at Events

Advocates publicize events, or more accurately, remind participants about related events—dates, times, and locations of advocacy activity—through group communication. In addition, advocates used networks of groups to increase the visibility of and participation in advocacy events. Discussion at meetings of other groups can be a venue for advocacy communication, according to advocates like Darlene, because intergroup networking increases the number of possible venues:

> The vast network of coalitions, like I belong to three different coalitions, so I go to one coalition, I hear about it, and then I go to my next meeting and something is brought up, I say, "At the Earth Day meeting we said this." Automatically, all those people are reminded of the event, they hear the plea for volunteers. That is just word-of-mouth. Word-of-mouth.

Intergroup networking provides an opportunity for people outside a particular advocacy community to discuss advocacy activities.

Some advocates view intergroup networking as an important ingredient for successful promotion of advocate activity. Joan, a longtime, internationally active advocate, explained how such networking contributed to the growth of the regional anti–death penalty movement:

> You have a Catholic church reporting it, mentioning it to the organizations. They actually mentioned the event at Mass. Which is nice. You have people who are in the Catholic workers community here. I've often noticed when there are visiting Catholic workers from out-of-town, they would come and join in the demonstrations. Amnesty International had it announced in the peace studies classes at the university, but not only the Amnesty International on campus but also the Amnesty International chapters in high schools, and the Fellowship of Reconciliation. So through these organizations working together, we can get the news out to all of our members. That is what really increased anti–death penalty activity recently, and will continue to increase it.

In the case of the universal health care advocates, often the responsibilities for cosponsoring organizations included communicating about the events and having members in attendance at these events. One hardcore anti–death penalty advocate, Joan, attributed the recent success on the anti–death penalty issue to this function of intergroup networking: "One of the reasons we have been successful is because of the intercommunication between organizations that are working on the [death penalty] issue." Joan perceived intergroup networking between small groups to be an important feature of successful advocacy-event promotional communication. Several of these advocates obviously perceive that such an intergroup-networking strategy increases the ownership in an event in cosponsoring organizations, and advocates perceive that such cosponsorship increases the attendance at advocate activities. Much of this intergroup networking occurred in small-group settings, although some was dyadic in form. The communication was primarily conducted to facilitate coordination between small groups, whereas intergroup communication networks were perceived to increase attendance at advocacy events.

Arranging Logistical Details

Small-group communication is the means by which the advocates studied here arranged logistical details as they formulated ideas, planned events, and volunteered for task completion. This is a necessary precursor for much advocate communication.

Advocates formulate ideas within their small group through brainstorming sessions and intergroup information sharing. Small-group communication allows for the exploration of possible advocacy activity. In the initial discussion phases in all three of the primary groups studied here, ideas were bantered about. Small-group gatherings allow the opportunity for brainstorming, or imaginative free variation of ideas about advocacy-communication possibilities, and these settings were opportunities for advocates to offer ideas for advocacy praxis. In the small-group setting, proposed ideas were evaluated and either rejected or embraced. For instance, at the meeting of a group dedicated to opposition to the execution of a journalist and an ex–Black Panther activist, Mumia Abu-Jamal, conversation often revolved around ideas about how to communicate to more people. In the case of the Earth Day committee, one of the decisions that must be made every year is the particular theme of each Earth Day event. Each year, a portion of an Earth Day–coalition meeting is dedicated to this task. Brainstorming, the nonjudgmental phase of formulation of ideas, was used to generate ideas. Discussion was then used to deliberate on the decision. In the first stage of deliberations, members are asked to offer all possible themes for the event, which are all recorded by a member of the group. In the second stage, members discuss the advantages or disadvantages of each of the theme ideas. A number of votes are taken to eliminate themes as discussion continues among participants. Themes are also modified to incorporate the preferences of group members. The group implicitly seeks a theme that all can accept, consistent with the consensus decision-making model. In this case, brainstorming is an important part of the function of arranging logistical details. Small-group discourse was often used for preplanning communication for the formulation of ideas for advocacy events.

In the case of the Mumia support group, after individual advocates committed to the achievement of communicative activity goals, logistical planning commenced, and local contacts to the advocates responsible for previous topical events were identified. Plans for intergroup coordination was arranged primarily in small-group meetings. These advocates then shared phone numbers for possible cosponsors as well as the best times to reach them. This sharing of ideas and information exemplifies the benefits of the use of small-group settings for formulating ideas for advocacy events, the first stage of arranging logistical details.

Group communication is a useful format for advocacy planning. This coordination of individual action performed a necessary, logistical function. In the case of the environmental coalition, the Earth Day committee used group meetings to coordinate the planning and execution of advocacy activity by individual advocates. For instance, at one point, group members decided that a large tent that had been offered for the event by a member of the community could be useful at the Earth Day event. I volunteered to contact this member of the community and arrange the particular details. Discussion in the small-group meetings was an opportunity to bring specific plans together. Planning was also a major function performed in the universal health care advocacy meetings. Plans were discussed for events, all of which would be opportunities to communicate about the plight of the uninsured. For instance, universal health care advocates often discussed panel presentations as an event format that could be used to inform the general public on the issue. The events were obvious attempts to inform people; communication was almost always the short- and long-term goal. Members discussed problems about procuring event locations, and times and dates were discussed and set. Small-group communication was a prominent venue for event planning for advocates. Thus, advocates used small-group communication to explore and negotiate such logistical concerns as event date, event time, and identification of potential cosponsoring organizations. Negotiation usually included group recognition that something needed to be done and the offers from volunteers to complete those tasks.

Small-group communication was also used by the environmental coalition to confirm logistical arrangements. At meetings of the environmental coalition, often the first ten minutes were devoted to confirmation. Much discourse consisted of questions such as "Did you [do what you said you were going to do]?" or "Did you call that person?" This assignment of responsibility and checking to see that tasks have been accomplished is an important function often performed in advocate-group settings.

Networking between small groups can also aid in the completion of logistical tasks. Intergroup networking can increase the resources available for advocacy efforts. Darlene, an active advocate for all three causes (organizes and supports four events a year, volunteers two to four hours a month, and attends another four advocacy events a year) suggested that the cross membership with other groups increases the resources at the disposal of the coalition:

> Also, intercoalition communications . . . [to communicate to a larger audience]. You tell someone at the Earth Day coalition that you need some kind of help, and when they go to other meetings, they say Earth Day coalition needs help, and then you might get a call because somebody there knows somebody who can help you.

The Earth Day coalition relied upon a network of organizations to connect with needed resources. For instance, city employees helped with setting up the stages for the event. In many instances, communication between organizations facilitated the completion of logistical requirements.

Cosponsoring events is a common means for fostering such cooperative efforts. In order to build such networks, many advocates decide in small-group meetings which organizations to contact, as suggested by Joan:

> And, when I heard about [a national anti–death penalty event effort], I thought, "Hey, there is no reason why with all of these wonderful artists that they have in Missouri that we can't do an event." I was a cofounder and participant of the Poets for Peace here in mid-Missouri. So we had kind of a vocal group, so we could do it.

Intergroup networking, which arose in the form of cosponsoring events in many instances during the course of this study, can provide expanded communicative opportunities. Joan suggested that cosponsorship facilitated more communication: "If you invite other organizations to be cosponsors, you activate their communication in the media networks." Joan explained how she perceived that intergroup networking helped disseminate information about advocacy events:

> The [networking] groups would be more likely to announce an event at their meetings, send out e-mails to their lists, activate their phone trees . . . , whatever way they have to get the information out. I think that cosponsoring events helps everybody all around. It helps divide out time it takes to put an event together, the labor, the cost of fliers, and it gives people an opportunity to get their message out. That forms a stronger movement.

Networking between small groups can contribute synergistic potency to advocates' communicative efforts. This increases access to communicative resources, according to Joan:

> In what ways can you cosponsor? To me when I've done organizing for a coalition, every little thing that an organization can do is vital. Whether it is helping put flyers up, or it's paying for flyers or contacting their members about the event, anything is so valuable. Every organization has their limitations and their availabilities of different resources, whether it is money or time, or people or whatever it is. Everything is valuable.

Small-group networking can more effectively spread the word about events. Joan explained that offering opportunities for other groups to cosponsor and contribute to the planning and execution of an advocacy event can increase a sense of ownership for the event, which will lead to more promotional effort from these cosponsoring organizations. When asked if she thought such a sense of ownership was important, Joan answered:

> Yeah, . . . it is absolutely incredibly important. If every organization contacted their membership and told them about it, then you would have turnouts in the hundreds to events. When you are talking about the Mumia 9/11 event, we had seven cosponsoring organizations. Within those seven cosponsoring organizations, like Mid-Missouri Peaceworks is one, they have how many people on their mailing list? In the thousands. 2,300 I think it is. And so even if 5 percent, even if 1 percent of those showed up, how much is 1 percent: 23 people? FOR [Fellowship of Reconciliation] has a mailing list, how many people are on their mailing list? And even if 1 percent showed up, and that adds up with seven or eight organizations you can easily have a hundred people there. Which is close to I guess what we had, it was quite crowded in there, where people couldn't get in.

The connection to characteristics of groups is that networking between advocacy groups increases advocate access to resources needed for other advocacy efforts. This synergistic potential for resource access is unique to intergroup networking. Offering the opportunity to cosponsoring organizations to communicate at the event increases their commitment to the event. In contrast, Joan speculated that the relative lack of success of an antideath penalty teach-in was partially due to the failure to invite cosponsoring organizations to have a more active role in organizing the program. This would have increased the sense of ownership in the activity in the cosponsoring organizations: "I am really certain it is. I really feel that was a downfall with the teach-in that we didn't give people enough of a sense of ownership." Thus, this function of small-group networking influences some advocates' desire to use this format. Some advocates perceive that coordination between several small groups facilitates arranging logistical details necessary for some advocate activities. This is particularly a function of networking between groups. Intergroup networking can increase access to logistical resources such as people power, or the numbers of advocates, time, and effort they are willing to commit to advocacy activity.

This small-group as well as networking coordination is important because it is a prerequisite for maintenance and execution of other forms of advocate communication, such as the use of events, mass media, paper communication, or computer communication.

Building Community

Advocates also use small-group settings for building community in several ways. Community building can be defined as developing professional and interpersonal relationships, a communal sense of belonging. Sharing information is a central feature of this use of small-group communication to build community because it is an important process in which the collective group understanding of advocacy issues and the factors that affect those issues are forged. As advocates reactively share information, they are negotiating the group's shared interpretation of the social world. This uniting of minds brings the advocates' conceptions of social reality in line with one another. As Anderson (1996) stated:

> Whatever the tension between collective meanings and local practices, the construction of reality is essentially a communication enterprise. The peculiar human character appears within this constructed reality through the practices of communication. For the hermeneuticist, our accomplishments arise out of our collectivity, not out of our individuality. Communication makes possible that collectivity. It is managed through the iconic, discursive, and the performative practices that are the resources of our communicative efforts. (p. 135)

This process, manifest in small-group meetings of advocates, also heightens the sense of collective identity. These are important factors in the process of building community. Group meetings are an excellent venue for advocates to share issue-related information. In the case of an anti–death penalty meeting, information shared in this way was of much value. Sometimes the conversations in these advocacy meetings can drift from the initiating topic. Meeting drift can provide a valuable opportunity for advocates to share related background information. For instance, at one of the Mumia meetings, there was also discussion of the case of Leonard Peltier, a Native American activist under a federal life sentence for his alleged role in the death of FBI agents. The conversation then drifted to other political prisoners being held in the United States. The group talked about the recent release of Puerto Rican independence activists by Clinton and the restrictions upon their activities imposed as conditions of their release. At that moment, Joan shared valuable information that answered some of the group members' questions. Joan had information about other political prisoners being held in the United States, particularly at Marion Federal Penitentiary in southern Illinois. Different activists may have access to different kinds of information. The sharing of such knowledge is part of the community-building function because it is through the group discussion process that group members forge a communally held understanding of social reality. In the above instance, an understanding of the location of political prisoners (the implied view of group members) incarcerated by the U.S. federal government was collectively decided (regardless of the actual location of these prisoners, who could in fact be at different incarceration locations, for instance, had Joan's information been outdated). Even the idea that Mumia was a political prisoner rather than simply a criminal was continually reaffirmed in the discourse between group members at these meetings. Field notes revealed that as the members of the Mumia support group discussed the most questionable aspects of the state's case against Mumia, a common perception was that the case was so weak that there must have been political motivations behind the actions of the prosecutors and the judge in the case. According to Lenny, a common understanding of the social world is negotiated through group communication:

> Well, it is good that it is real interaction between people. And . . . it is also creating, you also define yourself by . . . when you think about it, and you form an informed opinion. Personal interaction is normative; we can disagree about it and discuss it. This interaction can be part of a push toward positive social beliefs and actions.

This push toward positive social beliefs and actions refers to the negotiation over a shared view of the world. Advocates use small-group settings for this aspect of community life. The information shared at the meeting would also be conceptual ammunition for subsequent advocacy on these issues.

Advocates had emotionally binding experiences through group communication. In one instance, the related information was a source of strong emotions. There was great relief at one Mumia meeting because of the news that his execution was delayed for another six months. (Mumia Abu Jamal's death sentence was commuted in the fall of 2001.) The meeting almost had a happy, communal mood. I, as a very active advocate on all three issues (attends, organizes, facilitates approximately twenty-five advocacy events a year), felt that these small-group meetings were as much relational as functional. I knew I was going to be getting together with my friends, my comrades in the cause, and that these small-group gatherings would increase the morale of the group.

Advocates use small-group settings to nurture this camaraderie. The activists addressed one another as if they were brothers and sisters united in a good cause. There was a collective history for members of the group. The meetings were a way in which the advocates could acknowledge their common desire to do what they could to promote social progress. There was a feeling of belonging in the group. There was solidarity forged in the common identity of the advocates, evident in their willingness even to attend meetings. Darlene commented: "At the meetings [of the Earth Day Coalition], we were brothers and sisters in a cause. This wasn't just a social club; this was an important, righteous cause." Advocates use small-group settings for building community by sharing knowledge, experiences, and a communal consciousness.

The community-building function of group meetings is that they provide a social circle to which commitments must be kept, which can also bolster motivation. For instance, one very active advocate on all three issues reported that his real motivation was from the need to fulfill commitments made to other members within the environmental organization. As Darlene, a professor in physics, stated: "Saving the world is the last thing on my mind. . . . I said I would do it, so I did." Many advocacy meetings ended with each member reiterating what he or she would do to further the group's efforts. True motivation for completing the assigned tasks emanated, for this advocate, from a desire to fulfill commitments to the other members of that community. Thus, the community-building function of group discussion is important to advocacy efforts.

Lobbying

Advocates sometimes use small-group settings as a means for lobbying politicians. In the case of environmental advocacy, Abby explained that meeting politicians in this group format could be preferable to a one-on-one encounter or with interaction between the politician and the larger group. When compared with a one-on-one meeting, the group setting (in this case four or five individuals met with the politician) allowed more diversity of opinion than if just one advocate met with the politician. By inviting leaders of several groups: "There would be a variety of other constituents represented. This might allow the meeting to have more impact." Abby also suggested that the multiplicity of individuals could increase the propensity of the politician feeling like they were on the record with their statements. If only one advocate, or even two advocates, met with the politician, the politician might not feel the need to be straightforward; a number of participants could "corroborate" the statements made by the politician. On the other hand, Abby also suggested that having more advocates at the meeting, especially in excess of ten, might intimidate a politician. Too many participants in such a forum "could preclude real discussion," according to Abby. Group meetings with the politician (four or five) allowed opportunity for "intimate conversation." In another instance, anti–death penalty advocates were able to meet with the future governor in a small-group setting. Tony explained that this meeting gave a number of prominent advocates the opportunity to communicate their opposition to the death penalty to the future governor:

> We wanted a meeting with the gubernatorial candidate. We wanted to meet with him, our group, to talk with him about his views on the death penalty . . . so we lined up a meeting with a Methodist minister who had lost her husband to murder, but who was opposed to the death penalty. We also brought several prominent members of the anti–death penalty community from throughout the state.

Tony explained that even if the meeting did not convince the candidate to change his overall stance on the issue, advocates hoped that the meeting with them would evoke some introspection on the part of the candidate:

> So we . . . got a meeting with the candidate. He spent about an hour with us. He was very clear about saying that he supported the death penalty, but had some concerns about the legal problems, as far as adequate counseling offered to . . . fight that sentence. We were trying to make him think about these issues. I think it could help . . . it can't hurt. I really didn't hear either one of the candidates really go "rah rah rah" about the death penalty. You know, I mean, when questioned about that they said they supported it. But they would bring it out like a campaign theme for them, helping their electability.

Educating

Advocates used small-group settings of other organizations to educate, for instance, advocates for other issues, about their advocacy issue. Intergroup networking also allows advocates to communicate advocate issue positions to a larger audience than to the tighter community primarily focused on one particular advocacy issue. For instance, civic groups such as the League of Women Voters cosponsor activities organized by advocates for universal health care access. When the League of Women Voters deliberate over whether to support specific events, they also talk about the particular issues addressed in the event. In this way, intergroup networking is a way that advocacy groups can promote their issue stances. In the case of the Mumia group opposed to the execution of Mumia Abu-Jamal, advocates must invariably explain the case as they see it; a part of gaining the support of possible cosponsors is the task of convincing those possible cosponsors of the efficacy of action against Mumia's execution. In these instances, intergroup networking is a vehicle through which discussion of advocate-issue positions can be facilitated.

To summarize this section, advocates use small-group communication to perform a variety of functions and are critical venues for much advocacy communication. Small-group communication is important for increasing attendance at events, arranging logistical details, building community, lobbying, and educating the public. The potential communicative power generated through intergroup networking was also explored.

Factors That Influence Advocate Use of Small-Group Communication

Advocates' use of small-group communication is influenced by its characteristics: internal group factors and external factors. Advocates perceive that these factors influence their ability to create quality small-group experiences.

Characteristics of Small-Group Advocacy Communication

Through constant comparative analysis of interviews, field notes, and advocate literature (e.g., e-mailed minutes of meetings or reports of meetings addressed in newsletters), as well as analysis of emergent themes, several characteristics of advocacy group communication emerge, including presence of immediate feedback, multiple cues, language variety, and a personal character.

Immediate Feedback

There is much potential for feedback in organizational group meetings due to the instantaneous nature of group communication. High feedback, or immediacy, is a characteristic that increases the richness of the communicative exchange (as well as the other characteristics discussed in the following paragraphs), according to media-richness scholars (Daft and Lengel, 1986; Daft, Lengel, and Trevino, 1987; Rice and Shook, 1990; Sitkin, Sutcliffe, and Barrios-Choplin, 1992). In one instance, I, as a program planner for the Earth Day coalition, invited an anti–death penalty advocate, Tony, to speak on the main Earth Day stage. I had worked for weeks to arrange a prospective speaker's time and secure a commitment from the speaker. However, when the organizer brought this up in reviewing the planned program, other Earth Day activists instantly lodged a protest over uniting the issue of environmental advocacy with the issue of the death penalty, first with silence and negative nonverbal signals (e.g., frowns), then with comments. A representative of the local school district suggested, "I don't believe everyone in the coalition agrees with the anti–death penalty position." I suddenly realized that the range of groups involved with the Earth Day environmental advocacy, including, as noted, the public school system and officials representing the municipality, did not agree on the death penalty issue. This is also an example in which the social world, in this case the range of groups involved with Earth Day efforts and the issue stance that could be taken by the Earth Day coalition, was negotiated. My understanding of the reality of the situation was altered due to the collective discussion of composition and issue stances of the community of groups and individuals involved with Earth Day. I immediately amended my position and offered to negotiate with Tony, who is also an antimilitary advocate, to limit his comments to the environmental harm created due to the military industrial complex, or to withdraw from the event. In this instance, the instantaneous feedback from the other members of the group provided an opportunity for immediate negotiation of this logistical and substantive issue.

Small-group settings are similar to face-to-face communication in terms of communicative feedback. Small-group communication is a form of face-to-face communication, and, thus, is similar to dyadic face-to-face exchanges. One difference is that small-group settings may not provide the same level of immediate feedback available in dyadic communication, if only due to the multiplicity of participants in small-group communication. Group protocol, especially in highly structured, hierarchical groups, may limit these potential feedback opportunities, but in the groups studied here, meetings were saturated with opportunity for feedback, likely due to the consensus-oriented modus operandi utilized by these groups.

Multiple Cues

Group communication is also characterized by the presence of multiple cues. Multiple cues in group discussion include the presence of nonverbal and verbal communication and the ability of group discussion participants to incorporate literal communication in group meetings. First, as in the above example with Tony, when the other members of the Earth Day–coalition executive meeting heard about the invitation, there was initially silence coupled with many nonverbal cues from the other members participating in the meeting. One member frowned. Another member shook her head. Even the postures of some of the other members participating in the meeting appeared to stiffen, as if a gesture signaled a lack of comfort about discussion of the dilemma.

In another instance, at an anti–death penalty group meeting, a member of the group suggested a date for an event. Joan, an informal leader of the group, began shaking her head before the speaker was even finished stating a possible plan for an event on that date. After he was finished, Joan explained that the date of the event was inappropriate and that too many other events were happening around that date. While Joan did immediately provide verbal feedback, her nonverbal gesture communicated her initial reservation and was possible due to the physical presence of the participants at the anti–death penalty meeting.

Other cues can also be present in group communication. Often printed materials are used in advocacy meetings to supplement verbal communication. For instance, at the point in the year at which the specific entertainment plans for the Earth Day event were nearly finalized, I, as the entertainment chair, outlined the program after we handed out printed itineraries. This allows both aural and literal (e.g., printed texts) communication cues. In another instance, an anti–death penalty advocacy group proofed a flier that was going to be used to promote one of their events. Due to the physical presence of the participants and the presence of the flier prototype, members of the group could critically evaluate other printed visual cues, such as logo designs. In all of these instances, multiple cues were present: verbal, nonverbal, and literal (written or printed words).

Language Variety

Group communication can entail language variety such as formal or informal language as well as numerical data. In the first case, group discussion participants can engage in friendly, informal banter in meetings as well as more formal communication concerning logistical details. For instance, in one of the Earth Day meetings, a discussion centered on the theme for the 2002 Earth Day event. In the midst of serious suggestions in the brainstorming session, one of the group members offered the slogan "Why did we elect Bush?" Group members laughed and offered some other joke themes. In this instance, informal language was used as a friendly, joking tension reliever. However, the language did turn more formal when consideration of serious theme ideas recommenced. Numerical language can also be utilized in group-discussion settings. For instance, when the budget of the Earth Day coalition is discussed, numerical printed data provide additional language variety for the fiscal discussion. The possibility of the use of numerical data or conceptual themes constituted the language variety. The mathematical language of a budget report is different from language used in conceptual conversations in advocacy group meetings. Thus, the uses of formal and informal language as well as the presence of mathematical language in shared texts are sources of language variety in advocate group communication.

Personal Character

Group communication can have a personal element. The personal character of advocate group discussion is primarily due to the physical presence of participants that provides opportunities for feedback, multiple cues, and language variety. Group communication provides instantaneous interplay between the ideas of the group discussion participants. The personal character of many group discussions promotes dialogue. As evident in Abby's discussion of the appropriateness of group settings for the lobbying function, too many participants can preclude authentic personal discussion. Thus, group discussion can be characterized as personal, although not as potentially personal as some face-to-face discussions or telephone conversations because of the lower level of personal intimacy in an interpersonal conversation than a discussion in a group setting.

There are also symbolic characteristics of group discussions that intensify the personal character of group communication. The use of group meetings can facilitate a heightened morale due to symbolic convergence that sometimes arises as a result of group discussion. Individuals are often motivated after experiencing small-group meetings. Bales' (1970) studies of small groups reveal that if group members forge a communal consciousness that involves visualization of group goals, members experience higher levels of motivation. In some small-group settings, group fantasizing can be an exciting process through which task goals and commitments are solidified, as Sister Helen Prejean explained: "There is always someone in a group . . . it happens in groups, where suddenly it happens in your heart, 'We have got to do this [advocacy activity].' " If other members give approval and agree to expend people power, then the idea has a better chance of being nurtured to fruition. This is certainly people power, but some small-group settings allow a synergistic atmosphere that increases advocate willingness to expend people power, as Tony explained:

> The strength of groups rather than just individual activity is that, well, like I come up with this idea to flier at a public event. But are there people who are interested in doing it? We need to share that idea, and see if it's an idea that has validity with the whole group. It's hard to put the ego down a little bit, "hey, it's a good idea, let's do it" without consulting the whole group. I can't do it all on my own anyways.

Tony also explained that when the group relies too much on the efforts of one individual, it weakens the long-term strength of the group. Tony perceived that there is strength in the number of participants who are involved with the decision to enact a particular communicative strategy. While effectiveness is an illusive concept, Tony perceived that group efforts strengthened advocate praxis. In some instances, advocacy group efforts can be greater than the sum of the contributions of individual advocates. The collaborative nature of group efforts enables more advocacy communication than the efforts of an individual. Working within the confines of a group to make decisions was more effective than if individuals made those same decisions by themselves.

The symbolic aspects of group communication settings enables the community-building function of group communication addressed previously because the emotional bonds that constitute community arise from the symbolic personal investment involved with group communication. Symbolic convergence can contribute to the sense of community developed through group communication. In all three groups studied here, there was strength that resulted from the symbolic value of collaborative effort both in planning and in the execution of advocacy communication.

Internal Group Factors

Advocates' use of small-group communication is influenced by internal group factors, including people power, financial resources, knowledge, group history, and overlapping membership, all of which influence the ability of advocates to use group communication to engage others in effective communicative experiences. This is true for the use of group discussion by individual groups and the use of intergroup communication.

People Power

As noted earlier, people power, or labor, is required to arrange group meetings, network with other small groups, and arrange meetings with politicians. People power is necessary to coordinate schedules, to procure meeting locations, and to prepare and reproduce supplemental material (e.g., handouts, refreshments). People-power expenditure on the part of group-meeting participants is also required: Those that attend group meetings must be willing to take the time to attend the meetings and constructively participate.

Similarly, establishing intergroup networks requires an investment of time and effort of a number of advocates. Key members of possible cosponsoring groups must be contacted. Negotiation as to what these other groups can provide must be conducted. However, as noted previously, intergroup networking can also increase available people power.

Securing access to small-group meetings with elected officials also requires people power. Tony explained that much effort went into arranging a meeting with a gubernatorial candidate: "And so, you know, . . . I called them a bunch of times, and finally, you know, they said, 'All right, all right, we will talk to you!'" This illustrates the inherent overlap between advocacy media uses. Throughout this book, people power refers not only to strength in numbers but also to the personal initiative enacted by those involved in advocacy effort. The preparation for group meetings requires people power expended in uses of a variety of media that are necessary logistical precursors for group meetings.

This is relevant because, as in the example above, the expenditure of Tony's time and effort was required to arrange the group meeting with the gubernatorial candidate. In this instance, much people power was necessary to convince the politician (and/or his staff) that a small-group meeting with anti–death penalty advocates would be advantageous for the candidate. Tony had to expend much effort and time in virtually pestering the campaign. While quantification of the required people power is beyond the scope of this investigation, there was some point at which Tony and other members of the group exerted the necessary level of effort. Some advocates may have given up, but Tony did not refrain from exerting his efforts until the goal, a small-group meeting with the politician, was arranged.

Financial Cost

The financial costs of meetings are usually low. Because the Earth Day advocacy group had some affiliation with municipal departments, meetings were usually held in city facilities free of charge. Two of the anti–death penalty groups studied here were affiliated with a local university and could reserve space under the auspices of recognized student organizations. Meetings of advocates for universal health insurance coverage met at the home of one of the facilitators of efforts in the community. In these cases, group meetings required meager financial resources.

There are some financial costs of group meetings for some groups, however. For instance, the Fellowship of Reconciliation, a major anti–death penalty organization in the community, rented space for group meetings, initially from a local religious organization. When the religious facility raised the price to rent the room, the group changed the location of the meetings to a place that was less expensive. In addition, members of the group were encouraged to donate some funds to defray these costs. Overall, participants in organizational meetings must expend the capital necessary for their transportation to meetings.

Group communication is moderately efficient because it entails physical presence at a specific time, but also does not require exorbitant financial outlay. The personal presence in small-group interpersonal communication has more of a uniting power, even though other media uses (e.g., e-mail) can be more efficient. Abby, the leader of one of the largest social justice advocacy groups and a focal member of the Earth Day coalition, explained that the communal elements of the personal presence in small-group communication was lacking in computer communication: "So there's a continuum; on one hand there is solidarity and connectedness by people coming together, on the other hand communication is much faster with more people when you use e-mail. So there's a trade-off." Similarly, Abby also suggested that a characteristic of small-group communication is that it is not as efficient as e-mail. Small-group advocacy communication, however, according to these advocates, has a more communal character than e-mail. The most important point here is that small-group communication settings can be less convenient and less efficient than some other communicative media utilized by advocates.

Knowledge

Knowledge about how to facilitate productive group discussion and arrange group meetings can influence the use of group meetings by advocates. If advocates do not have the knowledge about the functions that can be performed by group meetings or how to arrange such meetings, possible avenues for advocacy activity are limited. Advocates' knowledge about how to conduct a good meeting can also influence advocates' use of the group discussion format. For instance, at the Earth Day meetings, Abby, the unofficial leader of the group, always starts meetings by constructing an agenda of items to be discussed at that particular meeting; this increases the efficiency of the meetings. The members of the group also strictly adhere to an hour meeting in almost all cases; this self-imposed discipline, according to my experiences, increases the efficiency of these meetings.

Knowledge about effective intergroup network building can contribute to a stronger coalition. A very involved universal health care advocate who is also a longtime union organizer in a major city suggested that knowledge about potential cosponsors in preplanning is an important small-group step for the construction of intergroup networks:

> One thing you don't do, I don't do, and I've seen people do it, I don't know if I want to comment on whether [Nancy or Wilma] would do it, what you don't do is you don't start building a coalition by having a big meeting where you say everybody who believes in health care come and help form your coalition. You sit down with a core of people that you know are basically on the same page and you make the list of needed resources and sources of power and the list of possible contacts and build outward so that you're inviting people in one-on-one knowing what they bring to the table, you know, you don't let the coalition grow up ad hoc because at least until we've got a strong cohesive core, you're inviting chaos.

Group History

The patterns of repeated use of group settings or networking between small-groups coordination influence advocates' use of group communication. If the members of a group are used to certain practices of group communication, they will likely use those practices again. For example, variations of the history of different groups influence the nature of their meetings; not all small-group settings are equivalent. The Earth Day coalition developed their group discussion patterns over thirty years of group meetings. On the other hand, the anti–death penalty group in support of Mumia Abu Jamal was an ad hoc group with a short history. Field notes reveal that the meetings of the Earth Day coalition were more efficient and adhered closer to time constraints.

One characteristic that influences the uses of the format by advocates is that some small-group meetings often have implicitly or explicitly agreed upon time limits that increase efficiency. Most of the other media examined in this study have explicit or implicit time and/or space limitations. Some small-group meetings have more rigid expectations about time limits than others. This necessitates brevity. Terse language is used to more efficiently communicate in the small-group setting when there are time limits. Ed, an environmental advocate who has been involved with several events a year for twelve years, suggested that the time limitations of small-group meetings can make planning communication more efficient: "Maybe having to get to a location makes the deadline issue more important. I'm here, only to be here for an hour, let's try to wrap this up." This advocate perceived that small-group communication settings with implicitly or explicitly recognized time limits could be more efficient than in group meetings with no assumed time limits. Not all advocacy group meetings have time limits.

One of the undesirable characteristics of advocacy use of the small-group setting is meeting drift. As noted in the discussion of community building in small-group settings, drift can have positive outcomes; unfortunately, it can also hinder the efficiency of small-group, goal-oriented discussion and leave some members disappointed with this lack of discursive decisiveness. There are two major factors that can contribute to such drift: One is lack of time limits and the other is the failure to establish and adhere to an agenda. For instance, in the Mumia meetings, the conversations skipped around a bit. Before one issue was resolved, another would come up. Closure on many issues was never reached. Before two previous events were fully discussed, an additional proposal was raised for a musical event between the local musician/activist group and an African American musical organization on campus. The possibility of holding a musical event in conjunction with a teach-in was raised, but the point was brought up that scheduling both events so close together might thin the audience for both. Plans for a future musical event were left open, and the conversation returned to the teach-in. Such conversational drift sometimes delayed prompt issue resolution in small-group meetings.

Group history also influences the ability of groups to network with each other. If a group has previously worked with other particular groups, this can influence the ability of those particular groups to work together again. If there is a history of intergroup networking between groups, relationships have been previously established and contact is less difficult. The fact that some members of the Mumia support group lacked a history of working with groups whose members were ethnically different from themselves may have precluded some intergroup networking, according to Joan, the hard-core, international advocate:

> In the case of Mumia, being willing to step over the bridge to organizations of other colors [would be more effective]. I don't know if this is just a personal thing that has come in to it, I'm really seeing something here that we still have a lot of work to do with the white activists feeling comfortable touching the black activists.

Networking between small groups requires intergroup contact. Another younger member of this particular group suggested that the lack of a group history of working through ethnic differences could hinder some intergroup networking. This advocate, Teresa, suggested that this might have been the case for the Mumia effort:

> Absolutely. I don't know why it happens. The one thing that I know is that the black organizations that sponsored Mumia, the people who volunteered to take on these organizations like the UMC chapter of the NAACP, they never got in touch with them. I'm wondering if because they were afraid to step over that one other bridge of going to a black organization.

If the members of the Mumia support group had a deeper history of working with these groups with different ethnic composition, intergroup networking could have been stronger.

Overlapping Membership

Overlapping membership can influence the use of group meetings by advocates. In one area, commitments to the group meetings of other groups could preclude certain meeting times for a group of advocates. In another area, when advocates are members of multiple groups, they can initiate the adoption of practices that they perceive as effective in another group.

Overlapping membership can facilitate networking between small groups. There is massive overlap of membership in various anti–death penalty advocacy organizations in this community. Many of the organizations that ultimately cosponsored the event shared members with the Mumia support group. Darlene suggested that overlapping membership of groups provided an opportunity for ideas and arrangements to be worked out in networking between small groups:

A lot of it is just branching off of ideas. Because you go and meet with other groups, and that can give you ideas about possible media uses. For instance, one of the members knows everyone in the whole world. We will bring up a person in a meeting, and she will say "I will be at a meeting with that person on Tuesday. I can talk to them. I can ask the mayor if she can speak at an event." And in that meeting, when she says that, she is telling that other coalition all about what the event is about. That is another media forum. Or advertising.

The fact that some advocates are members of several issue-related groups increases the propensity that ideas and logistical requirements can be worked out between groups. In the case of the Mumia event, the speakers and musicians were chosen based on the resources of the small-group network, according to Joan:

Yeah, that's the second part. The first thing was to target cosponsors and participants for the event, which entails communication. Consider Mumia: who can we think of that would be interested in cosponsoring the event? Like black studies, peace studies, and contact the key people in these organizations. Identify these people, on some of them we had an inside line. If nobody knows these key people personally, who would feel comfortable getting in touch with them, and I think that came into play in organizing other events around Mumia, for instance the teach-in. Because we have moved from having about half the number of people who worked on Mumia 911, moving into the Mumia teach-in. So, these are people who don't have as many contacts, and that don't have the comfort feel with reaching out to different groups. . . . it's like a two-step process. First of all, make a bridge to another organization.

External Factors

External factors, such as the community context, can influence advocates' use of small-group communication. In some instances, the community context can influence the planning process that occurs in advocacy group meetings. In the Mumia group, the group decided not to have the Mumia event on a particular date because many people involved in the local anti–death penalty effort were involved in a number of other events that week. The Mumia support group considered sponsoring such an event after the students returned from the Christmas break. The group seemed to lean toward having the event the week of Martin Luther King Jr. Day in January. That way the event could be promoted at related events. A Mumia event would also bring to the fore that there is still substantial progress to be made on racial issues.

External factors can influence the ability of small advocacy groups to meet. For instance, the community dwindles in the summer in college towns. For one anti–death penalty group, this created difficulties for establishing an appropriate small-group meeting time, according to Joan: "This was in the summertime, which in a community like [this town], the university campus, the summer is a real downtime. It's a hard time to get organized, because so many other community connections are with the university." Likewise, locations for these small-group meetings were often dependent upon external sources for meeting locations. The time and location of small-group advocacy meetings must be arranged. In the instance of the Mumia group, meetings were dependent upon the local university that had facilities where the group could meet. The environmental coalition conducted their small-group meetings at a municipal property, and was, thus, dependent upon an external organization, the city, for its meeting place. In the case of the universal health care advocates in this study, small-group meetings were often held at Nancy's home, so this group was less dependent upon external institutions for a meeting place.

It should be noted that, as with other forms of communication, advocates used small-group communication in concert with other media uses. For example, one of the environmental coalition meetings was confirmed by three telephone conversations, an e-mail message, messages on answering machines, and interpersonal communication (relational communication). Ultimately, as with other media, advocates perceive the use of various media in conjunction with one another as the most effective approach.

Conclusion

In summary, advocates use small-group communication to perform a variety of functions, including increasing attendance at events, arranging logistical details, building community, lobbying, and educating the public. Advocates' use of small-group communication is influenced by these characteristics as well as internal and external factors. Characteristics of advocate group communication include the presence of feedback, multiple cues, language variety, and having a personal character. Advocates' use of small-group communication is influenced by internal group factors, including people power, knowledge, group history, and overlapping membership, all of which influence the ability of advocates to use group communication to engage others in effective communicative experiences. External factors, such as the community context, can influence advocates' use of small-group communication. This theory of advocate use of group communication reveals that advocates perceive that effective communicative experiences can be evoked with advocates and politicians through group communication.

5

Communicating at Events

There are a variety of events that advocates can use as a forum to disseminate their advocacy messages. While events differ from other media in their diversity and nature, they are a venue through which advocates seek to engage others through communication. Events can be considered media when using the definition of media as any means, agency, or instrumentality: as radio is a medium of communication, or simply, environment (*Webster's New Universal Unabridged Dictionary*, p. 1118). Advocacy events are clearly consistent with this definition. While not traditionally considered media, this book would be incomplete without a discussion of events that advocates organize and execute. These events feature various forms of communicative action and can also perform a metafunction: The event itself communicates. The event suggests: "This is important to us. We are willing to invest our time in this event. This issue is important enough to justify the expenditure of our time and resources." Advocates hope to engage event participants in effective communicative experiences.

Events can be the life-blood of a healthy advocacy community. For instance, most advocate communication revolves around preparation for events. An event is a happening (from the Latin *eventus*, an occurrence) during which advocates come together to engage in collective communication. In this chapter, I explore the uses of events by advocates by identifying the types of advocacy events, exploring the intended audience of events, the functions advocates perceive events perform, and factors that influence advocates' use of events.

Types of Event Media Communication

Although different from other media, events are actions through which advocates communicate. In an effort to identify forms of advocacy events, I will first look at types of events, including educational, political, and community events, civil action, and socializing events. Next I will identify the forms of communication used at advocacy events, such as public speeches, musical performances, poetry reading, storytelling, multimedia presentations, guerrilla theater, and disruptive tactics. Finally, I will look at communication tools used by advocates at events, which include signs, candles, literature tables, and public address systems.

There are a variety of types of events that advocates can use to spread advocacy messages. These include educational, political, community, civil action, and advocate socializing events. The inclusion of narrative accounts enriches this explication.

Educational Events

Advocates often organized and executed educational events. For instance, the advocates of universal health care often held educational programs at schools (after hours) and at churches. These programs usually featured speakers, panels, discussions, slide shows, and music. Tables containing literature were also present. Speakers were brought in for some educational events. At one point, the universal health care advocates arranged a visit to the community by Dr. Quentin Young, president of the National Association of Physicians for Universal Health Care. In the larger process of coalition activities for the advocacy of universal single-payer health care, these events were typical. Educational programs comprised the majority of events sponsored by the advocates of universal health care coverage. The universal health care advocates brought outside speakers into the local area for the educational activities.

The advocates for the abolition of the death penalty also held a number of educational programs every year. In one instance, Tony, the legislative coordinator of a statewide anti–death penalty organization and a prominent local advocate, organized an event to educate people about a specific death penalty case. At the presentation, he provided background and explained specific case details. Tony suggested that the most appropriate sentence for the accused was second-degree murder, which did not entail a capital punishment. Tony contended that there was good reason to believe that the killing was not premeditated. Tony pointed out that the governor had stopped seven executions during his tenure, but it was also noted that he had come under serious criticism from conservatives. The governor faced a senatorial race with a conservative republican, and anti–death penalty advocates feared that this would affect the willingness of the governor to reconsider death penalty cases. Tony encouraged folks to continue to communicate on behalf of the accused and also encouraged others to join in protests at the courthouse and the governor's mansion on the night of the execution, if there was no stay of execution.

In another case of anti–death penalty educational events, the Journey of Hope members toured the local community, appearing at a number of speaking engagements as well as at a rally at the capitol in conjunction with legislative advocacy to educate people about their experiences. Appearances at educational programs were their primary means of communication, although they also spent a considerable amount of time attempting to utilize mass media outlets. Although all of the Journey of Hope members had lost loved ones to murder, they remained, or even became, antideath penalty advocates.

Advocates also conduct teach-ins, which typically, in this community, consisted of a number of educational programs held on a single day. The idea behind the teach-in was to provide "alternative" classes that would address various aspects of the death penalty. Various organizations in the community would focus on different topics. Each would be responsible for a specific topic. For instance, the antideath penalty advocates in this community held several teach-ins during the course of this study. The antideath penalty coalition's use of teach-ins is an example of an education program. They were held all day at a central location at the university. There were a number of programs held on different but related topics throughout the day.

Political Events

Advocates can also use political events to communicate. In one instance, the coalition for universal health care organized a rally and a lobbying day at the state capitol. The group reserved a room to gather in the capitol building. The event featured speakers including leading advocates and legislators who supported the general goal of more government-guaranteed health coverage. Advocates engaged in guerrilla theater tactics as well as singing. The event also functioned as a news conference.

Another rally held at the state capitol against the death penalty was held in conjunction with lobbying efforts. A few activists from the central community in this study were present, but most of those attending the event were from other parts of the state. Activists had gathered from around the state for the legislative activity. In another instance of a political event, supporters of a death row inmate held a rally on the front steps of the capitol and presented videotape that contained a documentary that questioned the charges against the death row inmate.

The health care advocates also held events at the state capitol to help foster political support for their position. One such event featured speakers and guerrilla theater at the state capitol. These instances show that advocates repeatedly use legislative-targeted events. These political events are a central part of the efforts of advocates.

Community Events

Some events sponsored by advocates are designed to bring the larger community together. These events are aimed at a more general audience than many of the other events used by advocates. Abby, the informal chair of the Earth Day celebration in the community for several years, explained that part of the reason to hold the event was to bring the community together:

> Earth Day is about gathering together community. It's fine if the media come out and cover Earth Day, but for Earth Day, thousands of people come, and they get to experience it. It's an experiential event rather than a media event.

Earth Day is a more moderate event than most of the events organized by the advocates studied. However, the communication generated at the community Earth Day celebration reached a substantial number of people. Exact attendance is extremely difficult to estimate. According to the community United Way representative who was part of the Earth Day coalition committee, approximately seven thousand people attend the event. The main event sponsored by the environmental coalition, Earth Day, generated substantial local media coverage and word-of-mouth about the event.

At a community event like Earth Day, there are a variety of possible communication forms. In the case of the Earth Day celebration in this community, there were speakers on the stage, a teach-in, environmental games for the younger attendees, and many educational booths. Musicians and entertainers wove proenvironmental messages into their presentations.

Civil Action

The advocacy groups studied here used a variety of civil actions that could be categorized as protests, demonstrations, and rallies. While there are certainly overlapping areas between the concepts, there are some useful analytical distinctions. Protests are usually considered to be acts in opposition to a specific action, policy, or general policy direction. Demonstrations, on the other hand, are the showing of a position, but not necessarily in response to something. Rallies are more celebratory, affirming rather than negating. All three are civil actions that advocates can use to attempt to engage others in effective communicative experiences.

The anti–death penalty advocates in the community held a demonstration every Saturday in front of a post office. In one instance, the demonstrators gathered on a dark and stormy Saturday morning. Eight activists joined together to protest violent policies, most notably capital punishment. We each held a placard upon which was written a message of peace toward other human beings, such as: "Killing cannot stop killing." The group was protesting government-supported murder at whatever level, from war to capital punishment. The group has met regularly for many years, ready to communicate their opposition to governmental killing.

Those gathered at the post office were communicating. Their presence communicated their stand against government-funded killing. Those gathered also communicated through the signs they were holding. As nonactivists went in and out of the post office, they read the signs held by the anti–death penalty advocates. Some of those who passed by would smile and wave, as if approving of the messages. Others would frown. Drivers passing by would often honk their horns. Some nonactivists who were taking care of post office business would engage the activists in conversation, either in support of the activists or in opposition. In either case, the activists would engage the citizens in positive conversation. Matt, a prominent peace activist since the early 1960s who was associated with the Quaker religious group in the city, was an informal but functional leader of the group.

Advocates use protests to engage others in communication and used protest gatherings to communicate opposition to governmental action. In several instances, advocates gathered at the county courthouse to protest executions at 5:00 PM on dates the state was scheduled to execute prisoners. Protesters often gathered in front of a prominent landmark on the university campus. This was a public space, so the location was also the site for much traffic at that time, both vehicular and pedestrian.

Vigils are another form of advocacy communication, a type of protest used by advocates in this study. Vigils are solemn gatherings in protest of some specific governmental action, particularly the execution of inmates. Anti–death penalty advocates held a vigil at the governor's mansion on execution nights. In one case, it was a beautiful day in February. A man was scheduled to die. Oppositional communication was prevalent. The execution was supposed to take place just after midnight at the state penitentiary. The total number of attendees rose to between thirty-five and forty-five and ranged from young college students to retirees. Signs were provided to give those driving by an explanation for our presence and to provide communicatively rich television shots. There has been discussion at group meetings about the atmosphere of the vigils and whether it should be lively or solemn. The consensus arrived at during the group meetings was that the last ten minutes of the vigil would be silent.

This is a typical description of an antideath vigil. We stood lined up in front of the governor's mansion. There was a somber mood, although small talk between vigil participants was taking place. I tried to keep my conversation on the death penalty topic. At ten minutes before the scheduled execution, Matt went up and down the line and reminded everyone, quietly, that we wanted to be silent, because the execution of the prisoner was ten minutes away. Participants became reflective. After the execution time had passed, Matt called us down to the corner. He made a short statement about how we were sad that this happened and that it degraded all humanity. Matt then gave anyone the opportunity to express him- or herself. One person asked: "Why do they use our tax dollars to kill people?" Such vigils were very common among anti–death penalty advocates.

Advocates also organize rallies in support of issue positions and involve a more active environment than vigils, often including speakers and music. An example was a rally promoting universal single payer health care with a press conference at the state capitol in Jefferson City at which legislators and mass-media representatives were present. In another example, opponents to the execution of a Missouri man held a vigil on the front steps of the state capitol before delivering a documentary on the case to the governor.

Advocate Socializing Events

Advocates can also communicate during events that are primarily for socializing among the core group of activists. These events provide opportunities for advocates to socialize and consolidate the particular advocate community. One example was a pro–universal health care luncheon with Dr. Quentin Young. A number of members of the local coalition met and ate in a large meeting room at the First Presbyterian Church in this small Midwestern city. This event provided the opportunity for key members of contributing coalition organizations to meet Dr. Young before his scheduled public activities. The observed event took approximately ninety minutes.

The community of progressive advocates coordinated another socializing event on the day of the 2001 inauguration. The event was called the People's Inauguration Ball. The event was designed to bring together the left-of-center advocate community. Abby explained the community-building opportunity the event provided:

> This was valuable because it was bringing people together, giving people a sense of solidarity and mutual support. A sense of solidarity leads to empowerment. That's part of the reason why we do events that are just media events.

Thus, the goal of the event was to provide an opportunity for the community of like-minded advocates to share time and an experience together rather than communicate to a larger audience: "The inaugural ball was an event in and of itself whether or not it got news coverage. We did get media coverage, which was cool." Such socializing events can help consolidate the advocates in a particular community.

The anti–death penalty advocates also held such events. For instance, when Sister Helen Prejean came to the community in conjunction with the Journey of Hope, key supporters were invited to dine with her at a community convent. This dinner was primarily an opportunity for those who had invested time and effort in the public events to share a relaxing time with Sister Helen and the Journey of Hope members. In another instance, after the public appearances of these anti–death penalty advocates, those deeply involved gathered at a local pub to again spend relaxation time with Sister Helen and the members of the Journey of Hope. The purpose of this gathering was to relax and share time together rather than engage in task-related communication.

There were other socializing events held by advocates in the community scrutinized in this study. One of the major environmental groups in the community holds an annual potluck dinner with entertainment to celebrate community activism. At the dinner, the group recognized major contributors to the organization's efforts. The target audience of this event was the most active core of this environmental group.

The Earth Day coalition also has a dinner once a year a few weeks after the event. The dinner gave coalition members a chance to reflect on the larger accomplishment of holding the event and the opportunity to congratulate one another for the successful execution of many labor-intensive tasks involved with holding the event. While the primary purpose of the gathering is to celebrate those who spent much time and effort on Earth Day, the dinner also provided the opportunity for debriefing. The core coalition members discussed what went well as well as what could have gone better. These advocates then discussed ways in which problems could be avoided in the future. Thus, this socializing event, like other such events, provides an opportunity for multitasking; socializing is combined with reflection on how logistical requirements can be better met.

Parties can also be the location for socializing between advocates. At one party, a fellow advocate and I just hung out and shared death penalty–related stories. This activist was also a musician. I broke out a guitar to provide him the opportunity to share some of his music. I asked him if he performed any songs related to the death penalty. He said that it was one subject that he had not written a song about. I played and sang a chorus of a song called "They Laid Jesus in His Grave" by Woody Guthrie. I suggested that Jesus was an early victim of capital punishment. The activist asked if I had seen the current Amnesty International poster that featured the figure of Jesus hanging on the cross with the words: "Maybe the death penalty isn't such a good idea after all." I then handed the guitar back to the activist. The activist/musician then stated that he had written a song about being in jail. The song was a firsthand interpretation of sitting in a cell in Leavenworth "and not counting the days." Loneliness and purposelessness were the dominant themes of the song.

Socializing opportunities are important to the community of advocates. The core advocates of all of the groups studied here work hard together; but playing together was also valuable for the nurturing and maintenance of rich relationships between advocates.

Event Communication Forms

Advocates use several forms of communication during events. Ed described the variety of communicative forms that advocates utilize during events: "We listen to speakers, listen to music, participate in marches, share literature, talk to people of ideas." These include public speeches, musical performances, poetry reading, storytelling, multimedia presentations, guerrilla theater, and disruptive tactics.

Public Speeches

Public speakers are featured at all of the advocacy events studied. Darlene suggested that a public speech is more formal than the other available communicative forms that can be used at events: "A speaker is probably more formal. Everybody is quiet, and everyone is listening. It is usually longer." Joan perceived that poetry was more interesting for the audience than public speeches:

> I think a lot of times people will just tune out somebody that is orating . . . and especially if they don't know how to orate. Sometimes they sit there and drone on and on and on and on. I guess you could say the same thing with poets. Some of it's about oratory skills.

Speakers must be succinct to keep the attention of the audience at advocacy events, as Joan explained:

> It is not very often that you see someone who is a really good speaker unless they are somebody that is absolutely incredible like Martin Luther King or Malcolm X or, god forbid, Hitler. His oratory skills people still recognize as absolutely awesome.

Yet, in the over one hundred events studied, oratory was the main communicative form used at advocacy events.

Musical Performances

Advocates use music at events to communicate. For instance, music was a key feature at an anti–death penalty event at a coffeehouse. A number of performers shared their music at the event, and the songs often had lyrics or subtext that condemned the death penalty, and more specifically, the possible execution of Mumia.

Anti–death penalty advocates also used music at several events at the state capitol. When Sister Helen Prejean and the Journey of Hope advocates rallied outside the capitol and presented speeches in the capitol-building rotunda, two musical performers were also featured. Lenny lamented that abolition advocates did not feature music more often:

> Song is another possible way to communicate. Song, music, any communal act, at the vigil, I believe, transcends the group. Standing there is one thing, but I would've liked to have group interaction, like through singing a song. You were talking [to] each other, we are seeing each other, and we could have been even closer together [with music].

At a rally at a national anti–death penalty conference, a song was featured before speakers began. A song was also played as the marchers started for a federal courthouse. One advocate suggested that the rhythmic character of music is uniquely useful, according to Lenny:

> Drums and social movements . . . there is a communal thing about drumming. And we were wondering how effective it would be at a protest. Just to have a human heartbeat of the drum pumping. Until the execution was over. At that moment. That might bring another level of awareness about what's going on that wasn't there without it.

Music can be a valuable communicative form for advocacy events. Joan explained that music could be used in conjunction with other forms of communication used at events to set a positive tone for an event:

> If you hear a song, people might start to get into it. They might start clapping, they might start dancing, and they might start singing along. Music can be valuable because it is a great opener. It gets people, it tells people, "We are about to start an event. Please sit down in your seats and be quiet." Because many of these people that belong to these groups . . . and other groups, at a large gathering, there is a lot of chitchat . . . that is how you communicate with each other. And so, if a song is played, it usually

gets people to settle down. It is a great introduction to the event, because it can be topical, and tie into the event, and lead into the speaker.

Poetry Reading

Poetry can also be used to communicate during events. Darlene, a very active antideath penalty and environmental advocate, explained why poetry can be emotionally compelling:

> Poetry can be very powerful for people. Well, first of all, usually it's a speaker who is . . . someone into his or her own poetry. And so they put a lot of emotion and feeling into the reading of the poetry. It is something that you get, yelling when you need yelling, or quietness when you need quietness . . . usually the poetry is topical to the event you are going to, and it is an art form.

According to Flanders, an advocate who attends three or four anti–death penalty or environmental events a year, poetry, as well as other art forms, can provide communicative variety: "But I think stuff like poetry . . . rap . . . it's another way to communicate. Or even music. Or dance. Any of the art forms. It's a different way of delivering with a message." The juxtaposition between speakers and other communicative forms at advocacy events is perceived to help maintain the attention of the audience.

Storytelling

Storytellers can also be effective advocacy communicators at advocacy events. One very active advocate suggested that storytellers are effective because they pique the audience's interest: "Storytellers are wonderful about that. You think about the message that they carry in those stories and how. They'll have an audience and attention."

In one instance, storytelling was a communication form used at an anti–death penalty event. A storyteller told stories that were not related directly to Mumia or even the death penalty, but were rather metaphoric in their portrayal of the unequal treatment afforded minority folk.

Multimedia Presentations

Multimedia presentations can also be a useful communicative form at events. All three of the advocacy groups offered presentations that combine video, music, and speakers. One advocate described the use by anti–death penalty advocates:

One example with poetry is in an event for Pastors for Peace there was a certain performer who I worked with. . . . And I read poetry I had written while in Cuba. And showed slides with it. And it really gave people a sense of how we felt about the death penalty.

One of the most active advocates for universal health coverage commented: "The multimedia presentations sort of gave them a motive to go. Whether it's the songs or poems, my dance, or whatever it might be." The entertainment value of audio-visual presentations is perceived to contribute to the attractiveness of an event.

Guerrilla Theater

Guerrilla theater is a stripped down theatrical presentation of dramatic texts in nontraditional settings, such as on the street. Joan explained why such theater could be effective, that by enacting theatrical statements at events she hoped to engage audience members in a effective communicative experience: "Again, because it kicks down people's walls of perception. Kicks down the wall of everyday life. And sometimes when we have a shock like that, it really implants the issue in their minds." Thus, guerrilla theater can be a tool for advocacy communication, according to Tony: "There are alternative forms of communication that can also be valuable. For instance, mock executions can be staged to bring out the ugly side of the death penalty." This alternative form can present traditional advocacy ideas in new ways.

Nonconventional communicative forms such as street theater are available to advocates. One advocate, Joan, who frequently participated in such theater, contended that the form was very effective for communicating advocacy messages:

I think it is extremely effective. For instance, with street theater, we call it guerrilla theater, because we use it as a guerrilla tactic. We would not forewarn before announcements of our performances. What is a guerrilla tactic? You don't announce it. Because anyone who wanted to stop that action would be able to. Another thing with doing theater as guerrilla theater is that it maximizes disruption of the wall. We all go around with these walls around us and it is very easy to block something out. But if we have a really strong kick to it, and something as unexpected as seeing theater or poetry being performed in a public place opens people, you don't expect that. It can have a greater impact on breaking through people's walls.

Disruptive Tactics

The advocates studied here seldom engaged in disruptive tactics, although some anti–death penalty advocates may choose this form, as Joan explained:

"People involved with [our group] may use disruptive tactics, but that has nothing officially to do with [our group]. But members may partake in disruptive tactics." On one occasion, two of the advocates referred to in this book engaged in vandalism related to advocacy efforts. In another instance, at an unrelated event that featured the governor, advocates in this study used disruptive speech tactics. However, these were exceptions. While I have intentionally decided to underemphasize messages and focus on means in this book, the messages intended through disruptive tactics are obviously those of extreme opposition to a policy or state of affairs.

Event Communicative Tools

There are several tools that advocates use in conjunction with advocacy events. They include signs, candles, literature tables, and public address systems.

Signs

Signs are often used at many advocacy events. These signs usually consist of a short message written on poster board. Anti–death penalty, pro–universal health care, and pro-environmental advocates at various events used such signs during the course of this study. As a moderately active antideath penalty advocate explained, short messages are better suited to signs than long messages: "Signs can be used to communicate short messages at events."

When I got to one event, I chose a placard (hand-held sign) from a stack that had been brought by another advocate. It said: "Executing human beings demeans humanity." All protest participants held a sign. Matt had a number of signs that he brought to such occasions with a variety of slogans. These gave those passing in cars or on foot at this busy intersection a clear idea of what we were protesting.

At another antideath penalty event, advocates communicated through a giant banner, which was to be sent to government officials and Mumia. Upon arrival, a key leader in the event approached me to sign it. She recognized me and invited me by name to sign the banner. While the banner signing may have been of low real politic value, it was a way to include me in the community of those attending the event, and the assumed hope was that Mumia's morale would be bolstered by the idea that we were fighting for him.

Some advocates believe that signs can turn some people off. Darlene felt that signs embarrassed some people:

> The general public is scared of people with signs. They are yelling at them. They are afraid of people with signs because they are embarrassed. That is why. They are

embarrassed because they think, we have been taught, and social norms, and you don't stand and hold a sign and chant a phrase. And it is embarrassing to people, and that is why they fear it.

Another advocate, Ed, doubted that complex issues could reasonably be simplified enough to fit on such a sign:

I think too often people can try to boil down any issue to sound bites. That can make the people involved look uninformed. Or reactionary . . . because it's difficult to talk about global warming on a placard. . . . I think I would be reluctant to try to encapsulate my views in such a limited medium. That I would want more space to define what I'm trying to get at; what I'm trying to communicate. I would rather be able to communicate in that.

The advocate was primarily referring to his environmental beliefs, and granted that on some issues, such signs may be effective:

But on the death penalty issue, it is a different thing. To say "We don't have the right to take someone's life," might be something you can put on a placard. That can be easy to phrase.

Thus, while there are some perceived limitations to the usefulness of hand-held signs, they can be valuable tools for communicating advocacy messages.

Candles

Candles are featured at some advocacy events, especially vigils such as those held at the governor's mansion to protest executions. Tony supported bringing a candle to the vigil, as it communicates a solemn sincerity.

Literature Tables

Literature tables were usually featured at the events sponsored by death penalty abolitionists, universal health care advocates, and environmentalists. They provided an opportunity to share relevant literature as well as establish new personal contacts, as discussed in chapter 6. There is almost always a table of literature at advocacy events. Field notes reveal that the presence of literature tables enabled more networking among advocates. Literature tables seem to be a necessary feature of activist events. They are a way to distribute more in-depth information about advocacy activities for those who seek it.

Public Address Systems

Public address systems were often used at advocacy events to amplify the audio components of event communication. For instance, at the events held by advocates of universal health care, some sort of public address equipment was also usually present.

The sound system is a vital element for any large successful advocacy event. The lack of an effective public address (PA) system can be detrimental to an advocacy event. The PA is a communication channel; if that channel breaks down, communication fails. Public address systems are often used at anti–death penalty events. At one anti–death penalty rally at the state capitol, Tony took the microphone and thanked all those who were in attendance. He then acknowledged the wide range of organizations involved in the event as well as the various locations from around the state from which participants had come. He then alerted those involved that there were prepared signs to carry and encouraged marchers to use one. The organizer then turned the microphone over to the St. Louis organizer. In countless instances such as this, advocates use electric PA amplification systems, rather than, say, bullhorns.

In summation, advocates use several forms of communication during events, including public speeches, musical performances, poetry reading, storytelling, multimedia presentations, guerrilla theater, and disruptive tactics. There are also various tools that advocates can use to communicate at events, including signs, candles, literature tables, and public address systems. These varying communicative modalities contribute to the formulaic richness at advocacy events. These communicative forms can be used in conjunction with one another to make events more effective in the evocation of emphatic communicative experiences.

Intended Audience

Intended audiences of advocacy events include other advocates, members of the general population, politicians, and media personnel. Advocates intend to communicate with other advocates at events. This is the primary audience of most events. Community events such as Earth Day are targeted to a larger audience than many other events organized by advocates. As a result, organizers attempt to avoid more controversial subjects in their programming. Nevertheless, these events provide an opportunity for advocates to communicate with large numbers of people. Political events are primarily targeted at government officials. As evident in the discussion of the function of facilitating mass media coverage, media personnel are also an intended audience of event communication. For instance, the pro–universal health care events were intended to reach other advocates. Advocates were the predominant audience at such events. The general public was the intended audience of vigils at the governor's mansion. Advocates intended to communicate to people who passed by the events. They hoped to reach this audience indirectly through coverage conferred by mass media outlets in the region. Politicians were also an intended audience of advocate events. For instance, a local state representative attended a screening of the antideath penalty documentary produced by Vincent, Sebastian, and myself, and spoke in support of the documentary after the screening at a local cinema. In another example related to the documentary, advocates hoped to gain the attention of mass media personnel through their delivery of the documentary to the governor and the rally that preceded that delivery of the tape.

Functions of Advocacy, Uses of Advocacy Events

Advocates perceive that events perform several functions, including arranging logistical details, educating the general public, recruiting other advocates, lobbying, community building, and facilitating mass media coverage.

Arranging Logistical Details

Advocates use events as opportunities to arrange some logistical details for future events. For example, some anti–death penalty protests were held between 5:00 and 6:00 PM at a county courthouse on a day that an inmate was to be executed. At these events, there was communication about logistical requirements for further communication. Some discussion centered on the carpooling to the governor's mansion at 10:00 PM.

Educating the General Public

Educational events are used to increase advocates' knowledge about their issues and activities. For instance, members of the Journey of Hope, while in this particular local community, shared their realization that forgiveness is a powerful emotion for healing. Through such local efforts they were likely educating millions of people a year about their experiences as they attempted to persuade the U.S. public to accept the abolition of the death penalty. In this community, hundreds of people were exposed to their messages.

Recruiting Other Advocates

Advocate events offer opportunities to recruit advocates. Joan explained that the use of literature tables at advocate events offered a communicative opportunity for persuading people to become involved in advocacy activities:

Well, one thing is to get their literature out. To make people aware of who they are, what issues they are working on, and to give them an opportunity to have new members. Have more bodies get involved in their organization.

In the case of citizens who expressed support at civil action events, the activist encouraged the supportive citizen to join in the protest.

Lobbying

Community events can also provide an opportunity to communicate with elected officials. For instance, elected officials who were sensitive to the environmental issue were visible at the Earth Day celebration and were approachable at this event. Darlene described the dynamic of this interaction:

> I do see a particular politician at many of the community events I go to. She seems like a great person. But every time I am with her, she is usually lobbying for a vote, and I'm usually lobbying for whatever the issue is, for that organization. So I have lobbied her informally, although I've never gone through her office.

Building Community

Field notes recorded during a number of such events indicate that participation is perceived by advocates to increase a sense of community. For instance, my field notes reveal that when I participated in a weekly demonstration against the death penalty on Saturday morning at the post office, a feeling of belonging did arise in me. I felt like I belonged, that I was united in purpose with these other people. Those who knew me expressed welcoming gestures, smiles, and a good word. When I apologized for showing up late, several comments were offered to make me feel as if I were totally welcome no matter what time it was. A prominent activist, an apparent leader of the group identified earlier in these notes, stated in a very sarcastic and supportive tone: "You have to be on time!" He had a huge, welcoming grin on his face, emphasizing his sarcasm. In a loose group of activists who are compelled to action by conscience, discipline-concerning issues such as tardiness was antithetical to the nature of the gathering. It would seem to require a strong resolution to stand in a small group, in the rain, on a cold autumn morning. This common will fostered a sense of community among the participants.

Advocacy events promote community. Many events contribute to a feeling of community between participating advocates. The community of likeminded activists is formed and strengthened through the different types of events used by advocates. An event such as the one opposing the execution of Mumia Abu-Jamal provided such a communal feeling. The community of death penalty opponents as well as Mumia supporters could gather together and participate in an event that allowed the communication of opposition to the death penalty. In addition, good turnout at events contributed to good morale among advocates. Thus, successful events contributed to communal resolve. One extremely involved advocate who was also a musician described the emotional impact of contributing her music to collective action in opposition to the death penalty:

> After one particularly effective rally, I felt a strong sense of belonging. Alienation was gone. I felt like a part of a community. I was experiencing what felt like an almost . . . spiritual calm. I spoke about the event at the other six shows I played that week, although they were all paying gigs in businesses, bars, and restaurants.

The interpersonal communication between participants in events such as the vigils at the governor's mansion fostered a communal sense between participants. Talking about why protesters participated in the event helps nurture a sense of camaraderie and community. It also provides opportunity for further communicative contact.

Other events, such as community events, can bring together larger segments of the community members who support a general idea. In the case of Earth Day, the general idea is that a healthy, natural environment is a good thing. The people in the community at large who found this idea agreeable gathered for the celebration.

Advocates perceive that there are effective communication strategies that can be utilized during coalition praxis in the form of events. Inviting as many key members as possible to communicate during events increases commitment to the event by that individual, and indirectly, their contributing organization. As Joan suggested:

> We gave organizations the opportunity to announce their upcoming events. When their meetings are. I've always believed that cosponsorship allows the opportunity for everyone to communicate more. It is absolutely a good thing. It may get more people involved. They may not believe that this organization, other organizations that are cosponsors in the event are necessarily for them, but other organizations participating may look appealing. It gives people more opportunity to choose from the groups. They might not decide to join *a, b,* or *c,* but [they] might choose over there.

Providing an opportunity for audience members to ask questions can be a valuable opportunity for more two–way communication. For instance, at an anti–death penalty teach–in at a university, a question-and-answer session was a valuable opportunity for audience members to express themselves. At the teach-in, more than half of the remarks at the panel discussion were statements rather than questions. At another educational anti–death penalty program, Tony opened the floor for questions. Question-answer sessions of such meetings are opportunities for people to air their opinion as well as solicit information. Question-answer opportunities are a means for people to express themselves, although the value of such communication may be expressive rather that valuable for information's sake.

Statements of acknowledgment and thanks to those who contributed logistical support are important during an advocacy event. Personal narratives can provoke emotive communicative experiences. Gathering member data at events can be used for future mobilization. Information concerning future activities can be effectively disseminated at an advocacy event.

Protests can bring advocates together, as Joan explained:

> Civil action is, supposed to be, a communal action between separate folks, who earned harmony about how they feel about the issues. This is democratic action and its route. This is people getting up and saying no.

Participation in protests can be a powerfully emotional experience and differs from writing a letter to your congressional representative, as Darlene explained:

> It is way different [from writing a letter to an elected official] . . . it is totally different. Because when you're protesting, you are so into it. You are feeling emotions, powerful emotions. It is like being at a revival! And you are . . . you are all stirred up and passionate. You are yelling, and you are chanting, and you have your signs, and you are walking and you're trying to convince people strongly, that is something you believe in. It is powerful.

Involvement in civil action can increase a sense of self-actualization, the feeling of advocates that they were enacting their opinion in an emotionally genuine and satisfying way. Ed, a truck driver who is an active participant in three to four environmental and anti–death penalty events a year, explained the emotionally compelling experiences of participation in civil action:

> We used protest as a means to communicate because it was fun. For a lot of people, it was very immediate. Direct and immediate and there was a feeling of self-gratification. To do the protest . . . you felt like you were really doing something here and now. Not just writing off some letter to some congressmen, just part of a letter tally, or in the recycling bin.

As advocates unite together in such self-actualizing praxis, strong bonds are formed between advocates.

Interpersonal communication between protesters can strengthen advocates, as Lenny (an advocate/sociologist) explained:

Interpersonal contact at the event . . . I think something happens . . . for me as a sociologist, it is Durkhiem's mechanical solidarity. When people get together for [a] purpose, a moral purpose, with reason, it takes action, you know, they're making a very clear and bold statement. It is very strong bonding. It's good for yourself too, because you have to make the decision, you have to make a commitment.

There was even community building going on in cars on the way to events, as advocates spent time building bonds through communicative interaction.

Facilitating Mass Media Coverage

Advocates perceived that events could facilitate mass media coverage. Protests are often deemed newsworthy by mass media personnel and receive coverage. One advocate believed that this expanded the range of the impact of the communication. An alternate image is being placed before the audience, which would not normally be there, that would not exist if it were not for this civil action.

For instance, anti–death penalty advocates held rallies and news conferences in conjunction with lobbying efforts. It was able to gain the attention of the mass media through the release of a study of the history of the death penalty in Missouri. The coalition organized a lobbying day as an opportunity to converse with state legislators and was able to promote the two events and gain the attention of local television outlets.

These signs were also a good way to communicate through pictures (television news or the newspaper). Sound bites are a prominent feature of television news. The best media advocate communicators are those who can provide cogent, informing sound bites. As sound bites are important, so are sign bites.

Sometimes protests can be successful with little publicity, as Lenny explained:

There wasn't much around campus [about the event]. I didn't hear about it until late in the afternoon. Even though there was not a lot of publicity about it, it was one of the biggest gatherings they have had for a while. Something is happening. There is a current that has not been there before, right now is present in the way that I haven't seen. I don't know why. People are acting.

On the other hand, there can be much mention of advocate events in the mass media news programming. The main event sponsored by the environmental coalition generated substantial local media coverage, according to Ed:

Protest provided a way to get the word out to people who wouldn't attend a press conference. If you walk into the student center, you couldn't help but see the protesters. You had no choice. If you can get the media there, all the better.

Protests can be a valuable tool for the dissemination of advocacy messages because they may attract media attention. This was the case for a protest against the execution of a prisoner at a county courthouse. It was fortunate I arrived early. One of the local television outlets was going to go live to a remote at the courthouse at 5:00 PM. Only a few of the advocates had gathered before 5:00, so my presence helped increased the number.

Matt was interviewed for the television news program about thirty yards from us and motioned for us to move behind him so the camera would pick us up. Matt perceived that by having the bulk of the group in the background of the television news shot, the advocates could better use the television to engage viewers in an effective communicative experience

One of the protesters mentioned that he hated when we had to adjust our activities to fit the media, rather than the media just covering what we did. But he also said that more people would possibly see our signs if we reacted to the location of the television camera.

At a protest vigil at the governor's mansion against an execution of a Missouri man, a remote television truck for a local station pulled up. In my mind, our efforts would be legitimized by the mass-media coverage. We would be part of the polis, the larger discourse of the regional community. Through television, our message would be amplified. People who saw us on television would again, hopefully, be provoked into asking themselves whether they supported the death penalty and why. Self-reflection seems to be an important goal of such communication. Through the mass media, maybe we can provoke such introspection.

The media personnel unpacked an extensive production set-up for a live remote at the governor's mansion at midnight. I was down at the opposite end from the reporter and cameras, so I didn't hear her words, but a member of a local Amnesty International (AI) chapter said she seemed to oppose the death penalty. For instance, at one point the report, according to the AI member, said: "Governor Holden had an opportunity to step up tonight . . . but he didn't." A larger number of participants displayed on television news programs may legitimize the action and the cause.

Factors That Influence Advocates' Use of Events

The factors that influence advocates' use of events include characteristics of events, internal group factors, and external factors. These influence the ability of advocates to engage others in effective communicative experience through use of events.

Characteristics of Events

Because events contain a variety of modalities of expression (including public speeches, musical performances, poetry reading, storytelling, multimedia presentations, guerrilla theater, and disruptive tactics, as well as various tools such as signs, candles, literature tables, and public address systems), advocates use events whenever there is adequate gumption and logistical resources. Because events can contain all of the characteristics discussed in this book, advocates' use of events is influenced by the rich characteristic potential of advocacy events.

Internal Group Factors

Consistent with the theoretical ideas explored in this book, internal group factors that influence advocate use of events include people power, financial resources, access to logistical resources, knowledge, group history, and overlapping membership. Advocates perceive that these factors influence advocate ability to engage people in moving communicative experiences through events.

People Power

There are a number of ways in which the planning, preparation, and execution of events requires people power. Several examples in this discussion reveal that people power is a necessary precursor to making advocacy events happen. All events require some planning, and planning requires people power and resources. In the preparatory communicative stages, communication reveals common ground among organizations. Effective communication is also dependent upon the people power required to reach out to other advocacy groups to make an event happen, according to Nancy, a leading universal health care advocate:

> We reached out to these groups, so you know that they are going to see some of the same things you do and feel the same way that you do about that. Now, like I said, it depends on the event that you're going to do and your timelines for those events as to whether you can have all of these groups [be involved].

People power is required to contact key advocates in the community in efforts to check interest, dates, and so forth. Key leaders on the issue in the community must be contacted in efforts to solicit interest. A number of advocates are often necessary to deal with logistical matters. Communication through community networks is an important advocacy communication channel. People power is required to procure a venue and get the word out. One advocate chose to participate in an event after an announcement of the Saturday morning gatherings in a local anti–death penalty newsletter provoked her interest. Communication of commitment to achieve an advocacy goal is a motivational precursor to expenditure of people power.

People power influences advocates' use of events. If there is not adequate people power, an event will not happen. Even one or two advocates can provide the people power necessary to initiate advocacy action. There are a variety of tasks to accomplish in preparation for an advocacy event. These include communication with other related organizations to identify appropriate dates, times, locals, and themes. Some advocates perceive that the amount of people power expended influences advocates' ability to effectively organize events. Matt said that he thought the recent success in mobilizing anti–death penalty advocates was the result of community communication. We talked about all the good communication that was going on, through press, e-mails, newsletters, phone calls, and other media uses. Matt said ads in several regional newspapers helped generate attention and thought the phone tree was most effective for getting out the more active persons.

Don, the Amnesty International member, said that the campus AI chapter learned of the execution and protests from Tony's primary anti–death penalty group newsletter. Matt was very happy about that. Often, the effectiveness and costs of such ventures like the newsletter must be considered. AI's comments validated the expense to Matt. He commented that Tony had sent out over one thousand of them, and it was good to know that the newsletter had real impact.

During the promotion of events, uses of some media snowball. Field notes indicate I received an e-mail from AI that mentioned an upcoming execution. According to the AI member, it seemed the newsletter led to AI's e-mail communication.

Matt commented at one point that the state capital had a strong Catholic community, and that there were many anti–death activists who traditionally participated in that denomination, so that helped explain the good number of folks that showed up at the vigil at the governor's mansion.

As outlined throughout the other chapters, a variety of media can be utilized to promote an event. One anti–death penalty and environmental advocate who attends four to five events a year explained how he heard about a particular event: "My neighbor told me about the event. I also think I saw an ad for it in the university newspaper. I also saw a flier on campus." People power was expended to spread the word. However, as articulated in those chapters, available people power can influence advocates' use of events.

Financial Resources

Financial resources are also necessary for some advocate events. The logistical costs associated with the tasks discussed in the section on people power also require money for gasoline, paper, permits, telephone calls, and so forth. At events such as Earth Day, sound equipment and personnel have to be hired. Financial resources influence advocates' ability to use events.

Access to Logistical Resources

Access to logistical resources can influence the ability of advocates to effectively use events to engage people in effectively emphatic, communicative experiences. For instance, public address systems can be a required logistical resource for many events.

At events, if the public address system is not properly operated, it can hinder event communication. One anti–death penalty event started late; public address equipment problems delayed the beginning of the event by thirty minutes. At the end of the wait, organizers did not get the PA running, but decided to commence anyway. Not only did the wait possibly harm the morale of the crowd, but also the lack of an effective PA made it very difficult to hear various speakers and performers. Some advocates perceive that adequate attention should probably be paid to the PA equipment before the event, so as to not derail the natural momentum of the event. At some events, audiotapes can be run through the sound system. At a rally in support of a death row inmate, organizers featured several types of communication forms. Initially, an audio tape was played on the stage that featured Mumia telling his story. This pre-taped message was about twenty-five minutes long and explained the dubious circumstances around Mumia's conviction and fight for appeals.

Access to logistical resources is required to provide the sound system at advocacy events. For example, I was responsible for the sound system at a number of advocacy events during this study. I had made a commitment to other activists. I felt that it was the most important thing at that time not to let my fellow advocates down, because I was the individual who had access to logistical resources. There was an element of peer approval. Commitments made to other advocates and a desire to fulfill those obligations can be an important source of gumption or the encouragement to follow through. While my conscious motivation to be involved derived from ethical considerations, during these moments, commitment to the community of activists was my primary concern.

PA problems can be significant for the effectiveness of an event. If the PA does not project with adequate volume, the speaker will not be heard. If levels are set too high, feedback may result. Few things disrupt the concentration of a group of gathered advocates like the piercing ring of feedback. Another significant issue is timing; the PA must be ready when an event is scheduled to begin. In this case, in which the rally was the first of a number of events, the delay in PA operation would have thrown off a whole day's scheduled events.

Knowledge

Consistent with the theory of advocacy media use, knowledge about required tasks is a necessary internal factor in the execution of effective communicative experiences. Allocation of other resources, particularly people power, requires knowledge of communicative possibilities and sensitivity to what has empirically been judged as effective. For example, the Earth Day committee based many of its decisions on what had worked or not worked in the past. While this was based on the sometimes flawed recollections, such intuitive empirical knowledge provided the basis of decisions about how Earth Day would be organized.

Group History

Group history is also a very important factor that influences how advocates utilize various events and is the source of much knowledge. The history of the groups that sponsor an event influences the execution of the event. Ed explained the habitual tendencies that develop within the institutional assumptions:

> The history of those members probably influences their use of protest. Certainly the choices that they made affected the membership of the group. There were some people who didn't feel comfortable in that environment. It may not have made them stop coming to all functions but contributed to decreases in attendance at some events.

Such events require planning, knowledge, and logistical resources. Previous experiences with these program forms can be a strong basis for effective education presentations. Experts with the applicable knowledge developed in previous advocacy efforts are necessary for the substance of the program.

Effective communication strategies for planning coalition events are perceived to require several things, including initial honest communication about goals and the resources available. Organizational roles are negotiated through communication in planning stages. Complete communication must be enacted in the final planning stages to facilitate maximum attendance. Adequate intergroup communication requires adequate time for planning.

Overlapping Membership

Interviews revealed that overlapping membership of groups involved in health care advocacy influenced the use of events. Nancy explained that the location of an event was influenced by other advocate activities of the health-care advocates:

> Because they had a 6:30 meeting with the legislators just down the street at the housing development corporation. They said you got to have it close by or we won't come because we will be cutting our meeting so close. We wanted to have a 7:00 meeting. Wilma said go to Douglas and then we'll zip down there two blocks and come in.

In this case, advocates who were involved in advocacy of universal health care had another unrelated advocacy meeting at a different location prior to the event in support of universal health care. The organizer of the universal health care event scheduled the meeting at a location close to the other event in an effort to accommodate these advocates who were members of both groups.

Teresa, an active leader of the university chapter of AI, explained that information she received due to her activity in the national AI efforts influenced her initiative to organize an event due to activity at the national level:

> Well, when I've worked on most events, it's usually with one group moving out to see other organizations to cosponsor. With the Mumia event, I actually found [out] about the Mumia 911 call of action, national day when I was in Cleveland back in June.

Advocates get ideas for events from networking with affiliated groups in other geographical areas. In one instance, Nancy, the leader of the local universal health care advocacy efforts, got the idea of sponsoring a national spokesperson on the issue after she learned through communication with universal health care advocates from other areas around the state that the national figure was touring through the region. In another instance, a member of the Mumia anti–death penalty group was informed about an idea for a local event from national communication: a National Day for Call to Action. This provided the impetus to reach out to other groups in an attempt to establish an intergroup network effort (coordination communication between small groups, much of it conducted in small group settings) in support of a man on Pennsylvania death row. Michelle, an undergraduate student and an officer in the local AI chapter, explained:

> We wanted to do a solidarity thing. What I started doing was throw the lines out to people that I know in organizations working on issues and death penalty and whatever

for instance like [Tony] with FOR. From there I began learning of other people
working in or who had an interest in, which had worked with Mumia's case.

In this case, an ad hoc small group was formed to focus on this particular case.
The initiating advocate learned about related national events from communicating with other groups. Joan, the intensely active advocate (fifteen events a
year) for a range of social justice issues, concurred with Michelle, agreeing that
the networking between the local group and the national organization was a
catalyst for a particular event:

> Well, in this case, we already had a date, the National Day for Call to Action, Septem-
> ber 11. So, we managed to get in touch with different people that we already knew
> or that had heard about it from other people. We just set up a time that would be
> good to get together.

In this case, networking with national organizations helped advocates come
up with a rationale for an event. Information sharing between organizations
contributed to preplanning advocacy activity.

External Factors

Communication among local, state, and national coalition units can facilitate
idea formulation. In one instance, a member of an anti–death penalty group
was informed about an idea for a local event from national communication, as
revealed in the above example. Don suggested growth in local anti–death penalty advocacy was partially the result of the recent shift in national politics.
Students who believed in this cause (as well as others) say that if they didn't
communicate for themselves, no one else would. He noted an increase lately
in AI attendance and activity.

　　In sum, characteristics of events, internal group factors, and external factors
influence advocates' use of events. Internal group factors that influence the use
of events include people power, knowledge, financial resources, access to logistical resources, group history, and overlapping membership. Advocates perceive that external factors influence advocate use of events. Advocates perceive
that these factors influenced advocate use of these communicative means.

Conclusion

In this chapter, I have discussed different types of advocacy events, event communication forms, and communicative tools, including signs, candles, litera-

ture tables, and public address systems, that are used by advocates at events. Advocates perceive that events perform several functions, including arranging logistical details, increasing awareness, recruiting other advocates, lobbying, community building, and facilitating mass media coverage. I also discussed the necessary resources needed to organize advocacy events. Internal group factors that influence advocate use of events include people power, knowledge, financial resources, access to logistical resources, group history, and overlapping membership. Political context was perceived to be an external factor that influenced advocate ability to use events. Advocates perceive that these factors influenced advocate ability to engage people in effective and emotionally engaging communicative experiences through the use of events.

6

Using Paper

It is just important to get information, to get thoughts in people's hands. A lot of times people leave an event and maybe they missed some of the key presentations or the whole event. The oral word in our society doesn't stay with people quite as long as the written word. So, just like if I have a choice of getting something in any medium, I would rather have them get a newspaper as opposed to others because the written word is just . . . you have a chance to transfer it on, people can pick up some literature, read it themselves, pass it on to someone else. If they feel moved by it they make copies of it and spread it around.

This comment from Tony reveals the perceived importance of printed communication in social and political movement campaigns. Since the invention of written language, and especially due to the evolutionary momentum of Gutenberg's printing press, paper communication forms have been important communicative media. This is not only true for communication in general, but also for advocates. In an effort to increase understanding of these uses, I will first describe the various forms of paper communication media that are utilized by advocates to disseminate their messages. I will then identify the intended audiences of advocates' use of paper communication. Third, I will explicate the intended functions of this use of paper communication. Finally, I explore factors that influence advocates' uses of paper communication, including use characteristics, internal group factors, and external factors. Consistent with the theoretical ideas presented in this book, these considerations increase our understanding of how advocates use printed communication to engage receivers in effective communicative experiences.

Forms of Paper Media

This construction of a theory of activist use of paper communication begins with an identification of the forms of paper communication used by advocates and discussion of the various means advocates use to disseminate their messages. Advocates use a number of forms of paper media to disseminate messages, including newsletters, fliers, handbills, pamphlets, letters, petitions, table tents, and adhesive stickers. Advocates perceive that in some cases paper communication can engage readers in moving communicative experiences.

Newsletters

The environmental coalition and the anti–death penalty advocates sent out newsletters to those who expressed interest in those issues. Abby explained he perceived that paper communication such as newsletters could be an educational tool:

> We send the [newsletter] out because it's a chance to reach people who are interested. A chance to change people's perceptions of issues, and get them information and hopefully, help catalyze transformation. It's an educational vehicle to educate people on our issues.

The anti–death penalty advocates also mailed out minutes from the organizational meetings. Rather than just a record of discussion at the meeting, the mailing was written in a newsletter form. This smaller newsletter, called "Meeting Notes," was on one side of a standard sheet of yellow paper folded into thirds. The newsletter featured news on upcoming events, news about legislative efforts, and featured five phone numbers, including the organizational headquarters and two numbers for the governor. The publication also listed a mailing address for the anti–death penalty organization and provided the Web site address. This was perceived by these advocates to be an effective reminder of upcoming advocacy events. The major organization in the Earth Day coalition also distributed a quarterly newsletter. The newsletter was sent to other related organizations.

Smaller newsletters were used to supplement the less frequent production and distribution of a larger newsletter. Tony explained that advocates' use of a smaller newsletter reflected perceptions about what readers wanted:

> We send out a smaller newsletter in between major mailings. Less information gets out this way. It is a ledger-size sheet of paper, with four pages, and is folded in half, so you have the front cover the back cover and the inside. And you keep it down to a lot less information, but we have found that a lot of people are more likely to read that than the large newsletter.

Advocates have a variety of forms for a newsletter. One choice is size. Ed, who participated in three or four environmental events and anti–death penalty events a year for the past fourteen years, explained that a newsletter can be small: "The newsletter can just be both sides of one page. It doesn't have to be big." This saves resources. It also makes it easier for people to read the entire document, according to some advocates. One characteristics of newsletter communication is that it requires reading time on the part of the recipient. This has influenced the decision by the anti–death penalty advocates to produce and distribute a smaller newsletter. Previously, they used large newsprint paper, as Tony explained:

> More people read this smaller newsletter cover to cover. It may depend upon the setting. But you have to be real devoted to make it through the longer newsletters. I never ever read whole newsletters that I get from another particular group. I never get around to all that, even if I am kind of interested. . . . I'll read it during an evening meal. I mean if I had the time I would. . . . The sad reality is that our lives do not afford us much time to continue to educate ourselves. We have to survive. People are out, typically, doing their minimum wage job, slaving away for corporate Joe, who really has no other option, and when they get home they are spent. They don't have time to do reading. Or they chill out with TV, or whatever.

The decision to use a photocopied newsletter rather than a larger newsletter on newsprint was influenced by the time constraints of the intended audience. Tony perceived that many readers did not consume the entire larger newsletter. Thus, smaller newsletter forms were sometimes used.

Fliers

Fliers were also part of the discussion in many of the small group meetings of the advocacy groups studied here. The environmental group wanted to make sure that fliers had been placed in all appropriate places and double-checked that all areas of the campus were covered and that other schools in the area had been "fliered." Darlene suggested such paper communication could be displayed in a variety of locations: "Posted fliers, at local businesses, on the kiosks downtown, at schools, at restaurants and other places." Fliers were often placed on kiosks in this community. These kiosks were column-like billboards at several locations in the downtown area that were designed as an appropriate place to post fliers. An announcement on a flier on a kiosk downtown contained the time, date, location, the primary organizational group, and very brief information about Mumia. The flier also contained information about who would appear at the event.

Fliers are usually 8½ by 11–inch posters that include information and graphics related to a specific event. For instance, Lana, a municipal employee and an environmental advocate, explained that fliers could be distributed in a variety of places, such as educational institutions: "We usually send out a batch of fliers to a number of organizations that we are in contact with, such as schools, pre-schools, and child care givers."

Leaflets

Leaflets, also referred to as handbills, usually take the form of smaller copies of fliers. They contain basic information about upcoming events and usually incorporate some visual variety.

Pamphlets

Pamphlets are usually a standard size paper that is folded in thirds and displays information on each side of the page. A pamphlet is often about more than one topic. There is obviously less space on a pamphlet than in a newsletter. Size is a factor. Ed explained that a pamphlet provided more information than other paper communication forms such as postcards: "You would have more space on a pamphlet than on a postcard." All three advocacy groups studied here used pamphlets at some point during the duration of this study.

Letters

Advocates also use letters to communicate. In this study, letters were used to contact politicians as well as inmates on death row. For instance, Josh, a lawyer for the IRS in Kansas City, wrote a letter to the governor of a state asking to stay a particular execution after learning about the case through a video documentary and discussing the case with other advocates. An Earth Day–coalition committee used letters to thank those who assisted with logistical resources.

Petitions

Advocates also communicate through petitions. For instance, during the premier of a film, *Unreasonable Doubt*, portraying a man about to be executed for a crime he likely did not commit, Amnesty International advocates solicited signatures for petitions to the governor to spare the life of an individual on death row. All three advocacy groups used petitions that gave signatories the opportunity to communicate with political officials.

Table Tents

Table tents are pieces of paper or cardboard that are folded into a triangle so they can sit up when placed on a hard surface such as a tabletop. An environmental advocate who was also a municipal employee described the utility of paper table tents:

> We used to do those little table tents. Those little foldouts on tables . . . , at the univer-
> sity. But it has not been happening lately. I think it was the student Sierra Club, or
> the Earth Day group, on campus that did that, then, and it might have been that the
> policy changed in the dining halls or something. The table tents could be good
> because you're sitting there eating, you know, you're kind of a catcher audience. If
> people are sitting around, and don't have something else going on, if they have some-
> thing in front of them [they] will read it. Even a soup can. The cereal box. It may not
> be interesting, but you are there, you're eating, you might as well do something, I
> guess we're all naturally multitaskers or something. And then they can take it with
> them too, if they really want to.

Table tents provided an imaginative way for advocates to reach audiences at unique times.

Adhesive Stickers

Other printed communication forms such as bumper stickers and other adhesive paper are perceived to be useful. Lana explained that these unconventional
paper forms could be a convenient way to reiterate advocate messages:

> Decals . . . I always think that it's good to have a little something that people can take
> away with them. So they can stick on the refrigerator, or put it in their pocket, or
> something like that, so that, when they ask, "When was that happening?" they can
> pull it out and have facts.

Advocates use such stickers to spread their messages. These messages are often
terse statements designed to communicate with fellow drivers.

In sum, a number of forms of paper communication that advocates use
include newsletters, fliers, handbills, pamphlets, letters, petitions, table tents,
and adhesive stickers. However, as discussed in the next section, there are a
number of ways that these forms of paper communication can be distributed.

Means of Distribution

Advocates can deliver paper communication through several methods. Abby
explained some of these:

> There are a bunch of advocate activities that are communicating to the public. For
> instance: literature tables on campus. If you're at a fair or any kind of public event,

being visible, going out with a petition on a clipboard on the street corner [can be useful]. Giving out leaflets can be good. Like going to the Memorial Day Parade, the downtown holiday parade, or other public events [can be useful]. Going out and giving leaflets to people and that kind of leafletting is a way of communicating with large numbers of people. In the course of an hour of a holiday parade we can give out 1,200 or 1,500 leaflets to people.

Advocates deliver paper communication through several means, including mail, handing out literature at public events, distribution from information tables, and a number of unconventional paper delivery means.

Mail

Advocates use a variety of postal means including the U.S. postal service and express mail companies to deliver a number of paper communication forms. Postage delivery of messages on paper are slower than some other media, according to Abby: "Here in town we have next day delivery, so it's not that bad. But it's still slow."

Anti–death penalty advocacy organizations often send periodic mailings. These can take the form of a single-page mailer and are often delivered through the U.S. Postal Service. For instance, Tony reported that the anti–death penalty advocates communicated with area religious organizations through mailed paper: "One of our members sends stuff out to churches. He has a database of churches." Tony perceived that such knowledge could increase the effectiveness of advocates' use of paper communication.

Distribution at Public Events

Printed information can be handed out at public events. This is a way that advocates can reach a large number of people. Tony explained some of the potential:

> If we were to hand out literature at a public event, like a basketball game, it would probably be paper communication size, half of a flier size. For cheaper expenses anyway. And with the picture for sure. There has to be a picture. For folks to tune in that's all. Maybe they're getting ready to go see the Missouri basketball team, as for twelve players, at least ten are black. And in the United States, 80 percent of the people that have been executed have been executed for killing white folks. There is value of an African American if they play basketball, but not if they happen to end up on death row. Forty percent of all the population on death row is African American.

Advocates have distributed large numbers of fliers at public events, like parades. Tony articulated a desire to distribute large numbers of fliers at sporting events:

The key is that you have to take the message to the people. Any kind of educational efforts are good. The sad commentary is that people are showing up to town hall meetings, or other city council meeting, or their school board meeting, or whatever else. They hang out at basketball games, the circuses of the modern day. Thousands of people gathered to see folks bounce a basketball across a wooden floor. It would be good to reach those people. You probably have millions of people watching on TV.

There are a variety of conditions that would have to be met for Tony to perceive that handing out literature in this fashion would be useful:

Well . . . to start with, to do a justice, we would have to get people power, a mass of people, at least twenty people, for five people at each entrance. We will also have to be prepared to expand and [have] enough money. It would take a lot of money to pull it off . . . to do [a] decent job, you would probably need at least three or four thousand. I need to find out what the capacity of the stadium is. I need to research it. There are pieces of information that are critical to that kind of endeavor. Then I find out what time the public event is, get there, now I have time. Ideally, you want to catch people well before they get there. Get there an hour ahead of time, so people are casual about the time. There may be folks that race into the stadium. Sometimes people just don't hear your other message. They have other agendas. Sometimes people don't want to hear your other message. Sometimes they have other agendas, like meet a date, or other people. The thing is, people always take something if you give it to them.

Handing out substantial numbers of fliers at public events is a possible, although difficult, way to reach a large number of people with advocacy messages.

Advocates sometimes placed paper communication into professors' boxes in hopes that they will announce advocacy events in class. Lana suggested: "That's a good vehicle." Potentially such communicative attempts could reach a large number of people.

Literature Tables

There is almost always a table of literature at advocacy events. Included on this table was literature that explained Mumia's plight. In addition, general literature was available on the death penalty. Also on the table was a petition to communicate to elected officials the displeasure of those attending the event towards Mumia's plight. Finally, there was a mailing list (while the mailing list sign-up sheet was on paper, it was not a message, but a way to send future messages). This allows organizers to continue to communicate to those who attended the event through mailings or phone calls.

Joan was the guide for the literature table at an anti–death penalty event. I had never been so well directed to the valuable literature on the table. She displayed gumption. In particular, she directed me to a current list of all appro-priate contacts, locally and for the Mumia campaign. Communication can facilitate more communication. That is the nature of networking in advocacy activity. Some advocates perceive that it is important for all participating groups at coalition events to be invited to have an information table so that people can learn about who these organizations are and help them build their member-ships.

Abby explained that literature tables allow people who are interested in advocate issues and activities to gain more information on how they can become more involved:

> Often we have petitions and that's a way for people to feel like they're getting involved with the issue and doing something. Here is a way you can take action, and with Amnesty we have letters that people can write or postcards that people can sign and [we] send for them, so a way that they can become involved right away. Then they can take the information on the fliers home and hopefully they can read them later.

Gathering contact information is another valuable function of the literature table, as Joe explained:

> It helps increase the number of people who are rolling up their sleeves and helping get this done. Every little bit helps, everybody helps. It is like what is one grain of sand on a beach, but when you start adding up those grains of sand, you've got a beach. Through mailing lists, and through inviting people to meetings. Inviting peo-ple to get involved however they can get involved in whatever their comfort level is. Some people have computer skills, some people have phoning skills, some people have fundraising skills, and every organization needs this.

Contact sheets allow advocates to be in touch with other advocates or pro-spective advocates. Tony explained how this information is valuable for later contact:

> Well, if you have your network using them wisely, they can be really incredibly valu-able for future contact, and you get on a mailing list. Again it is kind of hard to tell how effective mailing lists are. We get our newsletter out to 1,200 people; do we have 1,200 people turn up to any event? Yeah, right. We are pretty happy with twenty or thirty. That's pretty pitiful in some ways. When we send a newsletter out to that many people, I would like to think that a fourth maybe call, that's really way too hopeful, idealistic. But the contact lists are real good in that they can be used to identify people for phone trees or e-mail networks and see who can be future participants and helpers. The other day . . . our contact list I ended up using it to help identify a contact over at Hickman.

Unconventional Paper Delivery

There are several inventive uses of paper in the advocacy activity in this community. Placing fliers on pizza delivery boxes is one nontraditional use of paper communication. Tanya, an environmental advocate and professor of environmental studies at the area university explained that paper texts can be placed in unconventional locations:

> Putting fliers on pizza boxes is a different way of getting the word out. We take fliers to several places that do deliveries of food to homes, like sub sandwiches, pizza places. They staple them on the top of the box, like the week before the event. That's kind of a different way of getting the word out. It reaches a whole other segment of people. They may not see a flier, read the newspaper, watch TV. I hope that it is something that would catch their attention, because it is unusual, on top of pizza boxes.

Environmental advocates in this community also make arrangements so that a flier advertising the Earth Day event is distributed in the pay envelopes at two of the higher education institutions in the community. Fliers in paycheck envelopes reached different audiences than other advocacy communication forms.

In sum, advocates deliver paper communication through several means, including mail, handing out literature at public events, distribution from information tables, and a number of unconventional paper delivery means. Advocates hope that through these dissemination efforts a number of people can be engaged in emphatic communicative experiences.

Intended Audience

Advocates utilize paper communication to communicate to fellow advocates, to the general public, and to politicians. Ed explained that there are different target audiences for different forms of paper communication:

> Well, a pamphlet is for a specific issue. And I think you would use a pamphlet more for people who you were already not linked up with. You would send the newsletter to someone whose name you knew . . . you had their e-mail address. You use a pamphlet to communicate to someone who was walking by the booth. More to generate additional interest. The newsletters would be for the committed.

Fellow Advocates

Much paper communication is directed at other advocates. Ed explained that pamphlets might be more appropriate for people who already possess some interest in an issue: "A pamphlet would be useful to somebody who's already interested." The information about advocacy activity can be included in mailings of other groups. Joan explained that printed media can be used to announce events of other organizations: "You can also . . . send notices to other organization, besides your organization, send information to, say, the Sierra Club, and other organizations. Then they . . . send you their mailings." Mail delivery can be targeted to particular audiences, as explained by Abby:

> We send postcards several times a year when there are big events coming up. That usually goes out to a sublist. Not to our full list. Rather it's the list of people who are some way or another more interested than those on the big list. It might be a combination of people who have given us money, or got involved one way or another, and we get a sense that they are more interested and that's about five hundred.

Different mailings can be targeted for specific audiences, as Ed explained: "You would send the postcard to a smaller audience than you would for the newsletter . . . unless it was for an event."

General Public

Advocates also utilize printed media to communicate to citizens who are not active in these specific advocacy issues. For instance, advocates use posters to communicate to large audiences. Darlene explained that some paper communication offerings such as fliers can be useful: "We would use posters, fliers. Fliers are good because there are large letters and they have an immediate, simple, message, exactly what you want. A location, or a phone number, a contact . . . a contact!"

Politicians

Social and political advocates use paper communication to reach politicians. Joan explained she perceives that postcards are an appropriate paper media form with which she could contact politicians:

> I've written letters to politicians. I like to send a postcard because it's cheaper. And it's amazing how much you can get on the back of a postcard. If you get the one from the office of the post office you get the one with the address on the one side, so you get more room to write your issue.

Advocates, such as Tony, include information on printed media about how interested people can contact legislators and the governor: "We could dedicate half of an entire edition of our newsletter to information about how to contact congressmen."

Mail campaigns to elected officials can be planned for maximum impact. Advocates can target mailings to advocates in specific legislative districts to apply strategically coordinated political pressure. That pressure takes the form of communication between constituents who support various advocacy efforts and their elected officials.

> For instance, in a couple of days here, we're going to be sending out a letter to folks who have identified as interested, who are committed, to our organization. We've identified people in specific legislative districts, and people who are there, who lived in the districts of certain representatives and senators. We want . . . to get them to contact the representatives. And the senators. And get them to support legislation moving out of committee and toward the general House and Senate.

In this case, knowledge about how to reach certain constituencies was viewed by Tony as valuable for using paper communication to reach politicians.

Functions of Advocate Paper Use

Advocates perceive that use of paper communication can perform several functions, including increasing attendance at events, building community, educating, lobbying, and raising funds. Through these functions, advocates hope to engage others in effective communicative experiences through paper communication.

Increasing Attendance at Events

Advocates use printed media to disseminate the information necessary to facilitate attendance at advocate events. The newsletter offered the time, locations, circumstances of the event, and gave background into Mumia's situation. Darlene explained that the text of the newsletter increased her awareness of advocate activities:

> Normally, in the newsletter, as opposed to a card, is that I get more text. In the newsletter, I might find out a little bit more about it, instead of in the newsletter, where I might only get one line. "This particular event," whereas in the newsletter, there is a story about the person to be executed . . . it maybe makes more pull for me, to feel for this person. I might not know what it is, if I just see an announcement for an event. The newsletter gives me more text to read.

Newsletters are valuable for reminding advocates about advocate events, although advocates like Jossey find it difficult to attend all events highlighted in the newsletters:

I feel like when I have the newsletter, I know I should read it, I know it has important information, but it does mix with my other professional periodicals. Leading into something that I need to do and want to do, and it's important to do, but it's not easy to be engaged.

One advocate explained that a newsletter provided information about how to be active in an event: "Initially, I saw an announcement for an event in the local anti–death penalty newsletter."

Advocates use fliers to increase awareness about events. For instance, the production crew of the documentary studied in this community posted fliers around the university campus and downtown in order to attract attention to the screenings of the video production.

Postcards also perform a function of increasing attendance at advocate events. Tony explained that postcards present a reminder about events:

Postcards are wonderful, a great way of getting information out. It's better for an alert kind of a thing. Ideally, folks already have some previous information. The group works to get information their way. So there is a general understanding of a concept, or predicament or situation. The cards are a reminder. A card is a good way to reach out to the converted. You're not really being persuasive, as much as just informing them about an event.

Educating

Tony described the depth of information provided by the advocacy newsletter to increase awareness about advocate issues:

With the newsletter you can get more in depth. On the background of the situation, on the person who could be executed, that could not be communicated if you spend an hour talking with someone about the issue. You couldn't get that amount of information.

Recruiting Advocates

Tony explained that paper communication such as newsletters performs a persuasive function in attempts to recruit more issue advocates:

The newsletter is better for trying to build your case. And trying to convert. I have to avoid the costs and those kinds of things, but it boils down to the fact that we want people to come to our side.

Pamphlets can also be useful for getting people interested in an advocacy issue. Darlene explained that she would be likely to pick up a printed media form in order to learn about new aspects of advocacy issues.

I would pick up the pamphlet if it were something new to me. If it announced stuff, and it looked interesting. Hey, women's issues. Or hey, environmental issues. Let's clean up a creek. A pamphlet is easier to carry around. I don't have a backpack, I don't have a bag, I can slip this little pamphlet in my pocket. The flier is easy to carry around.

Advocates perceive that engaging people in effective communicative experiences through paper communication may help recruit new advocates.

Community Building

Advocates perceive that paper communication can serve a community-building function. For instance, newsletters can provide a valuable link between like-minded advocates. Although Tony wondered if the effort was really worth it, he explained the utility of the newsletter when asked about the importance of the anti–death penalty newsletter:

> Big question mark. [Laugh.] I mean . . . on the one hand I hope it's getting used a lot. You wish that you knew. I don't want to be like a big brother . . . but I'd love to be able to put a camera on every newsletter . . . do they end up in the recycling bin or canary cages, I wonder. I don't know, I mean sometimes I know people pick them up with a lot of enthusiasm and a lot of people are excited to get them in the mail and all and a lot of people actually . . . I don't know . . . I can't . . . tell you like what percentage of the people that get them read them and act on the suggestions. I don't know that, we ought to probably have some better tracking mechanism for that.

Tony explained ways in which a newsletter can be a valuable tool for advocacy efforts:

> I hope it mobilizes and activates and persuades people to act like . . . I know that there are some people who read it and say they are so grateful for our efforts to try to humanize individuals, especially those who are scheduled to be executed. They say they find that information really incredibly helpful to them and it is very moving a lot of times. So in that way it does some good. I would really like it to be a tool, I really want it to be, and I am feeling it more and more that you know it is becoming more of a tool as people are broader, you know more people, different voices are involved as far as writers, so there is some good in that. I would like it to be a tool.

Successful advocacy communication is a catalyst to the contribution and participation of coalitions of groups to a specific endeavor.

Lobbying

Advocates also perceive that paper communication can perform a lobbying function. Advocates like Tony believe that letters to politicians imply a strong conviction in the sender:

I think a letter shows more respect for that person, the legislator, whoever, the staff people. They see that the person that sent that letter is probably a little more concerned, a little bit more affected by this particular issue than somebody who makes a phone call instead. I think a letter shows a little bit more commitment on the issue.

Writing letters to elected officials is another way that advocates can communicate about their position, as Darlene explained: "Writing a letter to my congressman is very important. Otherwise he might not know how I feel. . . . I like that, because I'm busy, and I want to write a letter and support the issue, and I want my name on the letter, and I want volumes of letters . . . to be received by the public official."

Advocates perceive that other paper communication forms, such as petitions, for instance, can perform a lobbying function. Tony perceived that petitions communicate to politicians a commitment to an issue position by those who signed it: "Petitions helped to show that there is some passion on a particular issue. It shows that there are a number of people who will take that minimal snap of signing the petition. Not a whole lot. It is a step."

Darlene described her perception that elected officials react to the number of messages delivered to politicians:

> Elected officials are supposed to be working for the people. So, therefore, they want to . . . if they get fifty letters versus twenty letters, they are going to think that this is what the people want.

Advocates perceive that if politicians receive large quantities of paper communication, there is a greater chance that advocates can gain access for communicative engagement with politicians.

Fund Raising

Abby explained that environmental advocates used paper communication to solicit financial donations:

> When we send out a mailing we think it's profitable to stick donation envelopes in there. You have to have an envelope to give people an opportunity to give funds. You still do only get a very small fraction of the people that you send it to but it is definitely worth it. Giving them a vehicle to send their donation back is worth the costs. Most people won't bother to reply by mail so we [want] to send them a self-addressed envelope that they can put a stamp on.

Ed explained that his monetary donations to advocates was facilitated through advocate use of paper:

I donate money through the mail. I get [an environmental newsletter] through the mail. If they send out a yearly solicitation letter, then that is when I send them money. I'm not really sure about that. I'm still on their list, and I can't remember the last time I wrote them a check.

In sum, advocates perceive that paper communication performs several functions, including increasing attendance at events, raising awareness, building community, lobbying, and raising funds. Some forms of paper communication differ in their functional value. As Abby explained, not all forms of paper communication perform the same functions: "I think you would want to use a pamphlet to disseminate information about an issue, rather than just promote an event." There are two other functions that used to be performed through paper communication but have been primarily replaced by other media. First, advocates used to rely upon paper press releases to facilitate mass media coverage, but that use has been replaced by computer fax capabilities. Advocates do perceive that it is useful to have hard copies of press releases when talking to reporters in case reporters did not get a copy. Advocates also used to use paper to arrange logistical details; however, that function has been largely replaced by e-mail and advocate use of telephone communication.

Factors That Influence Advocates' Use of Paper Communication Forms

Consistent with the theory of advocate media use, factors that influence advocate uses of paper communication include characteristics of the media, internal group factors, and external factors. These factors influence the ability of advocates to craft effective paper communication.

Characteristics of Paper Communication

Advocate perceptions about the characteristics of their uses of paper communication influence advocate media-use decisions. These perceived characteristics include low feedback, multiple cues, information-carrying capacity, permanence, and, in general, a low level of personal character.

Feedback

Paper communication offers less feedback opportunity than other media. Feedback in paper forms is slower than with face-to-face communication, telephone communication, or e-mail communication. Ed explained that paper communication lacked the two-way character of other potential media:

You can get information from the newsletter. But if I'm talking to [you] about it, I can relay ideas, and work out ideas. Comment on it. I can think about what I'm reading, but there's no one to share that with. It's an issue of the communication being two-way verses one-way.

Multiple Cues

The multiple cues offered when paper communication forms include pictures are perceived to increase the effectiveness of the newsletter, as Tony explained:

> The saying is now so tried, but a picture is worth a thousand words. You can look at a picture, and people in their own minds conjure up all kinds of images from that. Especially if you have some keywords, and ideas, along with the pictures. If you can get them back together. You could say that this convicted murderer, who did awful stuff, was also the victim of some terrible things. It helps humanize them a little bit more. It's really important to recognize these human beings who are affected by these awful policies. To share their pain. It's very important for people to relate, and understand.

Pictures are perceived by other advocates such as Darlene to increase the effectiveness of the newsletter:

> Pictures help you personalize it. That makes a . . . big, big difference in postcards, because postcards are small. . . . I don't keep the whole newsletter. I recycle [throw away] the picture of the person about to be executed. But I usually keep the postcard around for while. And that's . . . because that's easier to put on the refrigerator.

Inclusion of pictures increases the personal character of paper communication. The incorporation of pictures in paper communication is perceived to provide a variety of cues that add a human element to texts. Visual images can be used to personalize those effected by advocacy issues:

> If you can show them as a real human being, they are a person . . . the image can be important. You know, and effective design might grab me, and I might pay attention. We don't often do a good design on some of the stuff. If it is a good visual, a good visual image, and I see it, and I react to it, and I don't even have to read it. I have already interacted with that material. In that sense, it is potent stuff. Very potent stuff, you know.

The presence of multiple cues in paper communication increases its effectiveness. Lana explained her belief that the importance of visuals was related to the fact that we live in a visual culture. She perceived that this increases our propensity to be engaged in visual communication:

The visual stuff is important, having a picture perhaps. Well . . . this is not a literary society. This is a media-savvy society. And they almost don't . . . look at words anymore. It's symbols, it's pictures, the brief little thing. They don't really want to read anything.

Logos that are incorporated into paper communication are perceived to increase its effectiveness. As an environmental advocate explained: "We use a visual symbol for our event. Because that is your visual, and that is why you want that to be spread all over, so people see that, they know immediately it is an event."

Information-Carrying Capacity

Tony explained that one of the benefits of the newsletter was that it had more information-carrying capacity than other media forms:

Newspapers are around for quite a while. They would be circulated among many people. They can be engaging if they are well done. By reading it, you can get a little bit more aware of a person, or a situation, of an issue. Trying to make a three-dimensional argument, or discussion, beyond the flat level, to share a deeper understanding of an issue. Other forms might be real limited.

Mail can be a valuable tool in the arrangement of logistical detail: for instance, when the Earth Day committee was arranging logistical details concerning the entertainment for the event. Letters from the bands are particularly useful as sources of information for promotional materials. Artists submitted demos and information about their acts when they applied for the Earth Day positions. These mailed items have been very valuable in coordinating this advocacy event.

Permanence

The permanence of printed text is derived from the physical presence of the artifact. Abby explained that the permanence of a hard copy of the newsletter increases the propensity of his group to communicate through a post-delivered newsletter:

There are a few reasons why we send the [newsletter] through the mail [instead of on-line]. One reason is that I think there is greater impact from any physically present printed newsletter. It's much more visual if there are pictures, something you can hold, something you can sit and read, or that you can take . . . to the bathroom with you.

Flanders, an infrequent advocate on the anti–death penalty and environmental issues, explained that this permanence increases the likelihood he will read the entire document:

> If the newsletter was only the e-mail, I would be less likely to look through the whole thing. I would be more likely to scan it real quick, and forget about it. In two weeks: up again, I already read that. But I get in the mail. I read it front to back.

Ed explained that the physical presence of paper communication forms increases the convenience of consumption:

> The physical presence brings convenience. I don't see . . . the computer at a certain time each day. But when I get it in the mail, it's out on the kitchen table where I sit down in the morning and have my coffee. I picked it out and I read through it. It's the right time and it's right there and it's convenient.

Postcards are perceived as different in some ways from e-mail because postcards have a permanent, physical presence. Ed explained that he believed that the physical permanence of a newsletter is more engaging to readers than computer communication: "If you reading the newsletter, at least you're investing the effort to open the page, to physically handling it. I don't think the e-mail is a good choice for trying to get people involved. I think it's so easy to just get rid of it." Tony reiterated his perception that in terms of physical presence: "I think generally, a postcard in the mail is probably better. It's in their hands, it's physical." Postcards have an often-effective physical permanence, as Joan explains, and can be placed in a prominent location in the home:

> With a postcard I would hope I would get a little bit of advance notice . . . a postcard is something I can post on my refrigerator and bulletin board for reminding me that [this] event is going to go on. I can slip it into my calendar; I can carry it around, with the information. I can have the information right there.

Personal

Literal communication (printed or written words, as opposed to spoken words) can be emotionally effective, as Joan suggested: "Words can be very expressive. Great poems or even in letters, or e-mails to each other, is an opportunity to personally express ourselves." However, some advocates believe that it is a less personal medium when compared to other media. Some advocates feel a postcard is less personal than other communication forms, such as Darlene:

I like being reached on a personal level better. At . . . getting a postcard, I still always read them, and, when I get [a] postcard, I put it on the refrigerator, and then I can be reminded about the dates.

For instance, fliers may not be as effective as interpersonal contact. Lana suggested that a paper announcement does not possess the personal commitment entailed in other communication forms:

I probably wouldn't be likely to engage in action. And I would have it socially affirmed from another source. We are, with face-to-face interaction, thinking about, "Where am I getting this information?" The source can lead us to stronger actions . . . involves more commitment.

Newsletter layout is also perceived by some advocates such as Joan to influence the effectiveness of the newsletter:

Like a newsletter. Anybody can put out a newsletter. Or your chances of putting out a newsletter that is going to be read by people, that's friendly to the eye, that's readable, readable not only on the page but in the mind. . . . If you follow the [newsletter form], you get more legitimacy.

Layout quality matters, and knowledge is necessary to create effective paper communication.

In sum, the characteristics of paper communication that influence advocates' use of paper communication include limited feedback, multiple cues, information-carrying capacity, permanence, and, in general, a low level of personal character.

Internal Group Factors

Several internal factors influence advocate ability to use paper communication including people power, financial resources, access to logistical resources, and knowledge. If advocates lack these resources, it limits their ability to use paper communication.

People Power

The number of advocates willing to invest their effort influences advocate ability to use paper communication. For instance, when environmental advocates deliver literature through payroll envelopes, someone must expend the necessary people power. Lana explained that someone has to invest the time necessary to complete this project: "Another member does that." In one case, about fifteen people met at the home of a key local organizer to prepare an anti–death penalty newsletter for distribution. The newsletter is put out by a coalition of groups who are sympathetic to the anti–death penalty cause.

The main headline of the newsletter concerned the date of the next prisoner to be executed in the state. However, there was a misprint that identified the date of execution as November 1 rather that November 10. This is a very important date for the activist involved, so the first order of business for the session was correcting the mistake by writing in a zero after the "1" on the headline, thus requiring more time.

Preparation of newsletters is a multistage process. Writing is obviously the first step. This requires knowledge of the subject matter as well as knowledge of appropriate writing style. Editorial decisions must be made. Layout must be designed. Proofing the newsletter is an important step. The master must be clean. All of these steps require knowledge about the publishing process. People power is also required to fulfill these tasks. Time is required, and the greater the number of those participating, the less the burden is, overall.

Financial Resources

Mail can be very expensive because postage costs money. Tony lamented: "We would send the newsletter to a larger audience if it wasn't for the money involved." This influences the use of mailings by advocates. Informative mailings are used as an advocate communication medium. Sent out periodically, mailings can inform advocates about meetings, events, or other business. Often, this may be the only source from which activists get their information. However, redundancy should be avoided in mailings. Also, there may be points at which an organization should review the mailing list in order to cut inactive people or those no longer available. In addition, return addresses and address-notification requests should be included on mailings in order to identify persons who are no longer reached. These steps are ways in which mailing waste can be minimized.

Paper communication preparation is time consuming and labor intensive and requires substantial people power. While talking to Tony on the telephone on another matter, he invited me to help get the newsletter together. This was a great opportunity to participate. In this instance, personal networking on the telephone aided in mobilizing the people power necessary to complete the time- and labor-intensive newsletter preparation. Another person who contributed time and effort for newsletter preparation said it was her first time helping out on it and that telephone calls made them aware of the mailer effort that night. The telephone is an important tool for communication, and in this case, use of the telephone was a catalyst for more communicative advocacy. Communication plays a central role in every aspect of the advocacy-organization process, including organizing newsletter efforts.

Abby commented that despite the efficiency of newsletter mailings, they do require expenditures of financial resources:

> We do our mailing now . . . we only do big mailings here. That is [the anti–death penalty] newsletter. Each one of those is a major undertaking, and we literally have five thousand names on the list. Or looking at printing costs and postage costs is running about $1,400 each time we do that. The funds come from our membership donations.

The newsletters sent out by Abby and Tony qualified for a lower postage rate in bulk because the mail was being sent by nonprofit organizations.

Access to Logistical Resources

One important resource necessary for effective paper communication is access to computer desktop publishing capabilities. Advocates use computer technology to increase the quality of desktop publishing and decrease the time necessary to complete the design and production of printed material. Resources such as a computer or a layout table (if it is not done with a computer program) are required.

Knowledge

When contributing advocates lend their knowledge to the design of paper communication texts, an increase in newsletter effectiveness may be a result. Joan explained that expertise increases the perceived legitimacy of the newsletter: "For one thing the quality of the research is higher, and the kinds of stories that are being done. It gives credibility to the newsletter. That level of expertise is the best way to report, very systematically." Paper communication design of artifacts such as fliers and posters is considered carefully by many effective advocates. Advocates perceive the quality of paper communication as important and reflected in the accuracy and aesthetics. What good is a great pamphlet with misspelled words? A letter to a congressional representative scrawled on the back of a paper sack with a crayon? With whatever medium, the quality of the appearance will likely increase the effectiveness of the communication.

Advocates perceive that knowledge can increase their effectiveness, as Joan explained:

Fliers and . . . within Poets for Peace, we have one woman who is a good graphics designer, that's her specialty, and that's the role that she plays in Poets for Peace. Sometimes she will read her own literature, but that is her main gift. She did that. And the owner of the venue printed up the fliers. So that cost was taken care of. And then, black studies also did a flier and passed them out to their people . . . and got them posted up around.

Advocates perceive that including interesting visual elements in literature increases its effectiveness. Lana, who had many public relations responsibilities related to environmental advocacy, explained her knowledge of how the multiple cues included in some paper communication added to effectiveness:

A symbol is good, because you want something that visually catches the eye. Then you have to be really careful that you don't give them too much, in the way of copy, because people aren't going to read it. You can put all kinds of things in there, and crowded so that, it just kind of puts them off. "That's too much. I can't handle that."

This visually interesting element may be necessary for advocates to attract attention above the clutter of the electronic marketplace of ideas:

All of this is happening in a split-second. People are deciding each moment, "I will read that, or I won't read that, I'll look at that photograph, I'll stay here to watch this TV saying, for two more seconds," or whatever. So you have to grab their attention and you have to recognize that you only have that attention for a very limited amount of time. Get in there, get it, and let them go on.

Proper literature design would include placing the necessary information in a visually stimulating way. Joan explained:

You just would include the basic information, you know, the "who, where, when and why," and then maybe something visual. If there is something that you can put as a hook, you know, some kind of thing that catches their eye, a headline, a band that kind of draws them in so they will look at the "who, what, where, and why."

These advocates perceive delivery of basic, necessary information in a visually interesting fashion as effective paper communication design. Tony thought that the anti–death penalty groups he was involved with did not adequately utilize paper fliers to disseminate advocacy messages: "Yea, I think we have been very weak on that. We had a couple people who were great at it, doing a really nice job of giving punchy ideas on them." Skill is required:

Some people do a really good job. I have a tendency of being too verbose and wordy. I have good things to say, but I need to be more like the seed and less like the plant.

Here's my place, here it is. You can open and you can feel its powerful force. Instead I put the whole thing out there. Its kind of nice if people gander at all the leads and such.

The visual design of paper communication is important and is perceived as a valuable talent. Lana explained: "I would think that the design is important. And effective design means a more effective communication. You can only sanitize state murder so much."

There may be members of local organizations who are particularly gifted in flier design and production. For instance, Joan explained that knowledge about graphic layout could influence advocates' ability to produce perceptively efficient fliers. Joan perceived that if advocates possessed knowledge about design and appropriate locations, fliers can be an effective way of promoting an event.

In sum, producing and distributing fliers requires the investment of resources. Several internal group factors influence advocate ability to use paper communication, including people power, knowledge, and access to logistical resources. These factors both enable and limit the ability of advocates to use paper communication to engage readers in communicative experiences.

External Factors

Political context and technological trends are external factors that influence advocates' use of paper communication. Advocates perceive that, as with other media, these external factors can influence their ability to use paper media.

Political Context

Some hold the view that the government can interfere with the use of the postal service, such as Joan: "We could use the snail mail, but the problem I have had with the snail mail is that twice I was supposed to have packets of information come to me and they never arrived." Advocates perceive that it is possible that governmental surveillance can influence their ability to use paper communication that is delivered by U.S. mail. In addition, the costs of postage as established by the U.S. postal service can influence the ability of advocates to use this medium. While financial resources are considered an internal factor, external factors, in this case increases in postage, influence advocates' use of paper communication.

Technological Trends

Ursula, an advocate involved with three to four universal health care events a year, summed up these helpful aspects of this technology:

Computer technology has helped advocates out with desktop publishing. It's much easier now, and much nicer. You can produce a nice product. If you will put out the brochure, the newsletter, a flier, or a pamphlet, you can do a job that looks super slick and professional and do it in half the time [with computer technology]. You can make it look ten times better than it did back in 1988 or 1990.

Another advocate, Ed, provided more specific instances of advocate use of computer communication technology: "Computers have been useful to put out newsletters, design fliers. But that newsletter was not online. The newsletter production was facilitated by computer technology at that point in time. . . . Copying centers like Kinko's have also been an asset to advocates. We were bad in the mid-1980s [about spending money at photocopy centers], but activists in the '70s and before certainly didn't. And now it's a much cheaper process, more economically viable, and more available, too."

As with other forms of advocate communication, combinations of uses are perceived to be most effective. For instance, Tony suggested that fliers work best when used in conjunction with other advocate media uses:

Fliers can be very good then. But it's better if you already have letters to the editor out. Things like that. Get the information . . . out [into] the people's minds and eyes so they are thinking about it. The fliers can be effective. If you just put the fliers out by themselves, it's unlikely that you're going to reach anybody but your core.

Advocates perceive the combination of the use of paper communication forms with other media uses as most effective. Abbey explained:

Fliers are used to get information to people. They can see it. Ideally, it's to be part of a larger presentation or strategy. We should use many different means. E-mail to your base constituency, people who are going to check their e-mail anyways. Newsletters go out a couple weeks in advance, to get people information [into] their hands. To get people aware. Make sure that they are aware, and start to get an understanding.

The effectiveness of media varies by audience, as evident in this quotation. As with other advocate media uses, combinations of uses are perceived as more effective than isolated, unconnected, sporadic media uses.

Conclusion

In this development of theoretical ideas about advocate use of paper media, I described the various forms of paper communicative media utilized by advocates to disseminate their messages, including newsletters, fliers, handbills, pamphlets, letters, petitions, table tents, and adhesive stickers. I also identified a number of ways that advocates distribute paper communication including U.S. mail, handing out literature at public event, distribution from information tables, and a number of unconventional paper-delivery means. I then identified the intended audiences of this paper communication, including other advocates, the general public, and politicians. Third, I explicated the intended functions of this use of paper communication, as advocates perceive that paper communication performs several functions, including increasing attendance at events, raising awareness, building community, lobbying, and raising funds. Finally, I explored factors that influence advocates' uses of paper communication, including characteristics of uses, internal group factors, and external factors. These characteristics of advocacy paper communication include limited feedback, multiple cues, information-carrying capacity, permanence, and, in general, a low level of personal character. Internal group factors also influence advocate ability to use paper communication, including people power, knowledge, and access to logistical resources. The external factors that influence advocate use include political context and general technological trends. These considerations increase our understanding of how advocates use paper communication to engage receivers in communication.

7

Disseminating Messages through Mass Media

The group would look at what their chances of success are. If they think they can get a couple column inches, by talking to some reporter, by making a few phone calls, by sending letters, they will do that if they think they can. With a good visual opportunity they can get on television news. Hold a demonstration. Call the media; tell them there's going to be a protest. If they think they can get coverage on TV news. Use that format.

This advocate, Ed, who lends logistical support to several environmental and anti–death penalty events a year, perceived that mass media affords several opportunities as a channel for the advocates of social or political change. History abounds with examples in which advocate use of mass media played this catalytic role in such change. One of the benefits of a corporate mass media is that producers can be persuaded to cover the messages of political or social reform advocates if the message is compelling. Advocates seek to offer communication related to their advocacy positions and activities to mass media consumers because they realize that these experiences are catalytic in the emergence of gumption, a necessary element in future advocacy. As with other advocate media uses, advocates seek to inspire future communicative activity. This is the essence of advocacy communication. In this chapter, I explore the phenomenon of advocate use of mass communication through explication of particular advocate uses of mass communication, intended audiences, functions advocates perceive these uses to perform, and factors that influence advocates' use of mass media communication.

In this section, I will describe uses of mass media by social advocates. I will focus on print mass media, radio, television, cinema, and video. There are a number of mass media that are used by advocates to disseminate their messages in efforts to motivate involvement and action. Advocates perceive that mass media experiences can foster action in those who consume the mass media messages. My study reveals that advocates perceive that effective and emphatic communicative experiences contribute to advocate gumption.

The separation of the various available media is my construct. Ideally, advocates would utilize any or all available media. Ed suggested, "I would think they would want to cover all their bases. They would want to use radio, television, or newspaper. We would appreciate any coverage we can get." Ed addressed the idea that advocates do not perceive mass media forms as competitive. The various available media, including mass media forms, can be used in concert to maximize communicative outcomes. This caveat could be applied to all efforts mentioned in this book to isolate a media form in order to better understand it and other media forms. When asked if he had a preference about which mass media representatives he would prefer to cover an event, Abby, the key leader in the environmental- and peace-related advocacy activity in the community, commented, "Hopefully all of them. I would want all of them to be there." Likewise, individual members of intended audiences have different media preferences; to reach as many people as possible, use of several media is preferable. Redundancy may also increase retention. Thus, advocates can use a variety of communication media to maximize the impact. Advocates in this study used several mass media, most importantly print, radio, television, cinema, and video.

Advocate Use of Print Mass Media

Over 79 percent of Americans report reading newspapers (U.S. Census, 2000). The activists who participated in this study, due to the emphasis on local advocacy, used magazines and books infrequently. National and international advocates were found to use these forms more than local advocates.

Newspapers

Advocates use a variety of newspaper formats to disseminate their message. Advocates use newspaper stories, both hard news and human interest. Op-ed pieces can also be viable outlets for advocates, as can letters to the editor. Advocates can also buy advertising space in print mass media outlets in order to give voice to their message. In addition, groups studied for this project utilized published calendars of community events.

Stories

Newspapers can present hard news stories about the activities of advocates or focus on the issues upon which activism is predicated. For instance, stories about artists participating in advocacy events were a source of news coverage received by environmentalists. In another example, a universal health care advocate recalled an instance in which the activities of a mother and daughter were used in a newspaper article to put a human-interest angle in a story. There is a symbiotic relationship between newspaper producers and advocates; advocates use newspapers to disseminate their messages, but newspaper producers also use the advocates as subjects for interesting, newspaper-selling stories.

Op-ed Pieces

Op-ed pieces also provide an opportunity to use column inches as a literal bullhorn for advocates. Opinion-editorial pieces are a form of editorial featured from a person who does not write editorials for the newspaper or syndicated columnists. Often from a prominent person in a community, op-ed pieces are more formal than letters to the editor, but are not an opinion endorsement from the newspaper. The largest newspaper in the community under scrutiny in this study often carries editorial pieces written by community advocates. Abby judged: "[One local newspaper] is really good about running op-ed pieces, much more so than major metropolitan dailies. They have never turned me down for op-ed." This advocate perceived op-ed pieces to be a viable communicative medium for advocate issue position dissemination. Op-ed pieces are usually printed in a more prominent position on the editorial page than letters to the editor.

Letters to the Editor

Letters from readers are often featured near the editorial section of many newspapers. This is a relatively simple way that advocates can disseminate their perspectives. An environmental advocate, Lana, who is also a municipal employee, noted the costs entailed are insignificant: "Letters to the editor are another way to communicate. It is a free, sort of, possibility." While these letters are usually not in as prominent a location within newspapers as stories or op-ed pieces, they do provide a way in which the thoughts of advocates can be disseminated to the public.

Advertising Space

Like any organization, advocates sometimes purchase advertising space in local newspapers. Ed commented, "In one environmental group, we spent money on advertising in newspapers." By purchasing advertising space in newspapers or other print mass media products, advocates have control over how their messages are presented to newspaper readers.

Calendars of Community Events

Many newspapers also feature calendars of community events. Newspaper calendars of entertainment also mentioned some events when they were held at locations such as bars that regularly listed events at the venue. The environmental group and the anti–death penalty group studied here utilized the calendars of community events in several instances.

Magazines

Advocates also use magazine coverage to get their message out, although local groups have less access than national organizations. During my study of these groups, an event that brought the larger local progressive advocate community together was listed in the national publication *The Nation*. The event was a satirical celebration of the inauguration of George W. Bush.

Advocate Uses of Radio

Radio is a pervasive communication form in the media consumption habits of Americans: 99 percent of U.S. households contain an average of 5.6 radios and 84 percent of Americans report that they listen to the radio (U.S. Census, 2000). Advocates use a variety of radio mass media forms, including coverage on mainstream news programs, radio talk shows, and public service announcements. Advocates sent press releases, made telephone calls, and engaged in interpersonal communication with radio personnel to facilitate the symbiotic use of advocates by radio personnel to fill airtime. This increases our understanding of how advocates use radio by illustrating how advocates gain radio access by expending people power in calculated ways.

Mainstream News Programs

The first use of radio by advocates involves getting time on radio news programs, primarily on news radio stations. For instance, during a protest at the governor's mansion in the state capital against an execution in February, a talk radio station from St. Louis sent a reporter to the scene. As in other cases, advocates sent a press release announcing the event to the radio station. One of the participating protesters commented that the specific station was very powerful and broadcast over a large area. Thus, advocates can attempt to draw the attention of radio news personnel to certain issues to get coverage.

Appearances on Radio Shows

Appearances on radio programs are also a way for advocates to use radio media. Advocates contact talk-show hosts prior to appearances to arrange the airtime. In this study, antideath penalty advocates made appearances on local community radio programs. It is important to discuss the active strategies that advocates use to gain access to radio shows rather than advocates being used by radio. For example, Joan, an extremely active advocate, used a local radio program to gain coverage of an internationally recognized death penalty case in Pennsylvania:

> And also I went into [the community public radio station] several times and just to tell [a talk show host], who does Straight Talk, one of the most important shows for the African American community in [this town], just to tell her about it, and she threw me on the air and we ended up talking not one Saturday, but two Saturdays total about the event and what Mumia's case was about and everything else.

This interview excerpt reveals that the host of the program was not only willing to allow the advocate to communicate to listeners, but the host also extended the invitation for another time that she presented a program. This appearance on a talk show differed from telephone calls from listeners in a call-in portion of a radio talk show program because the advocate got more airtime than if she had just called in, and the fact that she was in the studio increased her perceived legitimacy.

Public Service Announcements

Public service announcements are another way that advocates can utilize radio. For example, the environmental coalition studied here discussed ways to get free coverage of coalition events. Several radio stations in the area had carried announcements of previous coalition-sponsored activities. Thus, mainstream radio news programs, talk radio shows, advertisements, and public service announcements are formats that advocates use to communicate through the radio medium.

A hybrid of advertising and public service announcements was used by the environmental coalition. The coalition communicated with prominent stations in an effort to get radio voices to announce a big environmental event. The announcements were not formatted as public service announcements because they also promoted the station, but they were not advertisements either, because the coalition did not have to pay for the radio time. They did not differ enough from public service announcements to merit a separate category in this analysis. Such cooperative efforts can be a way for advocates to get word out about significant events while pragmatically utilizing contacts with radio personnel for maximum communicative reverberation. These were different from a traditional public service announcement because the sponsoring stations rather than advocates produced the spots.

Advocates' Use of Televisual Media

Advocates use a variety of televisual media, including television, cinema, and video, to get their messages to the general public in efforts to evoke emotionally engaging communicative experiences. Televisual experiences are a central feature of home entertainment in the United States, and advocates use the medium to disseminate their messages. There are 235 million television sets in the United States and 98.3 percent of homes in the United States contain at least one television (U.S. Census Bureau, 2001). Advocates in this study used several forms of television programming to communicate their messages, including television news programs, talk show programs, cable access outlets, cinema, and video.

Television News Programs

Television news programs are a venue for the advocates in this study to get access to television. The news programs of local network affiliates, featured at 5:00, 6:00, and 10:00 PM, as well as shorter, fragmented news program segments between network programs in the morning, sometimes featured advocacy communication. For instance, the vigils held at the governor's mansion by anti–death penalty advocates were covered by local news programs, as were the universal health care lobbying event at the state and the Earth Day environmental event. Advocates on all three issues studied here delivered press releases and used the telephone to get television news personnel to cover their activities. This is evidence that advocates used the media rather than the media exclusively using the advocates.

Television Talk Shows

Local television programs were sometimes used to communicate advocates' messages. For instance, a local television program is an outlet for the environmental coalition studied in this project. According to Sandy, an environmental advocate and an official in the local public school district: "I actually go over to a local television program every year and talk about our event. So we kind of cover TV that way." This program is a variety, human-interest program.

Cable Access

Some of the advocates in this study used an access channel provided by the local cable company for the community. Joan reported that the anti–death penalty community had used a local cable access outlet. Environmental and anti–death penalty advocates produced video segments on their issues and activities and delivered them to the local community cable access outlet. In this case, advocates were also engaged in activities at the managerial level of the cable access organization to gain more access for this type of video programming. One filmmaker and activist, Rose, who was involved in both the environmental advocacy and anti–death penalty and also an employee of the cable access outlet, was a main spokesperson for increased access for such groups. Advocates can also use cable access channels to distribute communicative texts. Anti–death penalty advocates, including myself, a university graduate student, Vincent, an undergraduate student of communication, and Sebastian, a video producer at a local television station, produced a fifty-minute film on a questionable case against a death-row inmate in this Midwestern state, delivered it to personnel at the cable access station, and the program was aired several times. In another instance, because Joan had access to a camera and the knowledge about the local cable channel, advocates were able to get an advocacy event distributed through cable: "And what I did in that case was then video-tape it [the advocacy event was a lecture/event with a renowned speaker on the death penalty]. It was then shown on the public-access cable station." Joan explained how the use of cable access opportunities could attract the attention of television viewers:

> And when you think about that, how many people are channel surfing, didn't know about that [event], and look at it because of the suddenness and the strangeness of that. And they continue to watch it, and it can begin to make them think about the issue.

The environmental advocates also used the cable access station by providing short spots that promoted the Earth Day celebration and longer programs that reported on the Earth Day activities after it was over.

Cinema

Several advocates used cinema to reach advocates and some members of the public on the local level. Three advocate/filmmakers, Vincent, Sebastian, and I, screened our film at a local cinema/café as well as several screenings at university campuses across the state. We were able to use a cinematic setting as a venue to air this anti–death penalty film.

Films can be an effective means for advocates to communicate to large audiences because of the proliferation of videocassette recorders, which has increased access to advocate films. One very prominent example was *Dead Man Walking*, for which Susan Sarandon won an Oscar for her portrayal of Prejean. In one case, anti–death penalty advocates (Vincent, Sebastian, and I) gathered to view the film as a source of inspiration for their work on a documentary about a death row inmate in which they were engaged. In another instance, the film production team gathered to watch the film *Thin Blue Line*, directed by Errol Morris, for the same purpose. Not only did these cinematic texts offer ideas about the available tools of filmmaking technique, but they also were proverbial software that inspired the filmmakers' efforts.

Local advocates also utilized the celebrity status of Sister Helen Prejean and her stature as the main character in the film *Dead Man Walking* to promote her visit to the community and appearances on the university campus. Local anti–death penalty advocates used the film and references to the film to promote local events in which Sister Helen Prejean participated.

Video

Video releases of films such as those previously mentioned provide more audience access to films that contain advocacy themes. The proliferation of eighty-three million home videocassette recorders has given viewers the opportunity to experience films no longer featured in cinematic release (U.S. Census Bureau, 2001). Television previously was the only media through which audiences had exposure to films after their first release. As Sister Helen Prejean explained: "People rent the film on video and they buy that film. And the [video] began that reflection process." This mass media form, according to this internationally active advocate, provokes introspection.

Video productions can also be distributed without ever being presented in theaters. Video technology has also increased audience access to films not released or exhibited in cinemas. For instance, advocates staged an anti–death penalty event featuring a video about Mumia Abu-Jamal on the campus of a large Midwestern university. The video was titled *Mumia Abu-Jamal: A Case for Reasonable Doubt?* The video was a Home Box Office production, a Time-Warner holding, and was likely originally featured on HBO.

Video can also be used to communicate to audiences and increase the gumption necessary for further communicative praxis. In a number of instances during this study, video presentations were a catalytic factor in creating the enthusiasm that precedes further advocate praxis. The anti–death penalty documentary produced by Vincent, Sebastian, and myself generated attention and contemplation that provoked further communicative praxis by those who experienced the televisual text. In one of many similar instances, a coworker of the person responsible for converting the documentary to CD-ROM format viewed the documentary and subsequently e-mailed the governor and requested him to stop the execution of Joe Amrine.

In summary, there are several forms of televisual presentation that advocates use to disseminate their messages to the general public and other advocates, including television, cinema, and video. Advocates use several forms of television, including television news programs, local television talk shows, and cable access outlets. These, along with forms of print and radio communication, are considered viable channels for advocacy communication.

Intended Audience

There are four primary audiences for advocate use of mass media: advocates, as they seek to communicate to the advocate community; the general public; politicians; and mass media personnel. Separation of these audiences is not useful due to the nature of the mass media audience. Overall, advocates perceived the general public to be the chief audience of the use of mass media.

The first audience advocates intend to reach through mass media is other advocates, although this audience is incidental. Second, in the case of the environmental organization studied, the mass media are used to communicate to the general public, according to Darlene:

> I think the environmental people . . . use the media that they do to communicate with the public, because they are trying to reach a very general audience, appealing to the average person. The big event is like . . . families, and get together[s], have a picnic, and throw your Frisbee.

Activists use newspaper mass media to communicate to a large audience. This is the case with other mass media forms as well. One environmental activist, Darlene, stated: "[To reach a larger, general audience] [w]e might use a newspaper ad." An example would be the efforts of Earth Day organizers to get media coverage of their upcoming event.

Advocates used radio to reach a large audience. There is not only a large audience for radio, but there are also distinct audiences that listen to different radio formats. For instance, the environmental coalition discussed a wide variety of radio stations from which to solicit help in spreading the word about a major environmental event. The group talked about talk radio, public radio, and a station that adhered to the adult alternative-programming format. One advocate at the meeting commented that the group should contact one station in particular because: "Our kind of people listen to that station." It was noted in this meeting that different folks listened to different kinds of radio. Another member of the coalition commented that the group should attempt to reach all possible audiences. Thus, attempts were initiated to get the radio stations to announce the event.

Advocates also use television to reach a large audience. For instance, a local television program can be an outlet to reach large audiences. As explained by one environmental advocate, Lana, who was responsible for the public relations duties for the Earth Day coalition, it is easy to underestimate the audience of a local television talk show program:

> He [a local television talk show host] is a nice guy, and, he had . . . sort of this . . . reputation of . . . a local celebrity, with seniors and women. Even the powers that be in the city don't think my being on [a local television talk show] is, like, "nobody watches that show." Well, surprisingly enough, they do. In this you cannot pay, we could never pay to have three or four minutes once a month on TV. That is a huge amount of money. A lot of people watch that. People come up to me and say "you know, I saw you on that local program." Older and young people watch that program.

This advocate not only believes that a large number of people watch this local program but that an appearance on this program is worthwhile for the group because the program fills an important role for the community:

> I mean, he really does a good job of having, like, a wide variety of what's happening in town. It is like five or six things every day that he is talking about with people, so you can really learn a lot about the community by watching that program. I think he does a pretty good job. It's a geeky local show, but you know . . .

Advocates can also use mass media to communicate to elected officials. One advocate also suggested that elected officials were watching television like everyone else, so elected officials would see some television coverage of advocate activities.

Community environmentalists also used cable access outlets. Lana suggested that whatever the value, it is better to use cable access than not:

> I have seen a television program about the environmental coalition on the cable access channel. I think they're great [laughter]. I don't know . . . because Channel 13 is kind of the low-production value channel. But it's on TV. It's like a commercial. It captures your attention and, he tries to convince you that you need this product, and you see it and it is like, "Hey yeah, Earth Day. It sounds like fun."

Advocates use cable access channels to communicate with large audiences. In one instance, a video piece was broadcast a number of times over a two-week period on a cable access channel. One person approached Lana in a grocery store and inquired about the program: "He probably would not have gone to an event, he probably didn't hear about the event happening." Obviously, in this case, cable access was a way to communicate to an individual who otherwise would never have known that an advocacy event that interested him or her had occurred: "Through cable access through the mass media, you can reach people that don't have the opportunity to go to an event." Cable access channels may not have the numbers of viewers enjoyed by commercial cable television stations. However, a prominently located cable access channel can draw some substantial viewer numbers, especially among channel "surfers," according to Lana:

> Surprisingly, a number of people see that. They would never watch it, you know, but I think they must be flipping or something, and surfing through the channels, and if that happens that for a split-second they see something that they want to, that they want more, they might hold there for a little bit.

Television offers the opportunity to reach a large number of people because of the large area covered by particular television stations and the high number of people who watch television. Tony explained that he perceived that during any given evening, a majority of people in the area were watching television:

> The thing of it is, is that the greatest number of people tuned into anytime and media, a plurality of them would be watching TV, the majority probably. If you're talking about ten thousand people who are paying attention across Missouri, to the media in general, at one time. Of those ten thousand, maybe seven thousand people are watching TV, on one of the three stations in the area. Maybe another thousand or two thousand tune into . . . cable. It does come down to numbers.

Abby stated succinctly: "More people watch TV than anything else so . . . the goal there is to reach as many people as possible." Obviously advocates perceived that mass media could be used to reach a number of audiences, including the general public. Advocates, politicians, and mass media personnel are secondary audiences of advocate use of mass media.

Functions of Advocate Use of Mass Media

There are several functions performed by advocates' use of mass media including increasing attendance at events, lobbying, educating, facilitating further mass media coverage, and legitimizing advocate issue positions and activities. Mass media coverage of advocate issue positions and activities can encourage further mass-media coverage, consistent with Noelle-Neumann's (1999) idea of a spiral of silence.

Increasing Attendance at Events

Advocates can use print sources to mobilize fellow advocates by informing them about advocate events. For instance, advocates arranging publicity for the Earth Day event sought to solicit participation from advocates. Advocates placed announcements in the local newspapers that provided information about how environmental advocates could get involved in the events.

Activists use coverage of community events in newspapers to promote events to the general public. Advocates can get their events published under the auspices of entertainment or simply community events. For example, a local radio program was used to spread the word about an event supporting an internationally recognized death penalty case in Pennsylvania. Advocates use mainstream radio news programs to reach potentially large numbers of people. As Ed suggested of a university environmental group in which he was active: "We would buy ad space to promote events." Advocates can purchase advertising space to promote advocate activities.

Lobbying

Mass media can be used to persuade politicians that advocate positions merit consideration. In one instance, Tony related the ease with which state-elected officials could be contacted through televised community forums:

> [Televised] public forums can be a good way to talk with elected officials. The senators and legislative tours have public forums where they talk to the public on occasion. I visited with our local congressman in his office, maybe four or five times.

In this manner, elected officials are communicated with at the same time that advocates' messages are broadcast to the viewing public.

Educating

Use of mass media can perform a function of provoking introspection, an essential feature of perceptively effective communication with the general public and other advocates. For instance, advocates use print mass media sources to disseminate their messages to newspaper readers in attempts to persuade those readers that advocate positions merit consideration. Because mass media print sources are distributed to people outside the immediate advocate community, advocates' use of print sources might persuade nonadvocates to adopt advocates' perspectives. For example, human-interest stories in television, radio, or newspapers can tangentially discuss advocacy issues. Newspapers can be valuable outlets for social or political advocates. Feature space can be an avenue for dissemination of social advocacy positions.

Facilitating Mass Media Coverage

During this study, I worked with local advocates to use the film *Unreasonable Doubt: The Joe Amrine Case* to draw attention to a case of an inmate on death row in a Midwestern state. Several articles were written in local newspapers about the making and release of the film. These articles discussed Joe Amrine's situation and drew additional attention to the case. Thus, in this instance, the release of the documentary attracted the attention of other mass media outlets. Mass media coverage is also a catalytic factor in the increase in coverage by other mass media news outlets.

Legitimizing Advocate Issue Positions and Activities

As one activist suggested: "Mass media coverage legitimizes." The articulation of positions in mass media confers the perception of acceptability of those positions (Habermas, 1973; Noelle-Neumann, 1999). When mass media outlets feature the perspectives of advocates, it confers symbolic legitimacy on their issue position.

Television is a powerful tool in the legitimization of social or political standards. As Ed explained, television news coverage of a certain perspective contributes to the perceived legitimacy of that perspective:

> The only thing I get out of television coverage on issues like global warming is a legitimization. It's interesting to see, when it comes on TV, it makes me think that the issue is going somewhere. It legitimizes it.

This advocate seems to perceive that articulation on television means that an issue is being evaluated in a certain way by a larger segment of the population. This, likewise, bolstered the advocate's morale. (Mass media likely also played a community-building function, but it was not pronounced enough to specifically identify.) In a particular instance of anti–death penalty advocacy, Lenny perceived that television news coverage legitimized the advocate position:

> There were media personnel there [at a vigil against an execution at the governor's mansion]. They legitimized us . . . they amplified our voice. Authenticated our voice. You're communicating that image. If you can't get that image to the people, they

never see it; they never have to deal with what they don't even know [opposition] exists. If it's not heard, then it's not there.

When Joan promoted an antideath penalty event, she perceived that the legitimacy of her views was increased because she was in the radio studio with the radio program host. Thus, if advocates seek public acceptance of their views, utilization of mass media is a valuable step. Television coverage is perceived to increase the legitimacy of advocate issues and positions. Many audience members view television as objective according to some advocates. Lana suggested the totality of the televisual experience confers a sense of legitimacy: "There is the illusion on television of objectivity. You get an image up there . . . there is an immediate image that is coming at you, sound, everything." The total visual and audio experience of television consumption, according to Lana, creates a sense that the viewer has an objective perspective or is in a position of privileged observer. This legitimizing function arises from the perceived symbolic characteristic of mass media discussed in the next section.

There are a number of functions that advocates believe the use of mass media performs, including mobilizing advocates, promoting events to the general public, lobbying, educating the general public, facilitating additional mass media coverage, and legitimizing advocate issue positions and activities. Advocates perceive that these functions enable mass media to be used to engage mass media consumers in communicative experiences.

Factors That Influence Advocate Mass Media Uses

As evidenced throughout this section, factors that influence advocate media uses include media characteristics, target audience, internal group factors, and external factors. These factors influence the ability to use mass media to engage others in effective communicative experiences.

Characteristics of Mass Media

My discussion of the characteristics of mass media forms is based on the characteristic similarities and differences of the three main mass media forms: print, radio, and televisual mass media. Several characteristics of print media influence advocate use. These include pseudo-intimacy, unique audience, and more issue depth than television coverage of the issues that were important to the advocates in this study. The characteristics of radio, including pseudo-intimacy, captivated listeners, a unique audience, story depth, sound bite importance, and lack of permanence influence advocates' use of radio. The characteristics of television coverage include a large audience, lack of issue depth, lack of permanence, an emphasis on visual elements, an appearance of immediacy, an appearance as objective, and the power to perceptually confer legitimacy. These characteristics are thus perceived as powerful tools by advocates and influence advocates' use of mass media by social and political activists. In an effort to critically explicate the characteristics of the uses of all three media forms, I will compare the characteristics of these mass media through analysis of differences of the characteristics of political and social advocates' uses of print, radio, and televisual media, which include permanence, multiple cues, information-carrying capacity, and personal character.

Permanence

There are differences in the permanence of the main mass media forms. Radio and televisual media are generally less permanent than print media. Print source texts are physically present when they are consumed, thus they possess a level of permanence; whereas broadcast audio and visual signals unfold in a linear fashion so receivers have only one chance to follow the story. Once it is finished, the story is gone. Recorders can capture the text for repeated consideration, but this is likely rare for local television news. With literal, printed texts (not aural), there is a physical presence. Darlene explained this physical presence of mass media print sources: "With a magazine or newspaper, I have it in my hand. There is a tactile thing to it." As a result, audience members can consume print mass media on their own terms. Flanders explained that he consumed print mass media based on his own preferences: "When I am reading it, I can take my time and dissect it. And if I have to look up the word, then I do. Because I am a real anal reader, I make sure that I understand everything as I read it through. So that way I can take my time and digest it." Print mass media allows more options for the receiver to receive in a manner that they choose. Another advocate, Darlene, claimed: "You can read it when and where you like . . . like in the bathroom. That is normally when I do read it, because my husband leaves magazines on the floor in front of the toilet." Some readers feel that they can avoid ads better with print, such as Flanders: "I like the fact that I can digest it on my own time. It's far better than listening to commercial radio because you don't have to hear the commercials." Thus, readers can spend more time on the aspects of the paper that they enjoy rather than on those aspects advertisers would prefer.

Radio does not deliver physical presence the way printed media do. Thus, the audience members do not control presentation of content, but rather the presentation is dependent on the speed that information is presented by the broadcasters. One advocate of the anti–death penalty and environmental protection issues, Flanders, suggested: "NPR sometimes goes a little too quickly for me. Or they use some words that I don't necessarily understand. So you don't always get the complete point that they are trying to make." Flanders compared the radio experience to a literary experience in abstract terms:

> With radio, there's no repetition. I can't go back and read a passage. I can't go back and listen to a passage again. If I miss something, or don't get the whole gist of something, it's gone. I'm a fan of print. You can go back in and look at it. Later on you can go back and reference it again. So that's a limitation of radio.

Television broadcasts lack a physical presence and are usually fleeting. As Tony suggested: "And [the television news story] never comes back again, unless someone happens to have their VCR out by accident. Nobody intentionally tries to save that, usually." For instance, television lacks the presence of print documents, which advocates like Tony may prefer:

> I don't think television is all that great of a means, personally. I prefer print. Because it's in front of the public's eye a lot longer. There is a chance the newspaper will get passed around. Among the family, couple households. With television, people might be playing a game of bridge, whatever.

The physical presence of the printed text allows for repeated consumption. A single printed text can also potentially be read by a number of people.

Multiple Cues

Media richness has explored the existence of multiple cues in various media. The number of cues refers to the presence of audio or visual signal availability (Daft and Lengel, 1986). This concept helps us understand the characteristics of mass media. While newspapers are primarily a textual form, they can also include pictures. This influences the consumption of print mass media by advocates such as Flanders, who enjoys the inclusion of photographs: "And in the magazine like *Mother Jones*, most of it is . . . text, and pictures that are there with the text." This excerpt reveals that pictures can supplement a text. Another advocate suggested that political cartoons are a form of press that can utilize the power of imagery, as Lenny explained: "Certainly editorial cartoons can be extremely political and solid. They can communicate on multiple levels." Thus, while press coverage is predominantly literal (of or related to the printed or written word), it can also incorporate visual elements.

An obvious characteristic of television coverage of the advocates in this study is that the communication has strong visual elements. Flanders explained that this visual character contributed to its power as a means by which advocate messages can be disseminated:

> The visual element is what is so powerful about television. It draws you in . . . the video along with audio are effective. We have evolved as highly visual creatures. That's why television is such a powerful medium. That's why there is so much trash on the air. I choose to not even watch it. Because I know how powerful it is.

Darlene, an advocate who is much more active, expressed a similar feeling about the visual character of television:

> Well . . . on TV it's probably more, . . . I was going to say it is more powerful on TV, but I mean that in very different ways. Television is more powerful because you get a visual image. We might feel outraged, or pity, or sympathy, or an immediate feeling, from the visual image.

This advocate believed that the visual character of television contributed to its emotional effectiveness. Mass media can broadcast the energy and commitment of activists, as expressed by Joan:

> The mass media provided a different frame. It is like you are still seeing the same thing. What is interesting about this, is energy, this purpose, created by this group, that came there and kinda solidified there, it is picked up by the cameras, and transmitted . . . outward images and symbols.

Advocates sometimes consider the most appropriate media for a particular event. Ed contended: "If you've got a meeting with the speaker, you might want to call the radio station or the print media. Or you might get these people's message out. Whereas those speaking to a crowd would not be good TV coverage." Events that have a strong visual component, such as protests, would be particularly appropriate for television, a visual medium. Ed endorsed adaptability among advocates: "Successful advocates use the media that reflect the strength of communication tactics." This also illustrates how this characteristic influences the use of media by astute advocates: If a story has a strong visual component, advocates seek to attract television coverage.

Information-Carrying Capacity

There are differences in the depth in which the three primary mass media forms can cover issues and events, including those promoted by advocates. For instance, the use of the inverted pyramid structure in newspaper writing, as well as more time/space than other mass media forms, allows print sources to go into more depth in stories. Ed suggested, "With a print media, you get more depth. You get more in-depth on what, and why. What studies have been conducted . . . what the consequences are." Abby stated: "Newspapers can generally give more in-depth coverage and analysis to things than TV news."

There are, of course, space limitations with advocates' use of print mass media. As an advocate of universal health care, Wilma, suggested:

> When you look at the A section of the *St. Louis Post-Dispatch*, it's mostly ads. I mean three-quarters of that newspaper is ads. Especially on weekends. Which means how much news can be put in there? Which news to choose to put in?

While print sources may afford opportunity for advocate communication, there are obviously limits to print sources. Newspaper coverage, like coverage from other mass media, can be incomplete. Darlene explained that the issues that were important to her were rarely featured in newspapers she read: "I rarely see things about these issues in the newspaper." This statement reveals that even though there are opportunities for advocates to communicate through print sources, print coverage of the death penalty, health care, or environmental issues in this community was perceived to be rare by some advocates. Kelly, an independent journalist and a veteran of the globalism protests in Seattle, Philadelphia, Quebec, and Washington, D.C., stated that because of the space limitations of newspapers, advocates used sound-bite statements to communicate with print mass media.

Some advocates who were interviewed and observed in the field perceived that radio went into advocacy issues in more depth than television news, especially public radio. Public radio is perceived by many advocates such as Ed to go into more depth than television:

> I occasionally listen to radio, [the university public radio station], NPR. Similar to the difference between television and print, public radio will do a three-minute, even a five-minute spot on an issue. Or on [the community public radio station], they will do a half-hour show on an issue. That is their niche I guess. That's the whole reason for existence. To get into issues a little more in depth . . . they're not just a regular news program.

This advocate perceived that the mission of public and community radio was to go into more depth in their stories than television or even corporate radio when Ed commented: "You can listen to the CBS News [radio], and get the same thing you get on TV." Thus, not all radio outlets are perceived to feature the depth afforded by public radio. Flanders voiced a similar sentiment:

> NPR goes into greater depth on the issues. They spend more time. I am sure NPR probably has more of a liberal perspective on the issues. It seems like there's more fair coverage on NPR. It seems like NPR does a better job of trying to present both sides.

Even though this advocate recognized a liberal disposition in the news coverage of National Public Radio, he still perceived that public radio is more objective than corporate mass media. Another advocate, Darlene, revealed this perception when she said: "But I love listening to National Public Radio because NPR is more bent [than other mass media] toward how I am politically." Ed identified depth on the death penalty issue when he said: "I hear a lot on the radio about the death penalty." These interviews revealed that many advocates believe radio explores issues, sometimes in depth, about which they are concerned.

Despite the depth that radio coverage sometimes affords, there is a limit to the time that radio outlets can spend on advocate issues. As Abby explained: "Radio . . . while there are talk shows and analysis shows, most radio is pretty similar to that in terms of sound-bite news." As noted previously, radio outlets differ in their inclusion of the messages of the advocates in this study. Corporate radio differs little from television news in terms of lack of depth, while public radio provides more opportunity for advocate communication.

One characteristic of television that several advocates noted was the lack of depth devoted to advocacy issues. Tony cited time limitations that contributed to the tendency for television news personnel to favor short sound bites: "And the television news story is five minutes tops. Probably only three minutes, maybe a minute and a half. A picture, you know, a picture, and then some two-sentence explanation." Other advocates also perceive that television affords less issue depth than newspaper stories. Abby suggested advocates must weigh the advantages of reaching large numbers of people against the lack of depth of television coverage: "Television is pretty much a *sound-bite* medium. So you get more depth in the newspaper." Ed expressed a similar sentiment:

> On television you don't get as much detail as you do from a newsletter, or newspapers because whatever you see on TV is usually not over twenty seconds. The latest study, what the U.N. has said, and it's just a summation, whatever they can fit into a twenty-second spot.

Advocates contend that television lacks issue depth. Darlene explained how this characteristic is manifest:

> But in a newspaper story, you don't get all of these little sound bites. On the TV the story is going to go really fast. In the newspaper, there will be more detail. In the newspaper, an interview with a person might be all there. On the TV, you only get a little bit of what they said. "The death penalty is bad." But, . . . I get more justification, and more reasons to take a stand from the newspaper.

Thus, television coverage of advocacy events and positions, especially on television news programs, lacks depth because of the high price of television time.

The importance of the sound bite is not lost on astute advocates. The increasing television news reliance on sound bites is a fact of which advocates can take advantage, as Tony explained:

> Ideally we had all of our [television] media sources. You need to be creative enough, and have to be real clear about the point you want to make. You need to think of a couple of very basic messages that you want to make sure you get across. Quite often, I don't do that too well. That's one of my shortcomings.

Tony recognized that those able to reduce their message to several short statements might be best able to take advantage of television coverage: "Sound bites are what they're getting used to. But something that catches the essence, the spirit of what you're trying to say. And what the action, or campaign is all about." The key to successful television communication rests in recognizing the formulaic tendencies of television journalism. Some advocates use the increased reliance upon sound bites by television journalists to their advantage. Advocates can formulate thought-provoking, terse statements to take advantage of the media's tendency to use sound bites.

Personal Character

Radio consumption is characterized by advocates as having pseudo-immediacy. Because audience members listen linearly to radio as the message unfolds, it is perceived as more immediate than print media, but is not as immediate as physically present interaction. On the radio, the announcer is talking in the now. As Darlene explained: "Though radio is something that I listen to in the car, I can hear that no matter what else is going on. That seems like more of a direct connection to me." This is not necessarily a characteristic of the media itself, but the context in which the media is consumed. This distinction is important. The personal character of radio differs slightly from a discussion of personal characteristics in the contexts of other media but merits noting. Another, more active advocate, Tony, suggested the intimate setting increased the impact of radio broadcasts:

> With radio, it can be a very intimate setting, like driving home from work. The radio is on, it's just a radio and you. It's kind of a unique situation. The oral word is powerful. If it's delivered in a concise and an articulate way radio can be very powerful.

Despite this appearance of intimacy, radio broadcasts did not have the personal impact for some advocates, such as Ed, as much as personal conversation. Ed explained this in hypothetical terms:

If I was invited to go see Howard Zinn on campus, by a person, I would be more
likely together with that [than] if I just heard about it on the radio. On the radio it's
just another thing that I would like to go to if I have time. Making the personal commitment to attend can be motivational.

Thus, while radio may seem to be more personal than print, it is not as immediate as interpersonal communication.

Television coverage of advocacy activities is perceived as more immediate
than literal text. Televisual texts create the illusion that we are witnessing a
phenomenon rather than just consuming someone's version of a phenomenon.
Consistent with Pirsig's (1974) theory of quality, televisual texts allow audience
members "to see and hear and feel the universe, not just one's stale opinions
about it" (p. 273). Because the audience members consume the event as it
temporally unfolds in televisual texts, it has more affective potential than other
media. Lana, a very active environmental advocate who is also a municipal
employee, explained the power of the immediacy of television: "We experience the television news immediately. Well, it is the trick of television. It is the
art. It comes to us as reality. We experience it as the now. We are interacting
with it right in the moment. So we are experiencing it." Thus, viewers feel as
if they are witnessing events on television due to the immediacy attributable to
the linear unfolding of a television presentation rather than reading about the
account from another who witnessed an event as in a newspaper.

The anti–death penalty film produced by local advocates communicated to
some viewers. Darlene explained that the film personalized the issue for her:

Well the films had actors in it . . . [it] made me cry. Although reading has made me
cry too, [in a film], you put a face with the name because you see a person up there
. . . as opposed to reading, where you don't.

A cinematic experience is different from an experience with written text:
There is a unique visual presence of film that literature can lack. Film, like
television or other televisual media, has an immediacy due to the temporal
illusion of witness.

Video can personalize the issue positions of advocates. One advocate, Flanders, wondered what he could do on Mumia's behalf after he viewed a video
presentation on Mumia's case:

I went to an event where they showed a video about a person currently on death row.
He is a celebrity of sorts. The video definitely made the issue more personalized.
Because I actually saw the condemned, and who he was, and listened to him speak.
That goes a long way compared to lecturing on his case.

This advocate raised an important characteristic of video: Video personalizes and humanizes. Flanders suggested that video provides a less abstract image of people than images evoked through spoken word: "Just knowing it was a real person that we were talking about. It was more than just words on a flier; it was really someone's life that was at stake. I felt that more with the video. The video personalized it. The video really brought it to life." Like television, when people watch video, viewers feel as if they are witnesses, rather than just consumers of someone else's account. In the instance of televisual presentations of *Unreasonable Doubt*, the cinematic presentation of Joe Amrine's experiences personalized the death penalty issue for some people.

The characteristics of these mass media forms influence advocates' use of newspapers, radio, and television. The characteristics of print media that influence advocates' use include pseudo-intimacy and more issue depth than television coverage of the issues that were important to the advocates in this study. The characteristics of radio, including a personal pseudo-intimacy, information-carrying capacity (story depth versus sound bite importance), and lack of permanence, influence advocates' use of radio. The characteristics of television coverage include a large audience, lack of issue depth, lack of permanence, an emphasis on visual elements, an appearance of immediacy, an objective appearance, and the power to perceptually confer legitimacy. These characteristics make these mass media forms very powerful media in the minds of advocates and influence advocate use of newspapers, radio, and televisual communication. The advocates studied during this research expended much effort to procure mass media coverage. When promoting events, advocates would, as a matter of course, contact mass media outlets in the effort to get their activities and perspectives discussed in the mass media.

Internal Group Factors

Internal group factors, including resources and group history, influence advocates' use of mass media, as has been repeatedly illustrated, analyzed, and emphasized throughout this study. Because these intergroup factors are similar for newspapers, radio, and print, they will be combined in this section. Internal group resources, such as people power, finances, and knowledge, influence advocates' use of mass media forms, as does access to logistical resources, the history of the organizations and individuals who are at the fore of those groups' advocacy activities, and interaction with other advocacy groups. These internal group factors influence the ability of advocates to communicate their messages through the mass media. A most important factor is available people power.

The *in vivo* concept of people power is critical for understanding how advocates gain mass media coverage.

People Power

As in all other media, the amount of people power wielded by advocacy groups has massive influence on their ability to maximize their communicative potential. People power is necessary to produce video on advocate issues and activities, write letters to the editor, and numerous other communicative tasks. In another case, access to radio broadcasts, as with other forms of mass media, requires what Tony called "people power." This term captures the various requirements necessary for any advocacy communication: numbers of members, time, and energy. Someone must devote the time necessary to get the attention of radio outlets. Someone must take the time to contact the press. What I have been referring to as gumption is part of people power, manifest in initiative by individuals or a group of individuals. Gumption is one aspect of people power, as opposed to numbers of people. One individual, filled with gumption, can provide sufficient people power for completion of some communicative tasks. Tony explained that someone has to expend the effort to get press releases to media personnel:

> I sent out press releases about four or five days ahead of time, to alert individuals about the protest. I've got kind of a standard format. I call the media folks up on the phone the morning of the execution. I ask them if they did receive the media press release. I try to make that personal contact. So I talk to someone and ask them if they had the press release in their hands.

Michelle, a member of a campus Amnesty International chapter, explained that someone had to take responsibility for expending the time and effort to contact the press:

> Somebody had volunteered to do that . . . [a group] volunteered to get the press releases out, so that was another way . . . and then [that group] and [another local advocacy organization] in their publications ran announcements of the event. So like I said before, each cosponsoring organization has their own resources that they can use to get help, to get an event going with the publicity.

Numbers of people committed their time and effort to advocate use of mass media. While advocates' use of mass media outlets is relatively efficient when compared to the other media considered in this book, it still requires expenditure of advocate resources, or people power. In one case, Joan contended that ultimately people power enabled advocate success in producing and broadcasting a cable access segment:

> We could produce a video, that we could maybe send to media . . . you would have to research that. It would be a lot more intensive. You know, we would probably have to pay something to get it, unless you have . . . volunteers . . . to do it, to produce it, to edit it, all that kind of stuff.

While there is potential to reach large audiences, people power, according to this statement, is a necessary condition for advocates to air their activities and perspectives on cable access channels, as with other uses of television. A key anti–death penalty advocate, Tony, identified that his organization lacked the people power necessary to get events on cable access channels:

> We have really neglected that. It's because of people power. Most of the reason that we don't do some things is because we don't have enough people to do them. A lot of people stretch themselves to their limits, and a little bit beyond. What is healthy? We all have our . . . healthy limits. [We have] people working too many hours doing stuff.

The number of active members, their energy, their time, and their talents have an impact on quantity, as is the case with other media. Tony suggested that few advocates underestimate the amount of time and effort necessary to formulate and deliver effective advocacy communication:

> A lot of people say they're willing to jump . . . but they don't understand all that it entails. [Producing a cable access program] takes a lot of commitment, and time. You have to put other issues secondary to it. It's not easy.

Sometimes there are more people willing to volunteer than there are folks who will actually deliver on their commitments. People power plays a key role in procuring cable access, as it does with all the other communication media.

For instance, Tony explained that an article should have appeared in a large metropolitan newspaper because of his significant expenditure of people power. He had dedicated a day to travel to the Kansas City newspaper offices with the wife of a man on death row. Tony has worked as a freelance reporter and has connections at various news outlets. This leader used his presence, his time, his knowledge, and his logistical resources for contacting the newspaper. He generated people power in an effort to use a large newspaper to communicate about the death row case.

Another element of people power necessary to efficiently reach a large audience is the time that these members are willing to contribute. A number of advocates cited time as a major resource, including Ed. Another environmental advocate suggested that volunteer time was the most valuable. Abby explained: "Personal contact is really key to getting media press coverage." That personal contact requires the expenditure of people power.

Advocates like Abby, however, perceive that computer communication has decreased the people power required to gain media attention. "Computer faxes have replaced all of our mail communication with media outlets. We don't send the media any e-mail—we send them a fax." (This is also addressed in chapter 8 on advocate use of computer communication.) This decreases the labor involved with this task. Lana explained that the Earth Day coalition utilized municipal computer resources to disseminate press releases to over thirty mass media outlets: "I believe . . . there is a very complete list that [a member] has, at parks and rec. So we just send her the press packet, and she faxes it out to all of them." Lana perceived that this use of computer communication made dissemination of press releases require less people power. Thus, technological advances had made advocate use of mass media even more efficient.

Lana implied that getting a press release to media personnel is a necessary precursor to gaining media coverage: "Well, we send press releases, press packets, out, several times. But then you're always, that's up to the discretion of . . . whoever, if anything ever gets in or not." Lana also explained that the Earth Day coalition used fax technology to communicate with media personnel: "Well, our press packets, our stuff is faxed." Abby also explained how he used fax technology to disseminate press releases to mass media personnel:

> I sent the news releases through computer fax. We used to mail the press releases. We get tied up with other things, so it's really nice to have that fast access that you get with fax. To the media outlets. Another thing about the fax, is of course, when I called to find out if they got the news release, and the answer is no, I can fax them another. It is a lot quicker means to try to get the press release in the hands of the media outlets.

Thus, while people power is necessary to deliver press releases to media personnel, the use of computer technology can decrease the people power necessary for this task.

Financial Resources

Members' financial resources can be particularly important when it comes to advertising in the mass media. This is the case with print advertising. Lana, who was also a municipal officer, lamented: "It costs a lot of money to put an ad in the newspaper." Newspaper advertising can be very expensive. Another advocate, Ed, explained that one organization he was in used much of their financial resources for buying advertising space: "But there was not a lot of money, because our newsletter chewed up a lot of the funds." As evident in this revelatory statement, resources expended on advertising are resources that cannot be used for other communicative activities. This is addressed more in depth in the discussion of finances as a factor that influences advocate media uses. This statement also implied that groups should be careful when purchasing advertisement in newspapers, advocates should be sure the benefit to the cause outweighs the financial expenditure.

There are costs associated with getting the attention of mass media. However, assuming access to expensive personal computers, contacting the media does not even require the cost of paper and postage. Letters to the editor are a particularly cheap way to gain access to print mass media.

Financial resources are critical for advocacy use of television advertising, as with other mass media advertising. The cost of radio and television advertising is prohibitive for the groups in this study. Advocates sometimes use mass media advertising, although advocates in this community did not often buy advertising time. The attitude was why spend money on ads when we are all trying to tune ads out? Tony explained: "Seeing ads all of the time on TV, they are kind of like. . . . You really try to tune that stuff out. You know, you're not really watching TV to watch the ads. . . . You're not really reading the newspaper to look at the ads." This antiadvertising view was an attitude of many advocates who participated in this study. Thus, advocates expended minimal financial resources to gain mass media attention. The advocates in this study had access to logistical resources such as computer Internet capabilities and other specific equipment such as video-production equipment, as well as other logistical support, which minimized financial requirements for some tasks.

Access to Logistical Resources

Logistical resources can also be critical for gaining the attention of the mass media. It is helpful, for instance, if someone in the group has access to fax technology. In another instance, because Joan had access to a camera and the knowledge about the local cable channel, advocates were able to get an advocacy event distributed through cable.

Expenditures in the effort to attract mass media attention require effort, time, and money, but the communicative payoff is perceived by advocates to offset these expenditures. Advocates perceive that the expenditures are justified for the large potential audiences. Lana suggested that contacting the media is a necessary precursor to coverage by mass media outlets:

> If you haven't sent a press release to the media, you haven't done step number one. Step number one is leading the media, the commercial media; at least [letting them]

know that this is happening. You cannot predict [if they have personnel they] can put on it, or, like, how much space or time you're going to get, but it should be the first thing that you do when you are publicizing anything, and if you can do it several times, if you can add a photograph with it, or if you can make it stand out, so that it catches some interest. Reporters are people. If it's anything that catches you, then you've got a much better chance of getting it into whatever media you are trying for.

People power, financial resources, and access to logistical resources influence advocates' use of mass media, but knowledge is necessary to utilize these resources in ways that are perceived as effective by advocates.

Knowledge

Advocates must possess basic knowledge of personnel procedures, contact information for specific mass media, knowledge about how events can facilitate mass media coverage, and knowledge about how to present an image agreeable to the general public.

A basic knowledge of professional mass media practices can influence advocates' ability to use mass media outlets to disseminate their messages. Advocates must know how to construct a press release, fax it to the stations, and personally contact the news director and reporters. The knowledge about how to communicate appropriately with mass media outlets is certainly a necessary condition for successful advocate use of mass media. An education in journalism can enable advocacy communicators, as Tony explained, since his university experience in journalism has been an asset in his advocacy activities:

Well it was my education, quite frankly. And that is a resource a lot of people don't have. My education was in journalism. At first I thought it was a real mistake to do it that way, when I got real close to graduating. I also got into counseling, something to do with people. Then I began to realize what kind of packaging machine the mass media is, or can be, you know. Corporate media especially. But there are cracks and there we can get word out. And a few work within the system; you have a certain degree of freedom, sometimes.

In this instance, advocates, who are outside the mass media business, possess useful knowledge about how corporate mass media operate to get mass media time or column inches.

There are other ways in which knowledge of media personnel practices influences advocates' uses of mass media practices. Media personnel must deem advocate activities and perspectives to be important or timely enough to warrant coverage. Some advocates emphasize elements in a story that provide an interesting newsworthy angle to a story. For instance, the fact that students contributed to the production of *Unreasonable Doubt* was an element of the story of the video that was repeatedly emphasized by the media. Despite the overstatement of the involvement of students in stories featured in the mass media, Joe Amrine's attorney convinced me to promote that aspect of the story. This knowledge was valuable in convincing mass media personnel that the story merited coverage. A hook to a story can help media personnel perceive it as newsworthy. Abby suggested:

> In terms of dealing with the media, you have to give them some kind of news peg, something that's newsworthy. If it's the old "dog bites a man," it's not news. If it's the same people and the same groups are [advocating the same positions] that's not news.

Advocates who seek a paradigm shift in society may find it more difficult to get media attention. Advocates who focus on incremental changes on one issue may find it less difficult to catch the proverbial fancy of a news-desk assignment editor, according to Abby:

> If you're working at making the underlying cultural change, it's very different than if you're working on trying to effect a specific decision that is the short-run decision, because it will be deemed less newsworthy. To try to make the systemic cultural changes, try to push a paradigm shift [it is different from] when you're trying to get change in a reformist way with one specific issue, like death penalty. Like the moratorium for the death penalty. That is something that is newsworthy. . . . Our media applies definitions if something is imminent; if it's present, if it's right in front of you it's newsworthy. Whereas if it's something long haul or something routine, they don't consider it newsworthy. You burn them out.

Press releases can be more effective if a news hook is developed and incorporated by communicating advocates. Tony explained that when advocates use their knowledge and present a story idea that has an interesting angle, news-media personnel may be more receptive:

> When you send out news releases, you always have to have a hook. Anything that can grab their attention, go for it. You've also got to concentrate on a couple main points. You can't try to present eight or nine hooks out there. . . . Then the media people will get to choose which issues to focus on, and they may choose one that you don't care that much about.

Some advocates perceive that their activities can lose news value in the eyes of media personnel if similar activities were recently covered. There are limits to the amount of coverage any advocacy group can receive. An advocate of universal health care explained: "I think in terms of mass media and overdoing it is . . . self-limiting because then mass media will only cover you to a certain extent." Thus, advocate knowledge of the editorial perceptions of sufficient coverage made by mass media managers influences the ability of advocates to use mass media news organizations.

Knowledge of available mass media is an important resource for advocates, as evidenced in the sections on specific mass media. Abby explained his preparation for media contact about a particular event: "And I went through a list of possible media." Another advocate, Lana, stated that conducting a mass media contact inventory can be valuable in initial promotion planning: "Step number one is probably making a list . . . of all the [mass media] possibilities." One advocate, Joan, explained how radio time was procured: "We call them on the telephone. We organized, and everyone just called them up and got them booked on [two commercial radio programs]." The important aspect of these statements is that the advocate knew who to call and how to talk to them in order to get radio time.

Knowledge of how events can facilitate media coverage can also be an important advocate resource. Some events can be planned that are designed primarily to gain mass media attention. "It depends on what you're doing. I don't let how I think the media is going to cover us affect what we do, but there is nothing wrong with trying to do a media event that's geared to getting media coverage." In this interview excerpt, Abby suggested that a group not pander to the media, or let coverage have too much influence on the activities of the group.

Advocate knowledge of how to control their image can be an important factor in long-term relationships with mass media outlet personnel. If a group is deemed too radical, it may contribute to the group's marginalization by mass media. Ed explained the concept in general:

> Some radical elements might scare people away. They can. I'm a little uncomfortable with people who are. I sometimes think that the people who are not certain of their cause are the most loud. The less sure you are, the more loud that you are likely to be. Sometimes I think that is the case.

Tony explained that not appearing too radical is valuable:

> Staying mainstream can help advocates get access to the media. Not being too radical. They might be less likely to cover somebody who is up there doing something that most viewers would find offensive. On the national level they might get more coverage. But the local news might not want to give you coverage.

Advocacy groups are well served by knowledge of image control. Advocacy communication is more effective when the images of advocates that are disseminated to the public are carefully controlled, as Lana suggested:

I think that one of the problems with social movements is keeping control of the images that we are putting out. Because, not necessarily, their problems with what SDS [Students for Democratic Socialism] had, image control, and all the stuff. It is important for the organizations to be more aware, I don't think, as a group, that we really planned for this event. We didn't think about what, how much more powerful or meaningful ways there might be to stage this. And in a sense . . . it is how you stage it. To have the right props. [Advocates should strive to communicate] a little clearer or a little stronger.

In the case of the environmental advocacy, one organizer, Darlene, expressed a belief that the group got media coverage because it was mainstream: The environmental group "is not in-your-face activism." This advocate associated this maintenance of a mainstream image with the high level of mass media access afforded the environmental advocacy group. One advocate, Ed, expressed skepticism for some of his comrades: "I think people sometimes enjoy delivering the message more than . . . what's behind the message. Do some join your group just to get out there and yell a message?" This interview excerpt reveals the lack of comfort many people have for advocates they perceive as too extreme or unreasonably radical.

Knowledge influences advocacy media choices. One advocate, Joan, suggested that the education of a leading member of the anti–death penalty advocacy community influenced media choices:

I think one thing that effects the way [the anti–death penalty group] communicates is that the main organizer was trained in journalism. I think that has a big impact on how [the anti–death penalty group] communicates.

Ed suggested that leadership in groups could be an important factor in the ability of advocates to use mass media outlets:

There were key individuals willing to put in the effort to lobby these news organizations. To work at getting their attention. And a small market helped as well. Key individuals would put out the press releases religiously. And learned what worked with press releases. And how to put them out, and who to send them to. And those individuals were responsible for the media relations. And those who put the message in a friendly format would get the media coverage.

In sum, advocates' use of mass media can be influenced by their knowledge of how to use newspapers, radio, and televisual mass media, including basic knowledge of personnel procedures, contact information for specific mass media contacts, knowledge about how events can facilitate mass media coverage, and knowledge about how to present an image agreeable to the general public. Praxis requires people power, financial resources, and knowledge, but not as much as other media forms to reach similar or greater numbers of people. Advocates' use of mass media is efficient in terms of people power and financial resources expended for the quantity of people contacted and the potential quality of the audience's communicative experience.

Group History

The history of personal relationships between advocates and television personnel influences advocates' use of television. What separates this discussion of group history from the discussion of knowledge is that the exploration of group factors that influence advocate use of mass media emphasizes developed personal relationships and the habitual patterns of praxis that arise as a result of protracted application of knowledge. Previous experiences of advocates with media personnel can be an important element in procuring television coverage of advocacy activity. For instance, during one protest against an execution, it was apparent that there was a relationship between members of the anti–death penalty advocacy community and the television reporter (a prominent news figure in the region). This helped Tony's ability to air his perspective on television. Communication between anti–death penalty advocates and the reporter was very cordial. Tony asked the reporter at one point if the reporter had heard any good news. The reporter said no, that the Supreme Court had turned down a request to commute the sentence. The reporter then attempted to make sure he had a close-up shot of Tony's sign. This example highlights the symbiotic relationship between television media personnel and advocates. Cooperation can result from this mutual reliance.

The frequency of relational interaction with media personnel can influence the ability of advocates to gain access to newspaper column inches through op-ed pieces. Abby pointed out he consciously tries not to submit too many op-ed pieces: "But I try not to wear out my welcome by giving them an op-ed piece every month." Abby wondered if that was the case with other community advocates: "I noticed for a while that Tony was getting an op-ed piece in any time there was an execution, and I do not know if they've ever said no to him, but I noticed they haven't had one every time an execution was scheduled of late." The important point raised by this statement is that advocates should not overuse their access to such media outlets, especially if timing is important. It desensitizes editors and lessens the chance that an op-ed piece will be featured when the advocates need them the most. If media personnel have a very dense recent history with advocates in a group, they might be less likely to cover the advocacy activity.

Group history can be an important factor in attaining access to television coverage. Previous practices and contacts can influence access to television news outlets. Relationships with mass media personnel are important factors in gaining access to television media, according to Tony:

> A thing about the media that I should mention is that the TV stations, all those other outlets, it's all about the people who are there. It is trying to build some kind of personal rapport with them. That personal rapport helps get coverage, and the longevity. I've known some of these people for twelve years, and it comes with roots, too, in a way. If you mess up, going ahead and apologizing, or if you have something that's bothering somebody about how it's been done. It is probably worthwhile to talk to them about it.

Thus, advocates must strive to maintain working relations with media personnel. Likewise, Tony stated that advocates should not exploit knowledge of the positions held by media personnel:

> And, you know, I'll never use the knowledge that some media person might be against the death penalty. That would be bogus. We have to remind you that it is not a "them and us" thing. These folks are dealing with these issues, reporting about these orders, and these other things. It's got to be tough passing on all the rough news and everything.

This interview excerpt reveals the importance of not abusing knowledge of the personal disposition of media personnel. Group history can be an important factor in attaining access to television coverage. Previous practices and contacts can influence access to television news outlets. Relationships, based on the history of interaction between members of advocacy groups and mass media personnel, are important factors in gaining access to television media. While such leanings of media personnel may be the necessary element needed to procure access to the mass media, such an inside perspective cannot be overused, lest the advocates lose that outlet. This knowledge can be a valuable resource to advocates if they preserve confidentiality. Thus, advocates must work to maintain working relations with media personnel.

In addition, communication contacts at mass media organizations are a valuable membership resource. Previous relationships with media personnel can influence advocate access to mass media coverage.

Overlapping Membership

Media uses of advocates are influenced by the media-use choices of other advocacy groups. Overlapping membership (cases where members are also members of other advocacy organizations) also influences the use of mass media by advocates. Scholars who advocate a bona fide perspective for the study of groups have emphasized these boundary issues. In one instance, I used contact information I had obtained from my involvement in environmental advocacy in my efforts to obtain mass media attention for the anti–death penalty film.

Internal group resources, such as people power, finances, and knowledge, influence advocate use of mass media forms, access to logistical resources, the history of the organizations and individuals who are at the fore of those groups' advocacy activities, and interaction with other advocacy groups. These internal factors influence advocate media choices in their efforts to present effective communication.

External Factors

External factors also influence the ability of advocates to use mass-media outlets. These factors include media-personnel decision factors, which involve interests of media personnel, density of newsworthy events, the general political context, and general technological trends.

Media Personnel Agendas

Mass media personnel must deem an event newsworthy before they cover it. The attendance of media personnel at events is a necessary but not sufficient condition for advocates to get, for instance, newspaper coverage. The editors also have influence in deciding how much access advocates have. Joan described negotiation with a newspaper editorial staff:

> I tried to help the [one local newspaper] . . . to advocate different angles to cover the story, with the editors. But there's a new cultural appropriations bill now . . . this is a policy that would be affecting Missouri farmers. The editors of the [local newspaper] won't even budge for that. Which is an argument that . . . makes perfect sense.

In this instance, the advocate attempted to suggest a useful frame in which the editors could justify a discussion of the issue.

During the time I studied these groups, there was dramatic growth in some anti–death penalty event participation. Instead of discussing these local events, the local newspaper only carried a wire story on specific information about the execution itself. Ed summed up the situation:

> In the local paper, even though there's a lot of local activism, the biggest local paper occasionally chooses not to cover locally initiated activity. It just pulls the national wire. It could be the political affiliation or the personal feelings of the editor of the paper, or the ownership of the paper. That would be my guess. Why would you fea-

ture a two-inch story that you pulled off the wire when there are local people who
are active and involved in it? You could cover it and bring . . . more local flavor to it.

When asked why the unprecedented turnout was not mentioned in the main
community newspaper, advocates brought up the editorial position of the
newspaper publisher. An anti–death penalty advocate, Tony, expressed disap-
pointment in the perceived motivations behind the editorial decisions made by
the community newspaper:

> I get disappointed by [a local newspaper] oftentimes. It's not as if they support the
> death penalty in theory, actually the position is to oppose it. The publisher's position
> is to oppose it. I think that if you're going to cover news, they should pay attention
> to what happens in your local community. I guess from their perspective they feel that
> individuals in front of the courthouse is nothing new. Is it news? They continue to
> cover each person that is executed. Which they should.

However, another leading community advocate, Abby, suggested that the
newspaper just failed to have a reporter on the scene: "I think they have relatively few reporters to go out, in [this town] they have a guy and [in the capi-
tal]." Another community activist suggested that they should have sent a
reporter: "The newspaper really should have had somebody at that last vigil. I
personally feel that anytime you kill a human being, there should be attention
paid by all the media. And it is worthwhile to know when the people are protesting it as well." Thus, advocates sometimes perceive that mass media personnel neglect advocacy positions and activities.

Another community activist suggested that mass media personnel might not
view certain protests as newsworthy because of the regularity of the protests:
"The thing is the [local city newspaper] generally doesn't cover demonstrations
that much, . . . unless it's something big and out of the ordinary. Since there
are protests every time there is an execution, it's assumed that it's probably just
a routine kind of thing." This statement reveals that this advocate perceived
that newspaper personnel had become desensitized to the news value of some
events. Several advocates attributed the lapse to the editorial position of the
publisher of a local newspaper: "I know that the owner is somewhat conservative. That can influence how they cover what story. In what manner they
cover it. The way they covered the recent death penalty issues, there was no
mention of local activity."

On the other side of the coin, the stance of the editorial staff can also benefit
organizing advocates. One longtime community activist, Matt, pointed out
that: "Both the *Kansas City Star* and the *St. Louis Post-Dispatch* are anti–death
penalty, and one of them runs a related editorial piece after each execution."

Thus, the editorial discretion of the newspaper can influence how much atten-tion advocate issues are raised in print sources.

External factors can influence advocates' use of radio. Public radio and com-mercial radio differ in their funding sources. According to some advocates, this creates differing influences of advocate access to radio outlets. Public commu-nity radio must have donors, and the most powerful of these donors may influence time afforded advocates. One advocate charged that a local commu-nity station was too willing to fold to the wishes of the most significant finan-cial donors. As a result, Joan perceived that the news managers of the community public radio station had become less willing to cover local contro-versial advocacy activities.

Community radio boards of directors also influence advocacy access to radio. Like any other enterprise that must stay solvent, local community radio managements must be concerned with the economics of community philan-thropy. Thus, those governing the policies of community radio may be suscep-tible to the influence of perceivably significant donors. Joan explained this situation in the community studied in this project. She perceived that major contributors can influence the access that advocates have to radio broadcasts: "In the case of [local community radio], the local news programming got can-celed, . . . apparently because some powerful people were getting a little irri-tated about the investigative reporting that was going on." The climate created by radio management can influence the ability of advocates to use radio.

University-sponsored stations are subject to different constraints. Joan explained that demands for radio production classes at the university increased advocates' access:

> In the case of [the university radio station], I've been told that the reason that they stopped doing [local news] is because there is less demand for radio journalism. And so they're teaching radio journalism less. And [the university station] was the lab for the journalism school, as such, as far as radio journalism was concerned.

Thus, coverage afforded by the university station to local advocacy activity is potentially limited by the student demand for radio journalism education. While neither university nor community radio managers needs to be con-cerned with turning a profit for a nonexistent owner, there are other consider-ations that influence advocate access to these radio outlets. This contextual consideration decreased the number of reporters at the university station and decreased the ability, according to Joan, to get the attention of reporters who remained at the university station.

Commercial radio stations, on the other hand, depend on advertisers to turn the necessary profit. If these advertisers object to the content of the news programs, this revenue source could be in jeopardy. Joan believed concern for advertisers kept a local commercial news radio station from covering some advocacy events. In addition, feedback from listeners might influence the coverage of advocate activities or issues. This concern is indirectly related to the desire to keep advertisers happy; if numbers reveal strong audience numbers, this can contribute to advertiser demand for advertising time on the station.

The personal perspectives of television news personnel can be important. This was revealed in a narrative provided by Joan, in which the personal interests of a particular reporter influenced the amount of television news coverage advocates were able to procure. Thus, the personal perspective held by a reporter can influence the kind of story that gets broadcast. The perspective held by media personnel can influence the access that advocates get in the mass media. Lana explained that the perspective held by a local television personality influenced the amount of access environmental advocates got on the program:

> Well, one, the host is . . . considers himself an environmentalist. And . . . so he is interested. So I have a monthly appearance. We talk about environmental and waste issues. And, so, if he didn't have that, he might not . . . the host is always looking for something to put on a show, of course, but it is nice having a monthly thing.

When asked why more advocates did not make use of this medium, the environmental advocate, Lana, replied: "Well, I think a lot of people think it's a geeky show. [Laughs]." Some advocates in this community underestimated the utility of the local television program. However, advocates recognized that the local television program afforded time that the environmental coalition could not afford, as Lana suggested: "It is impossible to pay for radio or TV, it's just way out of the ballpark of what our organization could . . . pay." Thus, through appearances on this local television program, the environmental advocates reached audience sizes that the costs of ads could have prohibited if the time had to be bought. The costs of television time can be avoided if advocates work with the staff of local television programs.

Any advocacy story on television must compete with the other newsworthy events of the day. This is likely true for other mass media as well. At one point, I saw a note on CNN that the state of Missouri was executing a person that night. Darlene stated: "It was media coverage . . . but I don't know why they covered it. Maybe it was the most salient news item out of Missouri today." The local mass media often focuses upon executions. Local television channels often broadcast news programs that announce the latest news on the night of an execution. In these cases, the number of other important events of the day can influence the time afforded advocate issues in the mass media.

Advocates such as Tony contended that the demographic composition of the television audience in the area in which this study was conducted made television access easier to get:

> The size of the market can determine access to mass media. In a smaller market town it was much easier to get on TV . . . the desire for local news coverage. When there's less competition for that local news coverage, it's easier to get on. In a bigger market, it's a little tougher.

The commercial television context in this community was favorable to advocacy groups seeking television coverage. The media market in a particular community can influence the ability of advocates to get the attention of mass-media outlets, as Tony explained: "We are blessed in some ways. We are in a media-saturated town, which is a blessing, good fortune. We have three TV stations."

Another external factor that could influence advocate use of television is the existence of cable access opportunities for members of a community. In the community studied in this project, there was more than one cable access channel, according to Lana: "I think in the past reviews, there is another, there is city cable access and then there is another, in addition to the school access channel, there is a community access channel." Some local cable service companies have provided the logistical support for community production efforts. However, that level of company support was not present in the central community studied in this project.

Political Context

The political climate can influence advocates' ability to get mass media coverage. For instance, some advocates believed that death penalty moratoriums in some states have increased the perceived salience of that issue and contributed to higher levels of mass media coverage of the death penalty issue. Tony believed there was increased coverage on the death penalty in the mass media because: "In Illinois they initiated a moratorium. In New Hampshire they passed some kind of legislation. And in Nebraska, there are moratorium bills, and the governor says he'll sign both of them." This national climate may also increase the newsworthiness of the death penalty issue for media personnel, according to Tony:

> That certainly allows for more access. [The national anti–death penalty climate] is a big media hook. It's too obvious of a hook. Legislators can't say . . . I don't want to tread on entirely new ground. Other people have been on this before, and talked about it before. And so for the media, it doesn't look so far-fetched. It looks like something that could happen. And the baseline at the state capitol of whether morato-

rium can happen or not, it is very much dependent upon the mass media, I think. It helps build good credence with your readers, and your subscribers, and your listeners, and your viewers.

Tony also perceived that presidential politics might influence the quantity of advocate media uses studied here:

I think that's kind of a mixed bag . . . because people are really pissed off obviously pissed off, because they voted for tweedledee instead of tweedledum, and the wrong one is in the office. Whoever they got. It has probably mobilized some people for sure.

This statement reveals that this leading community activist believed that the victory of Bush in the 2000 election, as well as the controversy surrounding the election, might have contributed to mobilization of left-of-center social advocates.

General Technological Trends

Obviously, the development of mass media technology was a necessary precursor for advocate use of these media. In another case, the growth of cable access capabilities has increased corollary opportunities for advocates. In the case of computer fax as the preferred way to contact media personnel, the trend within the mass media industry to rely on faxes pushed advocates to use this means as a vehicle for procuring mass media coverage of their perspectives and activities. In all of these instances, general technological trends have influenced advocates' ability to use mass media to disseminate their messages.

Before the personal computer surge of the 1980s and 1990s, advocates contacted media personnel through press releases that were either sent through the mail or personally delivered. The adoption of fax technology by mass media professionals led advocates to adopt the fax as the most viable way to contact mass media personnel, including television staff. The incorporation of computer-fax capabilities has increased the efficiency of obtaining mass media coverage. The adoption of fax by advocates to communicate with the mass media is an adaptation to changes in the practices of mass media personnel, as explained by Abby:

Well . . . we sent them by mail for many years, then we would try to follow up with phone calls. When we asked, "Did you get our news release?" I noticed that about five years ago, maybe six or seven years ago that when I called to do the follow-ups, I started to get the question, "When did you fax that? Well, can you fax one over?" Then I realized that the professionals were using fax machines for news releases. That's what news organizations were doing.

The adoption of fax technology has made the delivery of news releases a less laborious proposition, especially when computer technology is used. Lana explained that the computer-fax capabilities of a municipal office were used to promote the events of the environmental coalition for low expenditure of time (she could make it happen while on the municipal clock) and low financial expenditure:

> Before we had the computer fax capability, you had to . . . put it in the envelopes and mail it out. And here is . . . a touch of a button, and I think she's got it lined up so all she has to do is, . . . do it from her computer. I don't even think she has to go to the fax machine. Maybe she has to go to the fax machine and push one button . . . that goes to, you know, all of these organizations. It is very efficient. It saves you money. And it is probably the way they like it too.

Thus, the adoption of this technology saves temporal and financial resources. As Lana suggested: "I think you should really . . . try to do their work for them . . . send feature articles maybe." Due to the adoption of fax reception as the modus operandi of mass media personnel, advocates of computer-fax capabilities have made gaining the attention of mass-media news personnel less expensive and lowered the labor intensity of necessary task requirements; contacting mass media personnel has become more efficient. For instance, advocates like Abby perceive that computer communication has decreased the people power required to gain media attention: "Computer faxes have replaced all of our mail communication with media outlets. We don't send the media any e-mail—we send them a fax." This decreases the labor involved with this task.

Thus, advocate use of mass media is influenced by a number of external factors, including media-personnel decision factors, which involve interests of media personnel, density of newsworthy events, market factors, and access opportunities. The general political context and general technological trends are also external factors that influence advocate ability to use mass media. The factors can enable or infringe upon the desire of advocates to present emotionally engaging communicative experiences through mass media.

Conclusion

Advocates use the ubiquitous mass media in efforts to communicate. There are three forms of mass media used by advocates: Advocates use newspapers, radio, and television to communicate with their fellow advocates, the general public, politicians, and mass media personnel, although the general public is the most important target audience of advocates when advocates use mass media. The mass nature of the audience precluded differentiation. There are a number of functions that advocates believe the use of mass media perform, including increasing attendance at events, lobbying, educating, facilitating mass media coverage, and legitimizing advocate issue positions and activities. Characteristics of mass media include permanence, multiple cues, information-carrying capacity, and personal character. Activist use of mass media is perceived to be an important tool in advocacy efforts, although internal group factors and external factors also influence advocate use of mass media. Internal group factors, including people power, finances, and knowledge, influence advocate use of mass media forms, access to logistical resources, the history of the organizations and individuals who are at the fore of those groups' advocacy activities, and interaction with other advocacy groups. External factors include media-personnel agendas, the political context, and general technological trends.

8

Connecting through Computers

Before 1985, none of the groups studied here used computers in their advocacy efforts. Now all of them do, to a greater or lesser degree. In an effort to communicate, advocates perceive that computer communication is a valuable tool. The use of computers by advocates in this study is consistent with the massive growth in the use of computer technology in the United States. According to the U.S. Census Bureau (2001), over 40 percent of American households have computers and over 25 percent have Internet access. Millions of others have access to computer communication technology through school or work. In 1999, 57 million people reported having access to the Internet (Scenic Digital, 1999). There are at least 10 billion Web pages in existence (Swartz, 2001). Flanagan and Metzger (2001) pointed out that over 147 million people from many countries use the Internet—World Wide Web. Selnow (1998) explained the potential prominence of the role of computer communication technology in political advocacy efforts: "If it continues to grow as predicted, the Internet will soon stand alongside the conventional media and become an indispensable tool in political communication" (p. xxii).

Despite the financial setbacks in the computer industry resulting from market saturation and overvaluing the profitability of high-tech ventures, especially with Internet businesses (which has historically occurred with a variety of major technological advances throughout American history), personal computers will be a permanent feature of the media-consumption practices of many people throughout the world. As Benoit and Benoit (2001) postulated, "The Internet, does not reach everyone, but it is already beginning to exert its potential for disseminating information and affecting the voting behavior of millions of voters" (p. 3). As the use of personal computers has proliferated in other areas of human interaction, computers have also been increasingly adopted as a valuable medium in advocacy efforts. An anti–death penalty advocate who was extensively active (participates in over twenty events a year) explained the importance of anti–death penalty use of computer communication technology when she said: "The anti–death penalty community must learn to more effectively use computer communication. The other side certainly has. [One of the organizations with which I am involved] does whatever it can to connect people with computers." Advocates' use of computer communication technology requires academic exploration.

In this chapter, I examine advocates' uses of computer communication technology. I first outline types of computer communication technology advocates use. Second, I briefly discuss the intended audiences of uses of computer communication. I then identify the functions these uses perform. Finally, I list the factors that influence advocates' use of computer communication technology, particularly the influence of the characteristics of computer communication technology. In accordance with theoretical ideas that have emerged during the course of this study, this chapter reveals that advocates use media to perform a variety of functions, and these uses are influenced by a plethora of factors, most notably the characteristics of uses of computers as a medium for advocacy communication. Advocates hope to engage audiences in communicative experiences through uses of computer communication. I will first identify the forms of computer communication used and then the intended audiences of these computer uses. Finally, I identify the function of these uses.

Forms of Advocate Computer Communication

Advocates use a variety of computer communication forms, including e-mail, Web pages, and computer-fax capabilities. As with the general population, advocates have increasingly used several forms of computer technology to communicate. In 1980, none of these groups used computer communication; in 2002, all of them used computer communication.

E-Mail

E-mail can be a two-way communication channel, if advocates check and respond to their e-mail often. Within the e-mail messages issued by a university-sponsored chapter of an international anti–death penalty organization, suggestions and volunteers to help prepare for events are solicited. In these particular messages, a link to an e-mail address is provided, allowing for easy e-mail reply. Announcements of upcoming executions and related advocate activity are sent via e-mail by the local chapter of another international anti–death penalty organization. Earth Day executive committee members are notified of upcoming meetings through e-mail communication.

Listservs can also be a way that advocates use e-mail. Listservs are groups of e-mail addresses used to reach a certain audience. Abby practically defined the form of a listserv when he suggested that he had various lists of e-mail addresses grouped together so he could instantaneously e-mail a number of fellow activists with one send command: "I know . . . [of] a lot of activist lists where anybody or everybody can post the whole list." For instance, Lenny explained the university chapter of Amnesty International "has been working with an e-mail listserv." These examples provide ample evidence that advocates are using e-mail.

Web Pages

The advocacy groups studied also used Web pages. The Earth Day coalition launched a Web page in 2000. The page promoted the 2001 Earth Day event and the opening page featured the graphic logo chosen for the local event. Clicking on the large logo enabled users to access the Web site. The first page provided general information about the event as well as links to the entertainment stage schedules, information about booths, as well as links to eighteen cosponsoring organizations. In an effort to describe the Web page, I noted that almost all of the pages on the site were textual, with the exception of the initial logo/site entrance. Approximately ten months since its inception, the site reported 1,057 visitors. Links to coalition-member organizations were also offered, including a link to the national Earth Day organization, which also maintained a Web site.

The local chapter of a national anti–death penalty organization posted a rudimentary page in 1999 and updated it with impressive features and design in 2000. A description of the revised site noted it was all text and offered links to previous issues of the group's newsletter as well as links to an expanded explanation of the organization's perspective on a number of current events, including executions that had recently occurred in the state, scheduled executions, and legislation on the death penalty issue. Links to other relevant Web sites were also offered.

The local universal health care advocates did not maintain a Web page. Instead, they often referred people to several sites maintained by national organizations that advocated universal health care coverage.

The use of Web pages facilitates communication with people who look for information on the Internet, according to advocates such as Lenny: "The Internet is a great medium." Obviously, as Darlene explained: "they can go to a Web site and get information." Active death penalty opponents also provided information about future activities in conjunction with local efforts, as a national advocate, Helen, explained, was the case with her group as it worked with local advocates: "[Our group] also has a Web page that folks can interact with. As soon as we contact them with e-mail, we send them a link to our Web page." The Web pages maintained by these advocates offered communicative options for prospective advocates seeking more information about advocacy issue positions and activities.

Computer Fax Technology

Advocates also use computer fax programs, which send a photocopied facsimile of a printed document through telephone lines to receiving devices at other geographical locations. In the 1980s, advocates sent faxes through fax machines that were connected to traditional telephone-receiving technology, but advocates' use of fax machines has been displaced by computer fax generation due to the convenience of faxing through computer technology rather than telephone technology. This is also noted later as a factor that influences use of computer communication. For instance, I, as director and producer of *Unreasonable Doubt: The Joe Amrine Case*, used computer fax communication to contact media personnel at least ten times. The technology allowed a fax to be sent to over twenty mass media outlets.

In sum, there are a number of forms of advocate uses of computer technology, including e-mail, listservs, Web pages, and fax capabilities. While some advocates might use chat rooms, none of the advocates included in this study utilized chat rooms in conjunction with advocacy activity. One of the assets of computer communication technology is this variety in message form.

Intended Audience

Advocates use computer communication to reach several audiences, including advocates, the general public, politicians, and mass media personnel. First, advocates use computer communication to communicate with one another. For instance, several of the anti–death penalty advocacy organizations often sent e-mail messages to active members. A leading community environmental activist contended: "E-mail is especially helpful for alerting your base constituents. Your base activists can rely on e-mail for some communication." E-mail can be more effective if it comes from people the receiver already knows, as Lenny explained:

Well, with e-mail, it would depend or whether it was from a stranger, or whether it was from . . . someone I communicated with previously, or if it is someone . . . that you . . . take seriously, or respect. If it was from, just . . . getting e-mail in my mail, I would probably . . . if it was something I was already interested in, I probably wouldn't pay very much attention to it.

Core group members use computer communication, especially e-mail, to communicate with one another. Tony explained that e-mail could be particularly effective for communication between advocates who already share a relationship: "E-mail is handy, especially with people who are familiar with each other I think. You know, you already have a basis of knowledge about who the other person is."

Advocates who do not have computer access are an inappropriate audience for this media. Flanders clearly explained that because he was not online, computer communication was inappropriate to communicate with him: "I am not online. I don't have access, I don't have easy access." Despite the increasing number of individuals with computers, there are individuals who do not have access and they perceive access as difficult. One advocate succinctly stated the point: "E-mail is a technology that is only available to a few people. It isn't available to everybody."

E-mail is more appropriate for some audiences than others. Ed suggested: "It seems like e-mail is most valuable for people who are already involved. To keep them in touch with what's going on." Ed believed that while e-mail may be a great way for those most active to communicate, it may not be the best media for those only nominally active.

The general public is another intended audience for advocate Web pages. For instance, the opening sentence of the environmental coalition's Web page invites advocates and the general public to become involved in the Earth Day event. Because the Web page is targeted to anyone who downloads it, there is general information for those who have previously not been involved as well as for those who are currently involved or have been involved in the past.

Advocates also used computers to communicate with politicians. The producers of *Unreasonable Doubt: The Joe Amrine Case* included the governor's e-mail address at the end of the documentary to encourage audience members to use computer communication in advocacy. The producers also included a direct link to the governor's e-mail on their Web page to facilitate e-mail communication with the governor's office. As the director, producer, and writer of the documentary as well as the president of the Graduate Student Association of a large Midwestern university, I e-mailed the governor through our Web page at least ten times.

Media personnel are the primary audience for advocates' use of computer-generated faxes. Abby, an important member of the environmental coalition, suggested that when advocates perceived that media personnel had adopted fax machines as the primary channel for news releases, the environmental advocates began to send faxes via computer modem. The advocates studied here did not use faxes to communicate with the general public. Very rarely did advocates use fax capabilities to communicate with one another, although local anti–death penalty advocates did receive faxed information from an international organization that was planning several events in the specific geographical region studied here.

Thus, advocates use computers to communicate with several audiences, including other advocates, the general public, politicians, and media personnel. Advocates have adapted to changes in the consumptive tendencies of these audiences.

Functions of Advocate Computer Use

Advocates use computers to perform a variety of functions, including mobilizing advocates, arranging logistical details, building community, lobbying, educating, facilitating mass media coverage, and legitimizing advocate activities and issue positions. Flanagan and Metzger (2001) suggest that "examination of the functional images of communication technologies adds a great deal to our understanding of the current media environment" (p. 175). These authors were suggesting that perceptions of what computer communication does are a valuable aspect of analysis of computer communication uses. Computer communication is increasingly adopted as a tool for advocacy as personal computers have spread pervasively into people's daily lives.

Increasing Attendance at Events

E-mail is a communication channel that an advocate group can use to keep those involved with the group informed of affiliated activities. The groups included in this study used e-mail to announce group-sponsored events. Event purpose, time, location, and particular aspects of events can be communicated with e-mail. For example, one anti–death penalty organization, a local university chapter of Amnesty International, sends at least one e-mail a week to about 150 recipients who have expressed interest in the organization and who have provided their e-mail addresses in order to receive more information about the local chapter of Amnesty International. Abby, an informal leader of the Earth Day coalition, suggested that his experience indicated that advocate use of computer communication could aid in mobilizing advocate attendance at events: "E-mail is really good for notifying people about events. And giving people a reminder of something that's going to happen."

Arranging Logistical Details

Advocates use e-mail to confirm logistical details, such as the date, time, and location of organizational meetings. Minutes from meetings of organizations are sent via e-mail and typically contain much information about logistical details. Suggestions from members are requested in e-mail messages, and the most salient logistical concerns are discussed. E-mail was very valuable in the coordinating efforts of the environmental coalition. For instance, finalization of schedules of Earth Day activities were checked and confirmed through at least twenty e-mails in the week before the event. Several contributing advocates communicated exclusively through e-mail. E-mail responses were also used in conjunction with paper communication and telephone calls.

E-mail also offers the opportunity to coordinate local, national, and international events. For instance, at one point I received an e-mail concerning the impending execution of political prisoner Mumia Abu-Jamal. The e-mail explained that the governor of Pennsylvania had signed Mumia's death warrant and that his execution would take place on December 2. This e-mail requested a demonstration and explained plans for demonstrations in New York, Philadelphia, and San Francisco. The notice was forwarded through a local activist, and this computer communication was used to coordinate local and national activities.

In the meetings of the environmental coalition, e-mail was a key channel for construction of the Web page. The designer of the Web page contacted members of the environmental coalition steering committee to let them know that the Web page was online and requested feedback from the committee members via e-mail. Subsequently, advocates used the Earth Day Web site to learn more about logistical details necessitated for coordination of the event.

Building Community

As with the uses of other communication media, a communal sense can be cultivated through computer communication. If advocates invest in computer uses, it is perceived as real, authentic communication, according to Lenny. When asked if he perceived e-mail communication to be authentic communication, Lenny responded:

> People believe it's real if there are consequences. That is how I look at it. People kind of view it as all these fields that we interact in. And there are all the streams . . . going

out there and getting your voice authenticated. If it's an authenticated U.S. human being, if it promotes dialogue with others, and it is building community.

This activist suggests that if communicators personally invest themselves in the communication, then it is authentic, and this builds community.

Lobbying

Advocates who participated in this study also used computer technology to communicate with policymakers. As an extremely active anti–death penalty advocate, I used e-mail a number of times to communicate with policymakers. The link to e-mail the governor on the anti–death penalty group's Web page is an example of how advocates could use computer communication to express opposition to impending executions. Unfortunately, advocates perceived that e-mail communication with elected officials could be easily ignored. A universal health care advocate suggested: "In talking to legislators we found messages sent by e-mail don't carry a lot of weight. They dumped them real quickly. It's not really tangible, and does not really show that someone put in effort." Advocates only used fax capabilities to communicate to mass media personnel, not politicians. Computer communication is perceived as inappropriate for some functions. For instance, Tony believed that computers were not as effective for lobbying as some other media: "E-mail, however, is not useful for everything." Ed concurred: "There are some things that don't lend themselves easily to that. I mean you can't really petition on the Web. You have to hand-deliver those kinds of things." On the other hand, even e-mail communication to elected officials is likely better than no communication. Thus, there are limits to use of computer communication technology for lobbying.

Educating

Advocates also use e-mail communication as a news alternative to corporate-controlled media. An advocate explained:

> For example, Bush just tried to pass through legislation that would allow political assassinations. But you won't see that in the media. I think the only place I've seen that is in the e-mail. And I've sent that out to everyone I can think of.

One drawback of e-mail is that it is not always accurate, so research is sometimes necessary to verify information delivered through this source. Thus, e-mail can provide advocates with information they might not be able to get from other media forms. In an instance of anti–death penalty advocacy, an advocate said that she had received an e-mail from a listserv discussion list that announced news of positive developments in a death penalty case on which the group had been working. Nancy suggested that a federal judge had looked at the case and determined that there were some irregularities in the previous trial that needed to be examined. Nancy said she was not clear on the specifics, but that she had forwarded the e-mail to other group members.

The advocate Web pages studied here offered multiple communicative options for prospective advocates seeking more information about advocacy issue positions and activities. For instance, advocates used the Earth Day Web site to offer specific information about the event and the coalition, such as specific times and dates of activities and links from a list of coalition member organizations.

Advocates used Web pages as an educational medium to reach nonadvocates, such as university students, on activist issues and activities on the death penalty issue. Lenny perceived that directing his sociology students to Web sites that addressed incarceration and execution data was valuable as a venue for issue education:

> The Internet is a great medium. You can take the students directly to . . . the criminal justice page, and they can see the statistics themselves. Statistics on the death penalty, and they are not what people think. What has been happening with falling crime over the last ten years, it's falling like a rock. The students can start to get our real picture from the stats. They can get free access to the statistics through the Internet.

Web page links to other sites are also an important educational function when considering advocacy use of this medium. Advocate Web pages allow access for individuals surfing the net: "Then they can get other sites. They can go to pro–death penalty sites, and to antideath penalty sites, look at the arguments. So Web pages can be a wonderful tool." The focus here is not necessarily on the functions for advocates but for users. Some of the options offered in the Web pages of these advocacy groups were clearly an educational avenue directed to the general public as well as to other advocates. For instance, a page on the anti–death penalty group site offered a link to a section titled "How You Can Get Involved." This link was obviously targeted to people who were not currently active rather than to those who were. In the case of the environmental coalition, the Web page offered rudimentary information that anyone who had been previously involved with the event would know.

Web pages, however, are only valuable if people go to them. Wilma, an advocate of universal health care, suggested that this was a critical factor for Web-page success:

> Well, with the Web page, you have to get people coming to it. So that is another whole marketing and promotional thing to consider, which we really haven't consid-

ered yet. I mean, finding the Web page, you have to get people to come to it. It's not something you can just put . . . out there, and it's there, if they . . . come to it. So, the design of the Web page, it's almost like you need to hook them into doing that.

Design of the Web page is important to drawing surfers into the messages of advocates. This is a necessary precursor for successful performance of the educating function evident in advocates' use of computer communication.

Facilitating Mass Media Coverage

Computer fax capabilities can be used to communicate with media personnel, according to Ed: "Faxes have also been a technological advance that have [*sic*] been useful for advocates, to communicate with the press." While fax capabilities are virtually useless for communicating to the general public, they do facilitate communication with media personnel.

In sum, advocate computer use is influenced by choices concerning communicating to other advocates, the general public, and politicians, and media personnel. Computer fax capabilities are primarily used to contact media personnel. Abby explained how he uses computer fax capabilities for communication with mass media organizations:

> I don't send any e-mail to media folks. I do that through fax. I contact them through Internet faxes. I do that because I think that's what's generally done, and I think that is a little harder to ignore. You get a piece of paper that has to at least be put in the recycle bin rather than just reading any e-mail. Something that comes up on screen.

Computer fax technology is useful for communicating with media personnel because these media businesses depend on computer communication, according to Tony:

> We integrated computer technology into advocacy to make our communication quicker, to speed up our delivery. All of the mass media are computer friendly. You can mail stuff, that's all right. But if you're not at the point that you are working with the computer technology, then you're kind of screwed if they haven't received it. It is very often the case that they've lost the press release; you have to figure out another way to get the news release to the media person.

The environmental coalition never used telephone fax delivery, but rather only began sending faxes after they obtained Internet communication capabilities, as Abby suggested: "We've always used [computer] fax modem. We've never had a manual fax machine. We use fax modem." Some advocates use computer fax capabilities instead of traditional fax machines. The advocates studied here used fax technology only to communicate to media personnel and not other audiences. Anti–death penalty and environmental advocates used computer fax capabilities to communicate with mass media personnel, but the universal health care advocates did not.

Legitimizing Advocate Activities and Positions

Advocate use of computer technology, including e-mails, Web pages, and computer-generated faxes, is perceived by some advocates to reflect the strength of the advocate communities centered around a particular issue. Darlene explained that she believed that the lack of e-mail communication and the lack of a Web page for the local universal health care advocate community represented problems within the group: "When I never get an e-mail from the group and I can't see what other advocates are up to on a Web page, it starts to make me think that the group is not as healthy or active as some of the other groups I am involved with." Thus, for this advocate, the uses of computer communication media symbolize advocate group legitimacy.

The legitimizing function is related to the symbolic value of computer communication because computer use symbolizes technological proficiency and logistical competence. As addressed under the discussion of functions, advocates' use of computer technology, including e-mails, Web pages, and computer-generated faxes is perceived by some advocates to reflect the strength of the advocate communities centered on a particular issue.

Mobilizing advocates, arranging logistics, building community, lobbying, educating the public, facilitating mass media coverage, and legitimizing advocate activities and issue positions are functions that advocates perceive are served through computer communication. These functions are repeatedly present in this development of a theory of advocate media use. While advocates do perceive that use of computer communication can perform a variety of functions, advocates' use of e-mail and Web pages is not a panacea. Some advocates feel that e-mail use is not necessary for successful advocacy. One moderately active advocate, Jossey, stated she did not need to remain in e-mail contact: "I don't feel the need to use e-mail to contact the [anti–death penalty] organization, because the people that are most integral to my involvement, so far as I'm concerned, already know what my plans are." For some advocates, other means of communication are sufficient. The advocate, Jossey, however, did gather information about the activities of the group from its Web page. Nonetheless, this advocate perceived interpersonal communication and group-meeting communication as sufficient.

Factors That Influence Advocate Computer Use

Factors that influence advocates' use of computer communication include the characteristics of computer media, internal group factors, and external factors. These factors are similar in many regards to the influences on use of other media forms.

Characteristics of Computer Media

The characteristics of advocacy computer communication media use influence advocates' use of computer communication technologies. Some scholars have suggested that media-richness schemata are more useful for study of traditional media, but are less useful for studying computer media communication. I found media richness a valuable theoretical tool for the study of advocates' use of computer media. This affirms Flanagan and Metzger's (2001) suggestion that "perspectives that focus on media attributes in order to explain individuals' reasons for media use (e.g., media richness) remain important" (p. 175). These characteristics include feedback, multiple cues, language variety, personal character, distance, and permanence.

Feedback

Media-richness scholars have suggested that one aspect of rich media is rapid feedback (Daft and Lengel, 1986; Daft, Lengel, and Trevino, 1987; Rice and Shook, 1990; Sitkin, Sutcliffe, and Barrios-Choplin, 1992). For instance, this study revealed that feedback could be rapid if advocates regularly use e-mail capabilities. As Joan suggested: "And that's where e-mail can be very useful for getting [advocacy] information to people. Fast." One anti–death penalty advocate, Lenny, suggested that listservs could be used to generate discourse on a given issue due to the possibility of feedback. Listservs can provide a venue for the discussion of advocacy positions.

However, the instantaneous feedback in interpersonal, telephone, or group communication is not a characteristic of e-mail. Daft, Lengel, and Trevino (1987) suggest that, "Electronic mail has many characteristics similar to telephone or written memos, because it also has the capacity for rapid feedback" (p. 363). However, this study revealed that in several instances, those involved would have responded in less time if they had done so on the telephone. Fortunately, e-mails were usually responded to in adequate time to arrange the activities of advocates. As one universal health care advocate stated: "People can write back [through e-mail]." The speed of the feedback is determined by the e-mail use patterns of the communicators. This characteristic influences advocate use: The immediate feedback potential increases the propensity that advocates will use e-mail.

Multiple Cues

E-mail lacks some cues present in some other more immediate communication. Daft, Lengel, and Trevino (1987) contended that in e-mail, "cues such as eye contact, voice and body language are filtered out" (p. 363). When compared to interpersonal contact, Jossey suggested that e-mail lacks: "Voice quality, eye contact and intonation." E-mails studied here were composed exclusively of typed, literal texts.

There are multiple cues available on Web pages. For instance, the Web page of the environmental coalition allowed surfers to access photographs from previous events, an option that accentuated the language of images rather than text. In addition, the Web site of an anti–death penalty group includes pictures of members of Journey of Hope and pictures of people who had recently been executed in Missouri. One advocate, Lenny, indirectly recognized the multiplicity of cue types utilized in effective Web communication, typically chosen by the consumer of computer media communication when he said: "I like the visuals on the Internet rather than the printed page. Maybe it's because of my generation, I don't know . . . so I think the Web is great." This advocate appreciated the frame of the visuals provided on some Web pages, which is less similar to printed texts than a television screen, the preferred media of a generation that matured in the 1960s, 1970s, and 1980s' "TV babies." The movement of visual images offered in some advocate Web sites is also similar to movement offered on television, a comfortable feature of post-MTV media consumers. This advocate implied that the similarity between television and Web pages contributes to the satiation of some of his media consumption needs through use of computer media communication. Web pages entail a variety of cues, including visual elements, animation, written text, and audio options, among other variations, although such features were relatively rare in the advocate communities that I studied. This characteristic influences use: If advocates desire to include multiple cues such as photographs or video clips, they are more likely to utilize Web communication.

Language Variety

As with other media, there is some language variety available through computer communication. E-mail can be more or less formal, based on the relationship to the communicators. Also, numerical data can be communicated through e-mail as easily as conceptual text that incorporates literal language.

The choices offered on some of the advocate Web sites provided options that enabled users to choose the variety of the language used. This influences use by advocates because the language variety is not limited in computer communication. Advocates can use computer communication to include language variety in a single message.

Personal Character

Computer-mediated advocacy communication is perceived by some advocates to lack a highly personal character. When compared to interpersonal contact, Jossey suggested that e-mail lacks "immediacy." Factors that influence the personal character of advocate use include the lack of demand for personal attention, personalized reception, personal use preferences in Web sites, and relational context.

E-mail provides little demand for personal attention and is perceived by some advocates to be less personally intrusive than telephone communication. This is due to the lack of personal intrusiveness that is a result of physical presence of other media. Lenny suggested: "E-mail is less intrusive [than telephone communication], to me. I deal with forty or fifty communications a day." E-mail is less intrusive because the advocate can check e-mail accounts and respond to e-mails at their convenience. "E-mail is not like a knock on the door or a phone ringing. I was three weeks behind in e-mail. I missed a bunch of information I should have gotten." It can be easy to ignore one's e-mail account. This lack of personal intrusiveness may be less effective for gaining the attention of advocates than interpersonal communication or a telephone call. Lenny commented: "I get too caught up in immediate projects [when I use e-mail]." For this advocate, e-mail use got him bogged down in some communicative activity through his e-mail, but he also inadvertently ignored important advocacy communication disseminated through e-mail because it was not as personally imposing as advocates' use of some other media. If advocates need an immediate response, they may choose to employ another, more intrusive media form, such as telephone communication.

Personal use preferences influence computer communication through e-mail and Web sites. Some advocates use a number of e-mail lists to decrease the potential that receivers of e-mail correspondence feel they are getting too much irrelevant e-mail from an advocacy group. One advocacy group used this technique. Abby suggested that the best way to use e-mail is to put people on an e-mail list that is appropriately active for their level of desired involvement:

> You don't want to be bugging people, you know. People don't want to be continuously . . . some people want to be on . . . our high traffic list, like they're really

interested in an issue. But our event notification . . . will be about a week and a half between postings. We try to keep [to] that.

Advocates can also solicit feedback from individuals on the various e-mail lists in order to modify lists so receivers only get e-mails about topics they care about. Abby explained this process, in which receivers let the organization know how much e-mail activity is appropriate:

> Sometimes I have had people who are on one of the higher traffic lists request to be taken off the lists. Then I wrote back and said I will take you off completely if that is you want, but . . . I'd like to put you just on the event notification list. I think in particular one of two contacted me to be on the steering committee, and then she was too busy to be on the steering committee. She was still on the steering committee list, so she was getting everything I was sending out. She was getting inundated with stuff that was more than she can handle, and I gave her the alternative in just getting the event notifications. She found that to be preferable and she stayed with us for events.

Thus, the e-mail lists of this organization are based on what the receivers want out of the communication. Multiple e-mail address lists can be useful for these purposes, as Abby explained that the inclusion of advocates on each of these lists is dependent upon the desire of the advocates to receive more or less information. As previously noted, this precludes that feeling in recipients that they are victims of e-mail spam. Spamming can be defined as sending too many e-mail messages to the same receiver, especially e-mails judged as junk mail. Thus, advocates' use of multiple e-mail address lists, a form of adapting to various advocate audiences, is perceived to maximize e-mail effectiveness by tailoring e-mail communication to the personal preferences of the recipient.

One of the most unique and important aspects of website communication is that the interactive potential allows for individuals to choose the characteristics of the use. Computers are a master medium because the consumer can shape the experience to meet their personal communicative form preferences (Benoit and Benoit, 2001). Personalized consumption options on Web pages enables different forms of successful advocacy communication. Some advocates are more literal, some more visual. One advocate, Lenny, indirectly recognized the power of the adaptability of effective Web communication:

> I like the visuals on the Internet rather than the printed page. Maybe it's because of my generation, I don't know. My students like going out there and hitting a bunch of pages on the topic. They have five windows open; they can see what's going on. Whereas me, I grew up on written word. So for me the written word is so much more volatile. It is more effective human communication to me than it is for my students. So I think the Web is great.

Computer technology offers excellent personalized communicative opportunities. For instance, interaction with advocacy Web pages can be more personalized than consumption of printed newsletters. As Lana suggested, design is an important element that can facilitate or preclude interaction:

> While it depends on how well the Web page is designed, there are some Web pages that [are more] interactive, if you get them right. And if you get something interacting with the Web page, you get some dynamics of learning going on. . . . So I think it is a more active experience on the Web page.

The "dynamics of learning" referred to in this quote likely refers to the interactivity of Web pages that allows the user to access their choice of information when they want it. For example, the local anti–death penalty Web pages offered users a number of choices, depending on the information that the consumers wanted, such as back issues of the newsletter or specific pages about particular events. In one instance, Jossey used a link from the Fellowship of Reconciliation Web site to the Journey of Hope Web site in order to get more information about the advocates she would be logistically supporting by cooking for them and providing their local transportation. This interactivity increases the personal character of Web pages. Personal preference is the central determinant of the form of the interaction. Explicitly, if advocates have a history of personalized interaction with other advocates via computer communication, they will more likely use computer communication for similar uses in future interaction.

Personal character is influenced by relational context. As with the use of other media, the relational context influences the personal nature of e-mail communication. Lenny explained: "If I know somebody, and if what they say is understood, if we are on the same page, this is almost a conversation. It is real." This advocate perceived that computer-mediated communication is as authentic as the intentionality of those communicating through the medium. This is also related to the language variety possible in e-mail because the variety of relational contexts results in the personal character of e-mail language. The relationship between those who send and receive e-mail influences perceptions of its personal character. For instance, if e-mail correspondents have a history of a relationship through other media, this can influence the personal nature of their e-mail correspondence. In sum, the personal character of advocates' use of computer media is influenced by the lack of demand for personal attention, personalized reception, personal use preferences in Web sites, the lack of hierarchical restraints, and by relational context.

Distance

Computer communication technology also allows advocates to communicate over long distances. As Joan suggested: "And that's where e-mail can be very useful for getting [advocacy] information to people . . . over long distances." For example, when Tony was making logistical arrangements for the local activities of advocates from Journey of Hope, he used e-mail to solicit logistical preferences from members of the group. In another instance, Jossey was able to get information about Journey of Hope advocates by accessing a link to their national Web page. Computer communication, either with e-mail or Web pages, is similar whether the communicators are two blocks away from each other or across national boundaries.

Permanence

E-mail and Web pages lack the permanence of printed texts. There is physicality to mailed paper. Sandy, a university student and an active member in the local Amnesty International chapter, noted this permanence: "One thing is when you mail, it is something that is physically there." A postcard, for instance, is physically present, which may be more salient for advocates like Ed:

> The difference between the postcard and an e-mail would be that the postcard I could put on my kitchen table and that lets me think about it sixteen different times. With an e-mail, I probably won't pull it up again until it's time to get rid of it. The postcard sitting on my kitchen table, I'll look at it, I'll consider it, six, seven, ten times before making a decision to attend or not and throw it in the recycling bin.

E-mail is more easily disposed of than physically present media, according to Ed: "I don't think, even compared to getting the newsletter that the e-mail speaks to me. You have nothing invested, by looking at the e-mail—boom, delete, and it's gone." This is true of Web pages as well. Simply interacting with a Web page does not possess the tactile permanence of printed-paper forms. Thus, e-mail and Web pages lack the physical presence enjoyed by printed text.

E-mail can be more permanent than the telephone, according to advocates like Darlene: "I can save the e-mail and I can print it. And I have a record of it. As opposed to a phone call." Telephone messages can be erased easily but e-mails most often are automatically saved on a hard drive. Likewise, Web pages are recorded on the computer history record of sites visited, can be added to a list of favorite Web sites, and can also be saved onto a hard drive. These computer communication forms can have the permanence of computer information storage.

E-mail has a greater or lesser degree of permanence, depending on how the recipient uses the medium. If an e-mail is important, it can be easily saved or printed, and put in a prominent location as if to remind the e-mail receiver that that message is and was important. On the other hand, e-mail can also be deleted without being viewed. Permanence is underemphasized in the media-richness literature. E-mail can be physically present if the receiver chooses to print the document, such as Darlene often does: "For an important e-mail, I would tape it on my wall at work. I could print it out, and I have a wall in my office at work that I tape my e-mails to, and every week I look them over and take the ones down that I don't need anymore." The e-mail becomes physically present rather than in the less permanent form on the computer screen, as repeated by Lenny: "I print important e-mails, and tack them up." However, some advocates seldom do this, like Ed: "I almost never print out e-mails." Web pages also have a degree of permanence. Like e-mail, Web pages can be saved on a hard drive. They can also be printed so a hard copy can be secured.

Thus, there are several characteristics of e-mail that make it a valuable medium for advocacy communication, and thus influence its use by advocates. These characteristics include feedback, multiple cues, language variety, personal character, distance, and permanence. All of these features are beneficial, but the relatively low financial cost and the ability to send a number of messages out with little effort are very valuable features for communicating with advocates. The uses of computer faxes were observed more rarely. The use of computer faxes were similar in cost but lacked the feedback inherent in other computer communication forms.

Internal Group Factors

The internal group factors of computer communication include the people power available for advocate communication, financial resources, the knowledge possessed by associated advocates, the history of use of computer technology by the group and its members, and the media uses of other groups. Group resources, such as people power, finances, and knowledge, influence advocate use of computer communication.

People Power

People power is an important internal group factor that influences advocate use of computer communication technology. At a minimum, advocates must use e-mail for it to be effective. Some advocates neglect their e-mail accounts. As argued earlier, gumption is a part of people power. Some advocates do not devote people power to maintaining perceptively effective computer communication, as Tony suggested: "A lot of times people are not very good at getting to their e-mail." This decreases the usefulness of the medium. Someone must also expend the people power necessary to maintain listserv capabilities.

The people power available to advocacy groups influences uses of computer communication technology, as Lana explained of the environmental coalition Web page: "Oh, probably because there wasn't anybody that was interested in really doing it. And the right somebody came along and decided, you know, the time had come." People power then includes initiative of advocates as well as numbers of advocates in this group using computer communication technology. Use is also influenced by time devoted to computer communication by those advocates. Advocacy groups devote group resources and time to Web-page design and maintenance. One advocate suggested: "You have to also figure out different ways of packaging, looking at information you want to see, and figure out how you can integrate it into your computer use." This gumption in individual advocates is an aspect of people power. At many environmental coalition meetings, the group Web page was a topic of conversation. Many times, comments were made about developing a Web page. For instance, the designer of the Web page consulted the coalition committee about what external links should be provided, what the most appropriate artwork was, and what kinds of photos should be included on the page. Facilitation of inclusion of more information on their Web page was often a topic of conversation at the environmental coalition meetings. At these meetings of the environmental coalition, it was expressed that the important thing was to get other Web pages (like the municipal Web page and the Web pages of other local environmental organizations) to provide links to the group's Web page.

Financial Resources

Financial and logistical resources at the disposal of advocates also influence uses of computer-mediated communication. Once advocates have access to computer technology, computer advocacy communication has minimal costs. Initial expenses may be high. When asked what the impediments were to use of computer communication, Tony explained:

> Money was a big factor. It's not easy for a lot of people to [be able to spend the] money that it takes. That makes it difficult. So you have to rely upon the goodwill and charity of some of your constituents who are concerned about your social action to donate. You have to count on some sugar daddies. They sometimes keep this whole thing ticking.

If advocates do not have access to these resources, they will not be able to use computers to communicate. Once advocates obtain such access, the costs to use computer communication is low. For instance, Tony, the anti–death penalty advocate, wanted to know if he could use my computer. There was a picture of a man to be executed on the Net, but Tony did not have access to a printer that would produce a clear picture. An anti–death penalty advocate summed up the importance of financial resources for procuring access to computer communication technology:

> It's money. And you have to remember, there was a study released last year that showed the Internet access was only available for a little over 65 percent of the people in the United States. For people who do have access it is simply amazing but when you consider what it takes to get access, if you can afford to own a computer, can you afford the hookup for the computer for any Internet server, it can be tough.

This advocate clearly argues that financial resources are a necessary condition for the utilization of computer communication technology. An environmental advocate concurred: "The people who have a low income, they might be able to buy a computer. It is older computers which are slower when dealing with a server slow modem, [which] is going to affect their ability to get into the Internet." One advocate involved in local death penalty advocacy found himself responsible for sending faxes to the media, but he did not have computer fax capability. A local office supply store was an ad hoc armory in the battle to abolish the death penalty. The activist paid for a fax program with a credit card and was faxing mass media personnel within the hour of the purchase.

Donated computer equipment can be very valuable to advocates. Abby explained: "Someone donated the . . . Displaywriter [a word-processor], we were doing our word processing on that, for about four years. It was donated." The environmental advocate explained that financial resources were necessary to obtain the first computer for his advocacy group: "In 1991, we ended up getting a 386, our first computer. We took the money out of the organizational budget." This group was effective in fund raising, and that fund raising provided the necessary financial resources for the group to enter the computer age.

Even if advocates cannot afford their own personal computers or computers that belong to their advocacy organization, there are other ways that advocates can acquire access to this technology. Access to computers in other areas of activity can provide opportunities for activists to use computer communication technology. An example is found in further discussion of the acquisition of computer capabilities by the environmental advocacy organization discussed above. As members obtained personal computers in their homes, according to Abby, these resources were used by the environmental organization: "One of our members was keeping our database and our mailing list on his computer and we had everything over at his house." Abby explained that before the organization with which he was affiliated had obtained computer hardware, advocates used the computer facilities at an educational institution: "So I was using the university's computers until someone donated a dedicated word processor." When advocates do not possess adequate financial resources, such access opportunities are invaluable.

But increasingly, advocates have access to computer technology because computer technology has become ubiquitous, as Darlene explained: "Everyone has a computer at their home almost, now, or has access to it through the school, especially in this community." Another advocate explained: "It was easy to access information with the group because I already had e-mail access." Technology at the workplace can be used for advocacy communication, especially for advocates like Lana who are able to do advocacy work while at her place of employment:

> Yes, and in mine, it kind of crosses . . . barriers. My workplace, work, so directly is involved in environmental stuff that there is almost no separation . . . no delineation between the two, they kind of flow together.

Thus, in many cases, access can be attained without necessarily expending financial resources. Unfortunately, some Internet access locations require financial resources to a greater or lesser extent. The universal health care advocate explained that even municipal Internet access could incur some monetary costs:

> And even stuff like the [public access to computers and Internet] at the public library. They ask you to make a donation to help to pay for this year. And if you can't afford that donation, then they make it problematic.

Thus, even with the use of public computer access, use may still require expenditure of fiscal resources. Still, the cost of this access is far less than the cost of computer equipment. In sum, a problem with the use of e-mail assumes access to technology. Some advocate organizers may not have access to computer technology, and many advocacy participants will likewise not have access to required technology. The opportunities are not available to everyone. One advocate described the situations of two advocates who did not have computer access:

> One is an elderly woman, and she's . . . not in the workplace, she doesn't have computer access there, so a lot of people in her age group are not interested . . . not online. The other, I don't know. I suspect that her workplace is not, is a not-for-profit agency, maybe she just doesn't. . . . I don't know. It would be interesting to find out. I don't know if she just doesn't have an address, or . . . just about everybody has it now, if you have a workplace.

This is a disadvantage of looking at e-mail as a replacement for mail. Computer communication capabilities and traditional media forms, however, can be used to augment each other in advocacy communication efforts. A prerequisite for successful advocates' computer use is access on the part of intended recipients. There are several problems with e-mail, however. First, use of e-mail assumes access to technology. Some advocate organizers may not have access to the technology, and many advocacy participants will likewise not have access to required technology, a point worthy of redundancy. Lana, a very active environmental advocate and a municipal officer, pointed this out:

> I have an organization where the board and committee are all on the Internet except two, and so when I send out the agenda of the meetings or whenever, I have to send e-mail to everybody, and then I have to print the e-mail and mail it to those two people.

This is a disadvantage of using e-mail as a replacement for mail. The two should be used to augment each other in advocacy communication. If postal mail were eliminated in favor of e-mail, those without e-mail would be cut out of the advocate community constituted in communicative activity.

Access to computer technology may be expensive: Once it is obtained, use of e-mail and Web pages is inexpensive. The e-mail can perform the same function as regular mail, but with no postage cost or use of printed-paper products. E-mail is less expensive than traditional postage, according to Tony:

> E-mail can be better when you consider the cost of the mailing, e-mail is cheaper, if you have the initial investment, and the people who are receiving it have made the initial investment, if they have the accessibility.

E-mail is a very inexpensive communication medium. As Joan suggested: "And that's where e-mail can be very useful for getting this kind of information to people . . . at minimal cost. Yes, at minimal cost." Abby noted that the use of e-mail to contact media personnel is less expensive with computer fax-modem use:

> It's also free to send a number of faxes through a computer modem. The costs of mailings are pretty negligible but if you send out to twenty media outlets at 34 cents a stamp, you are talking about seven or eight dollars for postage. And it's easier to send a fax. The clerical requirements to send a fax to the modem are minimal. [The use of computer fax technology] saves us time and it takes less money.

Thus, e-mail and Web pages are more efficient than some traditional media uses. E-mail has replaced some telephone uses, such as telephone trees, due to the convenience of e-mail, as Ed suggested: "The Internet makes it much easier to communicate in mass. You don't need a phone tree. If you just want to get a short message out, or even a long message." E-mail takes less time and effort than making telephone calls, as suggested by Raymond, an advocate for universal health care who lends logistical support for three to four events a year:

> I remember having, trying to call lists of people and it just took so long and it was really . . . calling people was kind of an intrusion, but e-mail is less intrusive and you can convey more information and it's interactive, it's just a really easy way of organizing events and just getting information out.

E-mail is a convenient advocacy communication form; sending a number of e-mail messages requires minimal labor. Lists of recipients, once set up, can be used repeatedly with efficiency of reaching a number of advocates with a certain level of interest.

There are also negative implications that result from the minimal labor requirements sufficient for advocacy e-mail use. A problem with advocacy use of e-mail is the risk of having recipients regard the e-mail as "spam." "Spamming" is a new term that refers to excessive use of e-mail lists. Joan, an internationally active advocate on all three issues, complained about the problem of spamming with e-mail: "I can't believe how much junk e-mail that I get from people who are companions with the movement." Recipients tend to ignore mail coming from large lists if they get mail that seems inconsequential too often from the same source. It is important, therefore, to not send too much e-mail, and to only those who want it.

Unfortunately, listservs can sometimes overwhelm those "subscribers" to the listserv if contributors do not self-monitor. Joan lamented that some listserv arrangements allow advocates to post e-mails on issues unrelated to the primary issue for which the listserv was established:

> I am on several listservs. Sometimes I am inundated by them. There are some I just dump real fast. Because what happens is you are out on a listserv for a specific topic. And anybody can produce about whatever issues they want. . . . All this stuff . . . it is not directly related to what the listserv is supposed to be about.

Advocates who participate in listservs can attempt to persuade other listserv participants from engaging in these practices, as noted by Joan:

> I have complained to lists and I know that there have been a lot of other people that have complained, and I know a lot of people who have written in then said take me off because there's too much junk on their listserv. . . . I mean in like one day I got like thirty irrelevant messages.

Listservs operate better if advocates who use the medium refrain from dumping too much information about issues only indirectly relevant to the original purpose of the listserv.

Knowledge

Advocates' knowledge of computer technology influenced the environmental group's use of computers. Darlene, an active advocate on all three issues, explained that lack of knowledge precludes computer use by some advocates:

> I believe the greatest influence is knowledge. I think that the reason that more computer technology is not used in the coalitions is because of a lack of knowledge. People just do not know how to build a Web site. People don't know how to write a listserv. They only know how to type in everyone's name and send him or her individual e-mails. And as that knowledge increases, the learning curve on that is very . . . very steep. People learn it very quickly.

When a person who possesses the knowledge to put a Web page together becomes more active in the environmental coalition, it enables the Web capabilities of the group, as Darlene further explained: "It is the same for the Web page. We just didn't have anybody with the technological knowledge, until this year, to serve on the coalition, and do it." Tony suggested: "You need somebody who can be a resource person for you. We have been blessed with that. We have had a couple people in town that have been wonderful on helping us out with that." The lack of knowledge about computer technology can impede advocates' use of computers for some functions. For instance, Abby explained that the advocacy group he was most active in did not use e-mail for fund raising:

> We don't use e-mails for fund raising. I've learned a few things over the years about fund raising to increase response . . . we are basically a situation where we could do electronic fund raising but it would entail having a secure Web site. We haven't gotten to that level of sophistication with our Web site.

Abby's statement suggested that if there were people willing to help raise the Web page sophistication for the group, the Web page could be used for fund raising.

The base of e-mail addresses is an important resource that influences its use by advocates. Tony explained that his group: "gets the e-mail addresses from its members as soon as possible. That way we can contact them through e-mail."

Overlapping Membership

Overlapping membership influences the use of computer technology. For instance, Abby explained that he adopted e-mail communication practices when another group in which he was a member began to rely on e-mail:

> I was on the board for [a local community radio station]. . . . [T]he summer of 1997, and I was the only one on the board that didn't have e-mail. And everybody else was communicating by e-mail, but I wasn't, so I thought maybe I should get e-mail.

In this case, Abby's involvement in the management of a community radio station influenced his use of computers for environmental advocacy. He applied what he learned about computer communication in this other group to the environmental advocacy group. The uses of Web pages by other groups influenced the environmental group. Darlene explained that what advocates do in other groups in which they are members has influenced computer use by the environmental coalition:

> Because most of the people on the committee belong to other organizations, and they will be at that organization, and . . . they will hear, those organizations have Web pages. And then they will come to the Earth Day coalition, they say, "Hey! We should get a Web page." I didn't volunteer to do that, but I volunteered to find somebody that could.

External Factors

External factors influence advocates' use of computer technology to communicate to those involved in advocate activities as well as more general audiences. These include political context and general social trends.

Political Context

Governmental facilitation of the development of Internet technology has indirectly increased the availability of this technology to advocates. But, the use of computer communication technology may leave activists feeling vulnerable to government surveillance. Joan suspected government intrusion into her e-mail account:

> There are other problems with e-mail too. I had the e-mails delayed by even more than a week from organizations about immediate action that needed to be taken at our notes for meetings. I know that sounds absurd, but there could be problems if there are agencies that look into the e-mail. We do have to recognize that it is a very insecure method of communication. I think actually the access, then with a telephone,

because you have to go to the trouble of phone taps someplace around the line into the phone. Because Internet communications is on the often-public servers, it makes it easier for that kind of stuff to be tracked down.

Joan also discussed a computer program designed to cripple e-mail accounts: "And I don't know how much we will be able to rely on the Internet. There are computer programs that can kill your correspondence." This advocate was very sensitive to the threat of the use of such viruses by government agencies. (I am reluctant to use the term paranoid. As one influential, nationally prominent anti–death penalty advocate told me: "Just because you are paranoid doesn't mean [the other side] doesn't hate you.") The internationally active advocate asserted that the U.S. government had the capabilities to monitor the Internet activity of advocates:

> The U.S. government has a tracking system for e-mails and Web sites for surveillance. It can get in people's e-mail accounts, to see what they're sending, and to see the sites that they are visiting. Well already they can see which sites they are visiting with [a computer program]. The government can actually get in the people's e-mail accounts, address books, and everything.

These capabilities in the hands of government agencies could potentially hamper advocates' efforts to use computer-communication technology to communicate. Political context could chill advocate computer media use if a government decided to monitor computer communication, as Abby concurred:

> Also with e-mail, they can mess with that very easily and they will warn you when you set up your e-mail account that it is not secure, and it isn't. I don't want to be telling tales outside of school, but one day when I was active in my e-mail I had a block, a warning come up saying that someone was accessing my e-mail at that same time when I was trying to access it and put a block on me being able to access it. With what Carnivore [a computer program] can do . . . I can see very easily how e-mail [can be used against activists by the government], and I have come across a couple of cases of other organizations where I have wondered if the powers that be have not sent out inflammatory e-mails that would divide groups that ordinarily should be working together. Under the names of somebody within that organization. That would be extremely easy to do.

Computer technology has made activists feel more vulnerable to government surveillance as it has increased their communicative options. "I just recently began using e-mail and I will have to say it has . . . its uses and its abuses." This statement, from an internationally active anti–death penalty advocate who lost his daughter in the Oklahoma City bombing, reveals that computers, like all forms of technological advancement, present a double-edged proposition; throughout the history of human progress, every techno-logical advance has yielded liabilities along with benefits (e.g., those who fly aircraft into buildings or bomb hospitals are dependent upon the development of the wheel). This is invariably the case with advocates' use of computer com-munication technology, especially if use of computer communication media displaces advocates' use of other media.

General Technological Trends

An increasing number of people have access to computer technology. Joan explained that before the wide adoption of personal computers, the technology was not very useful for advocacy communication: "[The Internet] can be a wonderful form of communication, but if only a few people can afford it, what is the point of using it?" This cost impediment has been overcome because of general technological trends: Computer technology has proliferated. Advocates were obviously unable to use computer technology until it was easily available, as Ed explained: "The environmental group I worked with back in the late 1980s did not use the Internet, because the Internet was in its infancy. It wasn't developed, so you wouldn't have reached many people. There wasn't mass access. Who would you have contacted?" An anti–death penalty advocate con-curred: "If the Internet was then what it is now, I'm sure they would've used it." Technological and economic factors influence advocates' media-use choices. Ed explained that the two could be related: "Technological trends have made it easier for us to use computers. The price of the technology has come down to the point when so many people can own it . . . that makes it a viable form of communication." In this case, the more people bought comput-ers, the more they were produced on a mass scale. This is the essence of the personal computer revolution. Before computers were mass produced, the cost of the technology was prohibitive for most advocates. A nationally prominent anti–death penalty advocate suggested that his advocate computer use was influenced by general social trends of reliance upon computer communication technology: "I held off on doing e-mail for a long time. My life was busy enough and complicated enough without it. I did notice everybody was doing everything by e-mail. The general culture was moving in that direction, the activist culture was moving in that direction."

Likewise, Abby explained that his use of computers for advocacy activity was informed by his previous use of computer technology in the context of university coursework: "That was a long-ago decision. I started doing stuff on computers, besides what I was doing in school, I started to do stuff with the word processing back in 1985." Michelle, an anti–death penalty advocate who

worked with Amnesty International, attested to the general adoption that facilitated advocate use of computers to communicate:

> I think e-mail is great, I've seen sort of the evolution since I've been here from four
> years ago when I was a freshman a lot of people didn't use it, it was not a reliable form
> of communication to reach any kind of list or public because a lot of people didn't
> know about it.

Thus, shifts in media use in the United States and the world indirectly influence advocate media uses, as Abby explained: "There was a technological
transformation going on in our culture as people went from using typewriters
to using word processors. Before that happened, I used the typewriter. And I
wasn't a very good typist." This shift enabled advocates who were less efficient
with uses of precomputer writing technology. Abby suggested that advocates
needed to be online so when people search for advocate issue information,
they will find the advocates' messages: "There are lots of people who are looking for information on the Web now. We want to be there for them." Abby
explained that the availability of computer communication technology has
changed how many communicate: "For folks who use the Web a lot . . . it's
changing how they're getting their communication. It's shaped . . . how I get
my communication." Jossey, who is less active than Abby, is one of those people who has generally used computer communication more, and has, as a
result, increased her use of computer advocacy communication. Jossey
explained that her adoption of computer communication for other purposes
enabled her to use the Internet for advocacy:

> I have slowly been getting on the Net. I got on for general things, not related to these
> environmental efforts. I can get information on the Net. A map of the area, going on
> vacation information, things like that. So I was already on the Net. Before I got
> involved with these [advocacy] activities.

Conclusion

As noted throughout this exploration of advocate use of computer communication technology, there are limitations as well as empowerment capability in
advocate adoption of these tools. Some scholarship has suggested that e-mail
might replace other forms of communication. In many instances with advocacy
groups, it is an additional channel with unique characteristics rather than a
replacement. It may decrease the total time necessary to maintain commitments through interpersonal communication, but e-mail can also increase the
effectiveness of interpersonal interaction when used as a supplemental tool to

support interpersonal contact. For instance, the question was not how to replace telephone calls with e-mail communication, but rather, how e-mail can be used in conjunction with telephone communication to increase the effectiveness of advocacy communication.

In this chapter, I have explicated advocate use of computer communication technology. Rice (1987) suggested that in corporate organizations:

> [Computer mediated communication systems] have the potential to facilitate output processes, both as media and as content. . . . As an output medium, [computer mediated communication systems] can facilitate the diffusion of information to an organizational environment, both directly through interorganizational electronic mail networks and indirectly through electronic journals posted on text data bases. (p. 83)

This study reveals that advocates also use computer communication in the form of e-mail and Web pages and that use of computer fax capabilities is useful. The theoretical ideas offered here are multidimensional. Many advocate uses of computer communication media technology were described in the first section through analysis of the forms, audiences, and functions of advocate computer use. Forms of advocate computer use included e-mail, Web pages, and computer fax capabilities. Functions of advocate computer use included increasing attendance at events, arranging logistical details, building community, educating, lobbying, facilitating mass media coverage, and legitimizing advocate activities and issue positions. In the second section, I explained how characteristics of computer communication, internal group factors, and external factors influenced advocate use of computer communication technology. Characteristics that influence advocate use of computer communication include feedback, multiple cues, language variety, personal character, distance, and permanence. Internal group factors that influenced computer uses included people power, knowledge possessed by associated advocates, the history of use of computer technology, and the media uses of other groups. External factors such as general technological trends and political climate also influenced advocate use of computer communication. The evidence and analysis offered has suggested a theoretical idea: Advocates use media to perform a variety of functions in efforts to enact effective communicative praxis, and these uses are influenced by a number of factors.

9

Conclusion

The goal of a qualitative study should be the discovery of meaning for those who share a particular situated-ness. This book has explored a number of advocacy activities in the pursuit of emic knowledge of advocacy media use. I have focused on activists who organize to advocate their social and political views, and my aim has been to formulate a theory of media use. In this chapter I will review the media that are used by advocates, discuss the intended audiences for these uses, explicate the intended functions for these uses, discuss factors that influence advocate media uses, identify limitations of this study, and offer areas for future research. Many aspects of activist communication have been theoretically explored and clarified. Glaser and Strauss (1967) suggest that development of local theory is a validating outcome from such work:

> The pressure is *not* on the sociologist to "know the whole field" or to have all the facts "from a careful random sample." His [*sic*] job is not to provide a perfect description of an area, but develop a theory that accounts for much of the relevant behavior. (p. 30) [emphasis in original]

A theory has been constructed on the use of communicative media by the advocates studied here. This theory adds to our understanding of advocates' media uses.

As addressed in the beginning of this book, social and political movements are significant democratic forces that can influence public opinion, public policies, citizen access, and social consciousness. Advocates use communication media to increase attendance at events, educate, or lobby politicians. For instance, when anti–death penalty advocates used media to lobby, they attempted to influence policy formulation by communicating at legislative hearings. When advocates mobilized to oppose specific executions, they were lobbying politicians to influence the implementation of the death penalty.

Daft and Lengel (1986) suggest that reduction of uncertainty and equivocality were the two goals of information processing in corporate organizations. Uncertainty refers simply to what is unknown. Equivocality refers to a state of unwanted ambiguity that exists from multiple possible interpretations of a message. Daft and Lengel argued that face-to-face communication provides more opportunity for feedback, a useful tool for decreasing uncertainty about a message. They reiterated one of their earlier findings: "face-to-face media were preferred for messages containing equivocality, while written media were used for unequivocal messages" (p. 555). This book reveals that perceived levels of feedback varied in different media forms. Media with feedback potential were useful for decreasing uncertainty by providing information to advocates, members of the general public, politicians, and mass media personnel. Also evident is the idea that equivocality was not a major concern of advocates. As opposed to the corporate setting, in which managers use strategic ambiguity for some purposes, advocates seek clarity in their messages. Likewise, due to the nonhierarchical setting in which most advocacy occurs, ambiguity may not be as useful as in settings in which power positions are important, such as in corporate organizations.

To ascertain the emic knowledge shared by those who also share a similar life-world, several goals were set. In this conclusion I will explain how the data (texts) increase our knowledge and outline the resulting theory of advocacy media use. A number of media forms are used by advocates to reach several audiences. These media uses perform several functions, and their uses are influenced by particular factors such as characteristics of uses of a particular medium, internal group factors, and external factors.

Advocate Media Uses

Activists use a variety of media to attract, maintain, or mobilize those who support the advocates' causes. This book identified and generated a typology of media available to advocates (table 9.1). Advocates utilize face-to-face communication, telephone communication, group communication, event communication, paper communication forms, mass media outlets, and computer communication. Advocates use face-to-face and one-on-one communication in a number of settings: telephones, answering machines, and cellular telephones. Many if not most communicative activities are incubated and nurtured to fruition through advocate communication in group settings. Advocates can use a variety of events to spread messages, including educational events, politi-

Table 9.1   Available Advocacy Media

1. Face-to-Face Communication
2. Telephone
    Answering machines
    Cellular phones
3. Small Group
    Intragroup communication
    Intergroup communication
4. Paper Communication
    Newsletters
    Single-page mailer
    Fliers
    Handbills
    Pamphlets
    Letters
    Petitions
    Table tents
    Adhesive stickers
    Postcards
    Lobbying letters
    Fliers
    Unconventional paper forms (i.e., leaflets on pizza boxes; in pay envelopes)
    Literature tables: periodically, in public locations
5. Events
    Types of events
        Educational events
        Political events
        Community events
        Civil action
        Socializing events
    Forms of event communication
        Speakers
        Musicians
        Poetry
        Storytelling
        Multi-media
        Guerilla theater
        Disruptive tactics
    Event tools
        Signs
        Candles
        Literature tables
        Public address systems
6. Mass Media
    Commercial newspapers
        Stories
        Calendar of community events
        Letters to the editor

Table 9.1   Available Advocacy Media (continued)

Advertising space
Feature space (i.e., stories about participating artists)
Books
Radio
    Public service announcements
    Advertising
    Mainstream news
    Community radio
Television
    News
    Cable access
    Public service announcements
    Advertising
    Community calendars
Cinema
Video
7. Computers
    E-mail
    Web pages
    Faxes

cal events, community events, civil action events, and socializing events. Activists use multiple forms of communication during events, including public speeches, musical performances, poetry reading, storytelling, multimedia presentations, guerrilla theater, and, rarely, disruptive tactics. Those involved with social and political advocacy efforts use various tools to communicate at events, including signs, candles, literature tables, and public address systems. Advocates use a number of forms of paper media to disseminate messages, including newsletters, fliers, handbills, pamphlets, petitions, table tents, and adhesive stickers. Activists communicate through mass media such as corporate newspapers, radio, television, cinema, and video forms of mass media. Advocates use several forms of print mass media including, most frequently, newspapers and, less frequently, magazines. Advocates also use a variety of radio mass media forms, including coverage on mainstream news programs, radio talk shows, and public service announcements. In addition, advocates use a variety of televisual media, including television, cinema, and video. Finally, advocates use the computer communication forms of e-mail, Web pages, and computer fax capabilities.

Sharing knowledge of media between groups may be more prevalent among like-minded advocacy organizations than it would be in the corporate context, as Darlene explained:

> In the corporate contexts, I wouldn't think there is so much sharing. In your business, you really only go to the meetings for that business. If you did go to another corpora-

tion, you wouldn't want to share your corporation secrets. These are people that are like-minded. And the issues are very connected, and people know what Earth Day is doing. We are not in competition.

Corporations would be less likely to share media-use strategies that work with other businesses than advocates who share similar political perspectives. Corporations, as for-profit entities, would want to take full advantage of the development of new uses for media technology and approaches. Advocates in this study, on the other hand, were working exclusively for not-for-profit groups and were motivated by altruism more than personal or group gain. Thus, advocates freely shared information and knowledge of strategic media use.

Advocates such as Darlene perceive combinations of media uses are valuable for communication with core members: "By talking personally with them and communicating with them through e-mail." A combination of uses enables connections with multiple audiences, as Abby suggested:

> We would communicate with the larger public through newspaper ads. Or we might not use e-mail, because we do not have a listserv for all of the public, although the Web site is for the general public. That is what is really cool about e-mail versus the Web pages, you can reach more people with a Web page, sometimes, people who might be looking for something on your event.

The divisions between media uses established in this book are useful analytic constructs, but they often obscure the perceived importance of the use of a variety of media.

Audiences

Advocates communicate to several audiences, including fellow advocates, the general public, politicians, mass media personnel, or combinations of these audiences. Consideration of audiences inside advocate communities and outside those communities is a valuable conceptualization for the consideration of media uses designed to reach these audiences (see table 9.2). The first subdivision is thus intragroup or media uses designed to reach those within the advocate communities. Much advocacy communication is among advocates. I have attempted to draw a distinction between communication among advocates in the same group and communication among advocates who are members of different advocacy groups, although overlapping membership was very pervasive.

Another major division of media uses includes those designed to reach audiences outside of the advocate community. This study revealed that advocates

Table 9.2   Intended Audiences of Advocate Communication

Audience	Face	Telephone	Group	Events	Paper	Mass Media	Computer
				Media Form			
Advocates	X	X	X	X	X	X	X
General Public	X		X	X	X	X	X
Politicians	X	X	X	X	X	X	X
Mass Media	X	X		X		X	X

perceive some media forms as more viable for reaching some audiences. They use face-to-face communication to reach four primary audiences: advocates, the general public, politicians, and media personnel. The target audiences for telephone uses include other activists within the advocate community, elected officials, and mass media personnel, but not the general public. Intended audiences of advocacy events include other advocates, members of the general population, politicians, and media personnel. Advocates utilize paper communication to reach fellow advocates, the general public, and politicians, but not to reach mass media personnel. Advocates had previously communicated with mass media personnel through paper press releases, but the adoption of fax communication by media personnel influenced advocate delivery of press releases. The advocates I studied primarily used computer fax capabilities to communicate with mass media personnel. Computer communication was employed by advocates to reach all four audiences. Activists use the identified media forms to communicate to other advocates, the general public, politicians, and mass media personnel. Salient findings are that telephones are not used to communicate with the general public, and that computer fax communication has displaced paper communication with mass media personnel. Advocates do not use telephones to communicate with the general public because it is not perceived to be a wise use of resources.

Functions of Advocate Media Use

As evidenced throughout this book, advocates use media to perform a variety of functions, including increasing attendance at events, arranging logistical details, building community, lobbying, educating, recruiting new members, legitimizing advocate issues and activities, facilitating mass media coverage, and raising funds (see table 9.3). These functions are not mutually exclusive as there is some overlap of functions.

In my discussion of functions, I may appear imprecise in my reference to advocacy efforts within a single group (intra) and between advocacy groups (inter), but this is due to the artificiality of the conceptual distinction of a group in this advocacy community. This is also reflected in the discussion of bona fide groups (Lammers and Krikorian, 1997; Putnam, 1994; Putnam and Stohl, 1990; Stohl and Holmes, 1992). Most of the participants in this study were involved in multiple activities with a variety of groups. For instance, none of the anti–death penalty advocates studied here were members of only one anti–death penalty group. The dilemma of analytic choices, or defining the unit of analysis (i.e., individual humans, individual groups, or the larger community of networking advocates), could merit another book. I have done my best to retain the character of the massive overlap between groups while also utilizing some level of analysis (primarily the group). But how then can I consider advocacy effort that does not originate in a group setting, is not dependent upon any particular group, but utilizes the communicative resources of as many groups as possible? Another unresolved question is what is the most appropriate unit of analysis for studying local advocacy communication? Or rather is there a most appropriate unit of analysis? Throughout this book, and in the chapter on group communication in particular, I have employed analytical constructs (such as "group") in the Aristotelian effort to increase our understanding of advocacy media use, while still attempting to reveal the artificiality of such constructs in the lived experience of advocacy communicative interaction.

Increasing Attendance at Events

Activists use a variety of media to increase attendance at events. They are reminded about the dates, times, and locations of advocacy activity through uses of communication media. In addition, advocates use media to increase the visibility of and participation in events by advocates, members of the general public, even politicians and mass media personnel. This mobilization can be achieved through interpersonal communication, telephone communication, group communication, paper communication, event communication, mass media communication, and computer communication. Activists use these media to inform advocates about opportunities to be involved. Thus, all media were used to increase attendance at events. Advocates perceived that the various characteristics of all available media could be useful for increasing attendance at events.

Arranging Logistical Detail

Activists also use media for arranging logistical details. Those studied here formulated ideas, planned events, and volunteered for task completion. This logistical communication is a necessary precursor for much advocate communication. Confirmation is perceived to be a valuable communicative step in this process. Many media were used to arrange such details. Simply, advocates had to talk about what needed to be done and how to get those things done. Advocates perceived this arrangement as a result and a precursor to additional communicative experiences. This process is cyclical. Another audience of intragroup communication is marginalized members. The small-group setting was also used as an important venue for the discussion and arrangement for future communicative endeavors. Thus, advocates' uses of media to communicate with one another were important catalysts for other advocacy efforts. A single use of a communicative media form can be sufficient for arranging logistical detail. This may be in the form of interpersonal communication, telephone communication, or group- or computer-mediated communication. Small-group settings, in particular, provide a valuable venue for intergroup and intragroup communication. Advocacy groups must plan, commit, and confirm. The personal, immediate character of group communication contributes to the appropriateness of this function. Advocates did not use events, paper communication, or mass media to arrange logistical detail. Events did not provide a centralized focus and had less opportunity for immediate feedback and were inappropriate for arranging logistical detail. Likewise, paper communication did not offer immediate feedback opportunities and was inappropriate for the rapid feedback necessary for arranging logistical detail. Mass media also lacked feedback capabilities and was only quasi-personal rather than authentically personal, so mass media formats were perceived by advocates to be of no value for arranging logistical details.

Building Community

Activists also use media to build community. Community building can be defined as developing professional and interpersonal relationships. Sharing information is a central feature of uses of media in efforts to build community. This information can be used in further persuasive efforts, to help consolidate the opinions of advocates, and to help build community. Sharing of information is community building because it is an important process in which the collective group understanding of advocacy issues and the factors that affect those issues is forged. As advocates reactively share information, they are negotiating the group's shared interpretation of the social world. This uniting of minds brings the advocates' conceptions of social reality in line with one another. This process also heightens the sense of collective identity. Friendships that bind members of advocate communities are formed through uses of media, particularly though face-to-face communication, telephone communication, group communication, participation in events, and computer communication. These are important factors in the process of building community. Thus, another important role of intragroup communication is that it builds the community of advocates.

Advocacy media use can also help forge a larger community of advocates that transcends small-group membership boundaries. As I have noted before, most of the advocates who participated in this study were members of several groups. The groups to which each advocate belonged varied from advocate to advocate; communication through various media between these advocates often contributed to a sense of a large, left-leaning advocacy community. The bona fide group perspective (Lammers and Krikorian, 1997; Putnam and Stohl, 1990) has been useful for understanding the importance of interaction between advocacy groups and the fluid interaction of advocates within, often, several groups. The boundaries of the advocate community in this local area were fluid in the community-building process. Certain media were more useful for community building than others. Paper communication and mass media were not used to build community, although the legitimization conferred by mass media can contribute to the morale of advocates. As explicated in the discussion of characteristics, paper communication and mass media communication, because they lack feedback, were not used to build community.

Lobbying

Activists perceived that some media uses perform a lobbying function. They used several communication media to lobby politicians. Advocates perceive that communication with politicians can influence policy outcomes. Thus, advocates use all possible media for communication with elected officials. Activists perceived that such media use could aid advocacy efforts in at least three stages of governmental action: policy formulation, implementation, and public opinion (Berry, 1993; Chong, 1993; Duka, 1997; Garcelon, 1997; Hager, 1993; Kitschelt, 1993; Rochon and Mazmanian, 1993). Advocates can attempt to persuade public officials that support of advocate positions is the moral and ethical high ground, or that the policies endorsed by advocates is pragmatically sound public policy. The second potential goal, as outlined in the sociological and political science literature explored in the literature review, is to persuade policymakers that a substantial number of voters agree with a particular position. The goal in this case is to convince a politician that a course of action is politically astute, that a substantial number of voters and supporters would agree with a particular policy act. A third possible goal is to convince public officials that campaign resources (such as money or people power) can be mobilized if the elected official endorses a particular position. However, with these advocacy groups the procurement of substantial campaign (monetary) support was not prevalent. Advocates perceive that use of all of the media identified here can be used to lobby politicians and that this function was so important that the variety of characteristics of all media was perceived as useful for lobbying politicians.

Educating

Educating the public is another important function that advocates perceived was achieved through media use. Advocates use media in efforts to educate the public about advocacy issues. This entailed exposing people to facts and ideas that support advocacy positions in the hope that nonadvocates are persuaded to adopt advocate views. As Sister Helen Prejean, the author of *Dead Man Walking*, and an internationally recognized anti–death penalty advocate, repeated several times when discussing several media forms: "You have to get them to reflect on the issue." The power of provoking such self-evaluation has been historically proclaimed by many great thinkers. Certainly one of the most important goals of nonviolent protest methods by Gandhi and Martin Luther King, Jr., was to bring to the fore the violence inherent in unjust political and social systems. A worthy goal of advocates is to get the general populace to contemplate the relevant issue; advocate media use can provoke such introspection. This introspection is a form of intrapersonal communication. The goal of much advocacy communication is to get people to talk to themselves: "Yeah . . . how do I feel about this issue?" This requires communicative experiences. Thus, the most effective communication optimizes and provokes such thought within the confines of the available opportunities. The various media forms can be utilized in combination if resources are available to broadcast compelling messages that provoke self-actualization, or the decision to accept a given belief. All media were used to educate advocates, the general public, politicians, and mass media personnel, indicating that advocates felt that the various characteristics of all media could be useful for this educating function.

Recruiting Advocates

Activists use various forms of media to provide information about advocate activities and attempt to convince prospective advocates to engage in advocacy praxis. These included face-to-face communication, paper communication, event communication, mass media communication, and computer communication, but not telephone communication or group communication. Telephones were not used to recruit because the people power and cost involved were perceived as inefficient. Group communication was not used to recruit because the advocates who attended group meetings were already active participants in the advocacy activities of the groups.

Legitimize Advocacy Activities and Issue Positions

Advocates perceive that when their messages are delivered competently and are deemed reasonable by the audience, the legitimacy of advocates is bolstered. Advocates perceive that legitimacy is conferred upon advocate activity and issue positions through media use, although the Latin origin, *legitimus* (lawful) misses the essence of this perceived legitimization. Habermas (1973) wrote of legitimacy as the perceptual consistency between the values of an institution and the values collectively held by society. Thus, as evident throughout the discussion of advocate use of mass media, advocates perceive that the mass media are also accepting advocate issues and activities as legitimate enough, or consistent with general values held by society, to warrant mass media attention. Media uses that are considered incompetent can inversely decrease the legitimacy of advocates. If advocates are perceived to lack competence in their uses of media, advocates perceive that audience members will confer less-perceived legitimacy on the activities and issue positions of advocates. The characteristics of mass media contributed to this perception. The distance mass media covers was viewed as a characteristic that enabled mass media to confer legitimacy. Competent use of computer communication was also perceived to confer legitimacy, largely due to the external factor of general technological trends.

Facilitating Mass Media Coverage

Field notes revealed that advocates often used a variety of media formats to communicate to newspaper, radio, and television personnel. All media were used to communicate with media personnel except group communication and paper communication. The multitude of characteristics of mass media contributed to the perception that mass media could be useful for the fulfillment of many functions.

Fund Raising

Activists infrequently used media to solicit monetary contributions. When logistical costs required such periodic efforts, advocates used telephone communication, group communication, paper communication, and events to raise financial resources, but not face-to-face, mass media, or computer communication. Face-to-face communication was perceived as too personal for solicitation of funds. Mass media did not possess the feedback necessary for raising financial resources. The local groups did not possess the financial resources, access to logistical resources, or the knowledge necessary to solicit funds through computer communication.

Thus, activists perceive that media uses perform several functions, including increasing attendance at events through promotion, mobilizing activists, arranging logistical detail, building community, lobbying, educating, recruiting new members, legitimizing advocate issues and activities, facilitating mass media coverage, and fund raising. Advocates also perceive that these functions are better achieved through quality uses of media rather than media uses that lack quality (table 9.3).

The characteristics, internal factors, and external factors make some media more appropriate for the performance of some functions than others. Examination of table 9.3 reveals that advocates use some media for some functions, but not for others. For example, events communication, paper communication, and mass media communication are not perceived as effective for arranging logistical details. Paper communication and mass media communication may be inappropriate for building community. All identified media can be used to educate. Recruiting can be best performed through face-to-face communication, event communication, paper communication, mass media communication, and computer communication. Advocates perceive that all of the identified media can be used to facilitate mass media coverage, which, in particular, performed a legitimizing function. Fund raising can be achieved through use of telephone communication, group communication, and paper communication. There are differences between media in their usefulness of performance of various functions. This knowledge is valuable for scholars who study social and political movement advocates because it provides an embry-

Table 9.3   Functions of Advocate Media Uses

	Media Form						
Function	Face	Telephone	Group	Events	Paper	Mass Media	Computer
Event Attendance	X	X	X	X	X	X	X
Logistical Detail	X	X	X				X
Build Community	X	X	X	X			X
Educating	X	X	X	X	X	X	X
Recruiting	X			X	X	X	X
Lobbying	X	X	X	X	X	X	X
Facilitating Media	X	X	X	X		X	X
Legitimizing						X	X
Fundraising		X	X	X	X	X	X

onic conceptualization of the pragmatic goals of advocate media use. The knowledge is also valuable to advocates because it is a clear articulation of goals and audiences that they should consider when making communication-media choices to achieve particular advocacy ends.

Factors That Influence Advocate Media Use

Consistent with the theory of advocate media uses offered in this study, the characteristics of media, internal group factors, and external factors influence advocate media use.

Characteristics of Media Uses

Previous literature on characteristics of media such as the media-richness literature has focused on the qualitative differences between organizational communication media available to management in the corporate setting (Daft and Lengel, 1986; Daft, Lengel, and Trevino, 1987; Rice and Shook, 1990). The data-carrying capacity and symbolic meaning of media use in corporate communication have also been studied (Feldman and March, 1981; McLuhan, 1964; Sproull and Kiesler, 1986; Sitkin, Sutcliffe, and Barrios-Choplin, 1992). Much of this literature is written from a corporate managerial perspective rather than in the setting of political or social advocacy. My study adds to the understanding of other media characteristics that influence media use of advocates, such as permanence and distance.

In the case of advocacy communication media use, characteristics vary according to the particular medium, as explicated in specific chapters. This is synthesized in table 9.4. First, as with other advocacy communication, face-to-face communication can be influenced by the characteristic of the communica-

Table 9.4   Media Characteristics

Characteristics	Face	Telephone	Group	Events	Paper	Mass Media	Computer
			Media Form				
Feedback	X	X	X	X			X
Multiple Cues	X		X	X	X	X	X
Info. Capacity					X	X	X
Variety	X	X	X	X	X	X	X
Personal	X	X	X	X		X	X
Permanence					X	X	
Distance	X	X			X	X	X

tion form. This analysis reveals that the most salient characteristics of face-to-face communication is that the personal, physical presence allows much opportunity for feedback, nonverbal cues, and language variety that contribute to emotionally engaging personal quality. This is consistent with Rice and Shook (1990), who found that higher media richness is associated with "social presence" such as face-to-face communication (p. 200). My study has revealed that this is true in advocacy efforts as well. Thus, it is useful for increasing attendance at events, arranging logistical detail, building community, educating, recruiting, lobbying, and facilitating mass media coverage.

Second, telephone use is characterized by instantaneous feedback, lack of visual cues, language variety, a quasi-personal character, intrusiveness, and distance. Thus, advocates use telephone communication for increasing attendance at events, arranging logistical details, building community, educating, lobbying, facilitating mass media coverage, and fund raising, but not recruiting.

Third, group communication was characterized by the presence of feedback, multiple cues, language variety, and personal character. Advocates perceived that these characteristics made group communication useful for increasing attendance at events, arranging logistical details, building community, educating, lobbying, facilitating mass media coverage, and fund raising.

Finally, event advocacy communication was characterized by feedback, multiple cues, language variety, a personal character, but not information carrying capacity, permanence, or the ability to communicate across great distance. Because of these characteristics, advocates perceived that events were useful for increasing attendance at future events, building community, educating, recruiting, lobbying, facilitating mass media coverage, and fund raising.

Advocate perceptions about the characteristics of their uses of paper communication influence advocate media-use decisions. These perceived characteristics include low feedback, multiple cues, low efficiency, high information-carrying capacity, permanence, and, in general, a low level of personal character. Advocates perceived that these characteristics enable paper communication to be useful for increasing attendance at events, educating, recruiting, lobbying, and fund raising, but not for arranging logistical details, building community, facilitating mass media coverage, or legitimizing advocate activities and issue positions.

Overall, characteristics of mass media include permanence, multiple cues, information-carrying capacity, and personal character. Advocates perceived that these characteristics contributed to the usefulness of mass media for increasing attendance at events, educating, recruiting, lobbying, facilitating mass media coverage, legitimizing advocate activities and issue positions, and fund raising; but mass media lack the feedback necessary for arranging logistical details or the authentic, personal quality necessary to build community.

Characteristics of advocates' use of computers, on the other hand, include feedback, multiple cues, language variety, information-carrying capacity, a quasi-personal character, distance, and impermanence. Accordingly, advocates use computer communication to increase attendance at events, arranging logistical detail, building community, educating, recruiting, lobbying, facilitating mass media coverage, legitimizing advocate activities and issue positions, and fund raising. Because of the multitude of characteristics of computer communication, it is perceived as useful for all of the functions of advocacy media use. Thus, according to the theory of advocate media use, a variety of media characteristics influence advocate use of media to perform specific functions.

Internal Factors

Internal group factors also influence media-use choices, as outlined throughout this book. These internal factors include people power, financial resources, access to logistical resources, knowledge, group history, and overlapping membership (see table 9.5). These factors influence advocates' use of the identified media. Advocates perceive that those media that require the least resource expenditure and possess a high number of desirable characteristics are effective means for the achievement of functional goals.

For instance, internal group factors, including people power, knowledge, financial resources, and group history, influence advocate use of face-to-face communication. Advocates' people power, financial resources, access to logistical resources, group history, and overlapping membership influence the use of telephone communication. Advocates' use of small-group communication is also influenced by internal group factors, including people power, group history, and overlapping group membership, all of which influence the ability of advocates to use group communication for the dissemination of their messages.

All the internal factors I have identified influence advocates' ability to use events to perform several functions, including increasing attendance at future

Table 9.5 Internal Factors that Influence Advocate Media Uses

Factor	Face	Telephone	Group	Events	Paper	Mass Media	Computer
People power	X	X	X	X	X	X	X
Finances	X	X		X	X	X	X
Access to Logistics		X		X	X	X	X
Knowledge	X			X	X	X	X
Group History	X	X	X	X		X	X
Overlapping Members		X	X	X			X

(*Media Form* is the spanning header over Face, Telephone, Group, Events, Paper, Mass Media, Computer.)

events, building community, educating, recruiting, lobbying, facilitating mass media coverage, and fund raising. Events are not an appropriate locus for arranging logistical details because of the diffused personal character of events. Those studied here did not perceived events as valuable for legitimizing the activities or issue positions of advocates, likely due to the perception that anyone can stage an advocacy event.

Several internal factors influence advocates' ability to use paper communication including people power, knowledge, and access to logistical resources. Because paper communication lacks feedback and a personal character, activists perceived paper communication inappropriate for arranging logistical details and building community.

Advocates' use of mass media is also influenced by internal group factors, such as people power, financial resources, access to logistical resources, and knowledge, as does the history of the organization and interaction with other advocacy groups. Because of mass media's lack of feedback, language variety, and authentically personal character, advocates do not perceive mass media to be useful for arranging logistical detail or building community.

Likewise, a number of internal factors influence advocate use of computer communication technology. These include the people power available for advocate communication, financial resources, access to logistical resources, the knowledge possessed by associated advocates, the history of use of computer technology by the group and its members, and the media uses of other groups. Group history influences media choices, as Darlene explained:

> The history of the group does influence its media choices . . . they have contacts; you have people in the committee who know things that have worked. Through history, or you heard through the grapevine, how people heard about the event. Every year you can add a little more, because the committee knows more, and it works faster. You have twelve people trying to run this whole big thing, they can . . . and they only have so much time. But if they already have one contact, they can spend their time looking for another media method that works. So I think yes, throughout the years you will be able to add a little bit more, take away what didn't work, and add what does work.

This can be tied to the concept of norms identified by Sitkin, Sutcliffe, and Barrios-Choplin (1992). These authors suggest that norms guide many actions within corporate institutions. This book has revealed that while the particular norms may differ from a corporate context, group history nevertheless contributes to media use norms among advocates. Darlene explained that previous experiences are the basis for knowledge about what works and what does not: "[To reach a larger, general audience] you know who to talk to, because you have done this before." Thus, the theory of advocates' media use reveals that internal factors such as people power, knowledge, financial resources, access to logistical resources, group history, and overlapping membership influence advocate media use.

Media-use patterns are not a function of job categories and the levels of those categories, as opposed to corporate settings as suggested by Rice and Shook (1990). My research reveals less hierarchical media-use decision-making patterns in advocacy communication than corporate settings.

External Factors

External factors influenced advocate media uses, as displayed in table 9.6. The influence of external factors varied according to particular media, as explicated in previous chapters. For instance, external political factors influence activists' use of face-to-face communication with politicians. The political context influenced the ability of advocates to engage elected officials in interpersonal communication.

External factors influenced advocates' ability to use telephone communication. Advocates perceived that political context and general technological trends influenced their ability to use telephone communication to perform the previously identified functions of telephone communication.

External factors influenced advocates' use of small-group communication. Activists' use of paper communication is influenced by political context and technological trends, and their use of mass media was also influenced by external factors, including political context, general technological trends, and media personnel decisions. External factors such as political climate and general technological trends also influenced advocate use of computer communication.

Through inquiry into these areas of knowledge, the meaning of the uses of communication media by local social and political movement advocates is better understood. Qualitative methods have been invaluable for answering these questions because of the centrality of the intentionality of communicating advocates in the construction of this theory of advocate media use.

Advocates perceive that they should strive to utilize any and all available

Table 9.6   External Factors that Influence Advocate Media Uses

	Media Form						
Factor	Face	Telephone	Group	Events	Paper	Mass Media	Computer
Political Context	X		X	X	X	X	X
Technological Trends		X			X	X	X
Mass Media Decisions						X	

communication media when seeking political or social change. This includes interpersonal communication, telephone communication, advocacy event communication, paper communication, mass media communication, and computer-mediated communication.

Theoretical Implications

There are many theoretical concepts that have been raised in this book. Although these theoretical ideas are very narrow in their applicability, they do shed light on how advocates perceive successful phenomena of media uses. Some of the most salient findings are listed here.

Audience

Advocates are more successful in achieving effective communication when they adapt to the use preferences of their target audiences, because unless they reach their target audience, media use will not fulfill the desired functions.

Arranging Logistical Detail

Media uses designed to arrange logistical details do not require personalized characteristics to be successful because there is usually a prior relationship between those using media to communicate to arrange logistical details.

Because media used to arrange logistical details do not usually entail persuasion, less personal media uses are often sufficient for the function of arranging logistical details.

Knowledge possessed by advocates due to prior media-use experience is a valuable resource for coordination of advocacy-coalition efforts. Those advocates who possess such knowledge will be more successful than those advocates who do not.

Specific aspects about particular advocate activities should be negotiated through various media uses over a period of time, with room for modifications in planning in response to the desires and requirements of all sponsoring organizations.

If advocates use media to communicate and confirm specifics with speakers and/or talent who will participate in an event, rather than not using media in this way, there is a higher likelihood that logistical requirements for activities will be met.

Constant recursive use of multiple media with all concerned parties in preplanning and planning stages can increase the success of advocacy events. Events can be more successful if media are used to confirm specific aspects of activities with all participating organizations before plans are finalized. As the event nears, using media to confirm logistical arrangements can be very valuable in decreasing the destructive potential of unforeseen problems in the execution of advocacy events.

Logistical components are vital to the effective communicative value of an advocacy event, and advocates who do not use media forms for careful planning will not be as successful as those for which advocates use media for planning.

Advocates who contact all sponsoring organizations to ensure the activation of all related communication networks and mediums will be more successful than those who do not.

Promoting Event Attendance

Events must be promoted to be effective because having knowledge about an event is a necessary precondition for attending an event.

Advocates can increase the success of their efforts if they give as many organizations as possible the opportunity to use media to communicate about or at an event; as such, invitations to use media will increase the level of commitment within supporting organizations.

Fliers can be effective in the promotion of advocacy events when advocates seek to increase attendance at events by audiences other than other advocates.

The telephone is effective in increasing attendance among advocates but is not used to increase attendance among the public because it depends on a prior personal relationship.

Advocates who announce activities in the meetings of all participating organizations can maximize network potential.

Nontraditional forms of promotion (such as fliers placed on pizza boxes or enclosed in payroll envelopes) can be valuable because they can attract the attention of recipients due to nonconventional novelty.

Nonpersonal media uses can be sufficient for communicating among advocates who share common experiences and subsequent logistical and operational assumptions.

Advocacy groups who establish connections with other advocacy groups have more people power and will be able to generate more attendance at jointly sponsored events.

All related upcoming events should be announced during an advocacy event, as advocate media use supports future use.

Educating the General Public

Advocates perceive that mass media are effective for reaching the general public largely due to quasi-personal characteristics and the media's ability to reach large audiences.

Recruiting

Advocates recruit new advocates in face-to-face interactions at events and often provide these new recruits with paper literature to supplement these recruiting efforts.

Advocates and prospective recruits can enable future media use if advocates share media contact information, a form of knowledge, with all those who attend an advocacy event.

At events that feature a speaker, a period in which attendees have an opportunity to ask questions should be provided, as a way for those attending to express their viewpoint.

Lobbying

Advocates perceive face-to-face interaction as the most effective method but also the most difficult to attain for lobbying politicians.

Advocates perceive e-mail to be an easy but largely ineffective method for lobbying politicians.

Telephones can be used to lobby elected officials, but advocates perceive telephone calls do not have as much impact as other forms of contact.

Facilitating Mass Media Coverage

Local advocacy groups must interest news media in their events because they do not have the financial resources to buy space for their causes in the media.

Advocates who use telephone communication to respond to solicitation of information by mass media personnel are more successful than advocates who do not because of the immediate feedback between the advocate and the media representative.

Advocates who begin public relations efforts as soon as plans are finalized will be more successful at attracting the attention of mass media personnel than those who wait until the last minute to use media to contact mass media personnel.

Legitimizing Activist Efforts

At events, providing effective media tools, such as public address equipment and literature tables, are important ingredients for the effective delivery of advocacy messages because adept use increases the perceived legitimacy of advocate activities and positions.

Mass media, and television in particular, are the most effective methods for legitimizing the advocacy activities of an advocacy group.

Fund Raising

Fund raising is aimed primarily at advocates, and advocates use media for this function that will reach the advocate population (e.g., telephone, group, paper).

Building Community

Advocates can build community when all contributing organizations and key individuals are recognized and thanked through various media following an advocacy event.

Community building in an advocacy group requires repeated interactions among advocates and events and provides the venue for these repeated interactions.

Internal Factors

Activists can increase media-use success when advocates strategically consider their available resources, exploit their resource strengths, and attempt to bolster resource deficiencies.

Effective networking between groups can be more successful when informed from prior communication with other groups, as manifest through group history.

Advocates who use media to share their knowledge of successful media use can increase the effectiveness of future media uses.

Advocates who are receptive and respond to offers from others for contributions of people power can work with the synergy of efforts of a number of people to maximize the effectiveness of advocacy activities.

Advocacy groups who establish connections with other advocacy groups through the use of media have more people power and will be able to generate more attendance at jointly sponsored events than advocates who do not use media to establish these connections.

Advocacy groups who establish connections with other advocacy groups have more people power and will be able to share responsibility for logistical arrangements for events.

External Factors

Activists who have adopted computer fax to gain the attention of mass media personnel have more success that those who do not. Advocates who have not responded to this technological trend in the use patterns of this target audience and rely on traditional press release delivery means are less successful than those who have adapted to this technological trend. Thus, advocates who send press releases through computer fax will be more successful at facilitating mass media coverage than those who rely on other media to achieve this function.

General

Advocacy-event participants will be more successful in achieving a variety of functions if they discuss the relevant issue in interpersonal settings with all possible intended audiences.

Those participating at an advocacy event should be given adequate information to express their concerns to relevant policymakers through e-mail, telephone, or through the mail.

People power is a necessary ingredient for the achievement of any desired functions for which advocates use media.

Advocates who use multiple media for the accomplishment of a single function will generally be more successful than those who rely exclusively on one medium or a small number of possible media.

Advocates who seek emotionally engaging communicative experience use media that possess more personal qualities than media that are impersonal.

Advocates perceive they will be more successful if they utilize any and all available media forms because redundancy increases the chances to remind audience members of previous communication.

Unique media-form use can facilitate further advocacy communication more than media uses that are perceived by media personnel to be routine or old news.

These theoretical formulations are a beginning in creating transferable abstract knowledge of advocate media use. While the transferability value may be limited, the abstractions are useful for understanding the range of the phenomenon of advocate media use.

Areas for Further Study

The theoretical concepts developed here could be used to study advocates in other issue areas. The study of the media uses of world trade protesters, for instance, would be a valuable area of future inquiry. The theoretical constructs could be tested and refined in this as well as other advocacy settings.

Further exploration is warranted on the nature of experiences that advocates hope they evoke through use of communication media. I have learned that advocates seek to engage in communicative experiences with other humans about activities and issue positions of advocates through the use of the explicated media. This is true for all media forms, for all intended audiences, and for all functions. The ability of advocates to use media to engage others in effective communicative experience was influenced by a number of factors. Quality is experiential and beyond definition, although comparison to other concepts is useful for understanding it. The Greek concept of *arête*, which means to strive for excellence, to reach, to do the best one can, for the sake of responsibility to one's self, is similar to the concept of quality. However, the experiential nature of a quality communicative experience cannot be reduced to signifiers without losing much of the affective force of a quality communicative experience. One can have a quality communicative experience and be unable to fully articulate the totality of the experience. Thus, a quality communicative experience is impossible to define, but must be experienced to be understood. The difference between the French concepts of *connaître* and *savoir* is similar to the sociological differentiation between etic and emic knowledge; both words mean to know, but *savoir* refers to an academic, intellectual knowledge, while *connaître* refers to knowledge of experience. Quality cannot be known through *savoir*, only *connaître*. This is also a central difference between Platonic and Aristotelian thought: Quality cannot be defined, categorized, and classified, as Aristotle would desire. The holism of Plato is a necessary epistemological precursor to consideration of the concept of quality communicative experiences. Even this Platonic conception in its usual consideration misses the experiential essence of a quality communicative experience. Plato did not see the good (virtue) as a static ideal, but good is the quality that results when individuals conscientiously act with emotional attachment and engage one another in ways that allow them to see the world in a new way. A quality communicative experience that possesses *arête* cannot be defined; it can only be experienced. Pirsig (1974) describes an extreme interpretation of this idea through his main character in *Zen and the Art of Motorcycle Maintenance*: "Anyone who cannot understand [the meaning of quality] without logical *definiens* and *difinendum* and *differentia* is either lying or so out of touch with the common lot of humanity as to be unworthy of receiving any reply whatsoever" (p. 340). While Pirsig's main character is displaying unreasonable hubris and delusions of grandeur at the time that he states this, no definition can approximate the experiential reality of a quality communicative experience.

As I have grappled with increasing my understanding of the media uses of advocacy for the past several years, a realization dawned on me many times: The "gumption" factor is the most important determinant of advocates' use of communicative media. Advocates who have gumption act; advocates who lack gumption do not. But what creates gumption? Advocates perceive that the answer to that question is that communicative experiences, created through the uses of media I have outlined throughout this book, create advocacy gumption. One does not follow the other; rather, the interaction between quality communicative experiences and gumption are reciprocal. Advocates perceive that quality communicative experiences can instill issue-relevant gumption in those who consume advocate media messages. Advocates perceive that the only way they can contribute to such an experience is through communication. Gumption refers to advocates' will to act, the enthusiastic initiative in the enactment of advocacy communicative praxis. Pirsig (1974) offers an operational definition of gumption: "A person filled with gumption doesn't sit around dissipating and stewing about things. He's at the front of the train of his own awareness, watching to see what's up the track and meeting it when it comes. That's gumption" (p. 272). More importantly, Pirsig offers a description of the experience of gumption in which communication is central: "The gumption filling process occurs when one is quiet long enough to see and hear and feel the real universe, not just one's own stale opinions about it" (p. 273). Theoretically, quality communicative experiences provoke gumption, the desire in advocates to act on certain issues. Advocate gumption, a result of emotionally engaging communicative experiences, is a catalytic factor in future advocates' communicative praxis. The ultimate goal of this praxis is to provoke gumption in others, which symbiotically leads to additional communicative praxis and, advocates hope, additional emphatically effective communicative experiences. In the case of advocacy, it is communication that enables individuals to "see and hear and feel" experiences of those most affected by an issue. The theory of advocate media suggests that advocates use communication media to engage others in communicative experiences, because advocates perceive that those experiences contribute to advocate gumption, a catalytic factor in the public dialectic at the center of the process of human progress.

These theoretical ideas about advocate media use expand the exploration of the essential characteristic differences and similarities between various communication media. Besides the work of McLuhan (1964) and extensions of that work, as well as the research of media-richness theorists, discussion of the essential nature of communication through various media has been neglected. Thus this research represents a step forward in understanding the multiplicity of communicative options in a postmodern, cable-connected global village.

As addressed in the introduction to this book, clear distinctions between the larger movement and the particular groups working toward movement are illusory (tools for scholars). The purpose of this study has been to look at the media uses of bounded groups that are part of larger social and political movements. This proved somewhat problematic, but I studied groups within social and political movement organizations. Again, Griffin (1980) suggests that rather than debating the limits of which social phenomena could be considered movements, communication scholars should utilize an inclusive definition in efforts to study a wide range of situational activism under the rubric of social movement theory and methods. This book has revealed that there are differences in levels of communication between advocates and variance in the commitment of individual advocates. Traditional definitions have tended to focus on groups to the exclusion of between-group advocacy and advocacy efforts of individuals under no group auspices.

During the course of this project, it has become obvious that constant comparison is not exclusively inductive. Rather, the process is continually recursive, according to Glaser and Strauss (1967), as the scholar engages in "inspecting data and redesigning the developing theory" (pp. 102–3). Specifically, Glaser and Strauss contrasted the development of theory through the constant comparative method to methods that were exclusively inductive (p. 104). In addition, researching in the field and writing the results of research are two separate stages of this research process, although there is some overlap. Theory is primarily developed in the analysis of data before the final write-up of research results. Thus, concepts that are developed inductively can recursively be applied to other topical substantive areas as theoretical ideas are honed and written.

In efforts to engage others in communicative experiences, advocates use a number of media forms to reach several audiences and perform several functions, and these uses are influenced by several factors, including characteristics of the medium and internal and external factors. This study reveals that social and political movement advocates use various forms of a number of communication media, including interpersonal, telephone, group, events, paper, mass media, and computer communication in an effort to facilitate effective communicative experiences. Advocates perceive that these uses perform a number of functions, including increasing attendance at events, changing attitudes, raising awareness, arranging logistical details, building community, lobbying, facilitating mass media coverage, legitimizing advocate activities and issue positions, and raising funds.

The findings in this book offer a challenge to scholars who study activists to apply the topologies to activists in other substantive areas and to test these local postulates. Quantitative application of these typologies would reveal the extent of general applicability. Scholars would be challenged by sampling issues, but the revealing analysis would move our knowledge of the communicative practices of activists further. The typologies could also be applied to other organiza-tional communication such as in corporate settings. Finally, this book studied perceptions of advocates. Those who study activist communication can check these perceptions against the perceptions of nonadvocates.

Advocates could use some of these ideas to increase the effectiveness of their media uses. Communicating our political opinions is a duty in a democratic system and provides an opportunity to engage in community and actualize our personal participation in the polis. Opportunities have been defined, functions have been suggested, and the factors that influence advocate ability to use media have been identified. Advocates can use this knowledge to more pro-ductively use communication media to engage others in effective communica-tive experiences. Advocates can communicate more with one another through the means identified here to organize and motivate other advocates. Advocates can also use the communicative means and tactics to increase communication with nonactivists in efforts to educate and recruit. The real limits of activist potential exist only in the minds of activists. Strategic application of the find-ings in this book can facilitate liberation from the self-imposed limits on activist ability to engage others in quality communicative experiences. Exercising gumption by applying these practices could help activists more effectively reach targeted audiences.

The book opened with a story of advocates working for legal relief for Joe Amrine, a man on the Missouri death row despite no evidence or witnesses against him. On April 30, 2003, the supreme court of Missouri decided that there was not enough evidence against Amrine for him to remain on death row. Amrine became a free man on July 28, 2003. Efforts described in this book were helpful in the effort to free Joe Amrine. Hopefully advocates can learn from the experiences of these activists and others and engage in commu-nication that can make our world a better place to live.

Appendix A

Advocate Participants

The three advocacy communities I studied were in support of environmental protection, abolition of the death penalty, and universal health care. The environmental advocates were from several environmental protection groups that joined together to organize the community Earth Day celebration. Earth Day was a large event in this community with an estimated attendance of several thousand people. The anti–death penalty advocates I studied belonged to several groups, including local chapters of two international anti–death penalty organizations, a state-wide organization, and two ad hoc groups that advocated clemency for two different inmates on death row, one in the state of residence of the advocates and another inmate in another state. I also studied advocates of universal health care who were affiliated with a national universal health care organization.

There were at least thirty advocates who contributed to this research through interviews and allowed me access into advocate groups. Leaders of the groups were very helpful. They included Tony, a leading state advocate of abolition of the death penalty as legislative coordinator of a statewide anti–death penalty organization. Abby, the key leader in the environmental and peace-related advocacy activity in the community, was also very helpful. A leading advocate in the universal health care community, Nancy, added valuable perspective. Joan, the internationally active, hard-core activist on a variety of social justice issues (a self-labeled "rad"), added a more radical perspective in many instances. Other participants were active, but played less leading roles. These included Darlene, a college professor and an active advocate for all three causes (organizing and supporting four events a year, volunteering two to four hours a month, and attending another four advocacy events a year), who was

231

a valuable source of ideas. Many excerpts came from Ed, a truck driver who is an active participant in three to four environmental and anti–death penalty events a year and who has been involved in advocacy efforts for over fifteen years. Lana is an environmental advocate who is also a city employee. Lenny, a doctoral student and an important personality in university politics who was involved with several anti–death penalty events a year, was also a useful source of information. Advocates like these provided rich sources of data on advocate media uses.

There are several strategic benefits of the study of these three groups, which became more apparent as research progressed. First, these groups differ in the amount of time that the groups have been active. Differences in the length of time that the groups were in existence and differences in media use make comparisons between these sample groups theoretically valuable. The primary anti–death penalty group was originally formed in the 1950s. The environmental group was started in the early 1970s, while the health care advocacy organization was organized in the late 1980s. A second reason that these groups provide theoretical diversity is that they differ in their uses of various media. For instance, the environmental group has integrated computer technology the most, the anti–death penalty advocates used some computer capabilities, while the health care advocacy group used the least amount of computer communication, although all three increased their use of computer communication during the period I studied these groups. There are many differences in how these three groups communicated. In another example of the diversity afforded due to inclusion of these three groups, the patterns of telephone use differed between the three groups, as explored in that specific chapter. The differences in communicative practices enabled rich comparisons of the media uses of these three groups. The last reason these groups were chosen is one of access, an important factor for ethnographic investigation. These groups offered access opportunities. Media use is a prevalent activity of these advocates. Planning and executing opportunities for political praxis is a central feature of this advocacy. The distinct separation of available media is analytical. In the field, media uses are intertwined. Different media are used to reach particular audiences during various event-planning and execution stages, and communication is necessary in preparation for any of these stages. The overlap in membership of these groups also provided an excellent opportunity to examine diffusion of tactical knowledge between linked groups. These people were very generous with their time and willingness to share their perspectives.

Appendix B

Research Method

The goal of this study has been to understand advocacy communication from the perspective of those who use these practices on a regular basis. In an effort to develop theory about advocacy communication, this study entailed analysis of responses and activates of those who communicate to advocate their political and social views.

At the most basic level, rational choice theory implies that those who participate in social movement praxis are motivated by the possible impact of social movement activity (Olson, 1971). The aim of social movement communication is often an alteration of substantive policy or governmental structure. However, methodological difficulties confound scientific attempts to ascertain the structural or substantive consequences of such praxis. Social movement communication does not operate in a political or social vacuum. There is contextual impetus for those with access to institutional power to work outside social movement organizations in efforts to alleviate the conditions that necessitated the emerging social movements. The political climate influences and is influenced by social movement communication. While social scientists would likely grant such a proposition on an intuitive (and nonacademic) level, there is a lack of opportunity in constantly transforming social life to identify statistically significant effects of social advocacy communication. This methodological difficulty should not preclude assumptions about the importance of advocate media use. Such commitment to positivistic assumptions ignores the catalytic factors that give rise to social movements as well as cultural and political reverberations that emanate from social movements. Such a position would entail ignoring valuable avenues of research.

In this study I was interested in the pragmatic considerations of advocacy communication. The focus of my inquiry was to identify patterns of media uses of activists for a variety of functions. Through a constant comparative analysis of field notes gathered from over two years of participant observation with each group, interview transcripts, and texts produced by advocates, I identified categories of media available to advocates, and I developed theoretical postulates as a result of recursive consideration of composition of categories and the relationships between those categories. Advocates' perceptions were used to analyze media uses. I developed theoretical propositions as a result of my work to develop grounded theory (Glaser and Strauss, 1967; Strauss and Corbin, 1998). The rationale for using Glaser and Strauss's method of theory generation is that it allows for the inductive generation of theory. Theory arises from the analysis of data, particularly through the use of the constant comparative method. My ultimate aim has been to develop theory grounded in analysis of qualitative data generated from ethnographic investigation of media use by social advocates.

The meanings attributed to communication media by advocacy activists are the most important data of this study. Advocates' understandings are key to interpretation of the meaning of media-use choices. The most important source of such emic data is the activists themselves. An important aspect of qualitative research is the search for emic knowledge (the understanding of events from the perspective of those who live the events) as opposed to etic knowledge (knowledge that can be gathered from the outside looking into a scene). This emic knowledge is the advocates' understanding and interpretation of their media uses or "the sense that actors attribute to their communicative action" (Lindlof, 1995, p. 83). Thus, ethnographic methods of data collection are most appropriate. Analysis of data gathered through observation, interviews, and advocacy literature will be used to ascertain the meaning of advocacy communication.

Qualitative Approach

A qualitative approach was most appropriate for this project because of the type of knowledge I sought. Advocacy communication can be productively studied within the understanding of the participants. In addition, the intended impact of media uses by those who participate in advocacy activity can be ascertained from those activists. Analysis of this emic knowledge to generate theory about advocates' media use is the ultimate objective of this project.

Consideration of meanings, for which a qualitative approach is particularly useful in research, is also very important to my research project. As such, qualitative methods were useful. Those involved in the advocacy activities constitute meaning of their media uses. One of my key assumptions is that meaning does not reside in a message, but rather in the interplay of media use with the collectivity of past experiences of communication participants. The triangulation of methods (e.g., interviews, study of artifacts, and participant observation) and member checking provide other ways to gain information about motivations. Member checking was conducted by revealing results of my investigation to key participants and incorporating their input before the final write-up. As I honed this analysis, I contacted key participants at least twenty-five times to check my theoretical developments. I would subsequently modify my analysis based on their input. This is their story, and I privileged their voices in a cyclical fashion in an effort to inform development of this theory of advocate media use. Qualitative methods were most appropriate for this research.

Access

Access to activities of groups advocating abolition of the death penalty, universal health care coverage for all U.S. citizens, and for environmental protection was easy to gain. As a contributing actor in related activities of the community, cooperation was very easy to secure because of my previous involvement in other advocacy activities with members of the pertinent groups, especially key leaders and gatekeepers.

Initially in this study, I was not known to the group as an investigator, but as a participant in the planning, promotion, and execution of public advocacy events. The move from participant to participant observer was a personal evolution. The implications of such an evolution presupposed a trust between the researcher and key members of the coalition, and entailed acquiring informed consent from participants. As research became more focused, similar to the funnel analogy of the research process suggested by Lindlof (1995), and as interviews became necessary, consent was formally procured from interviewees. Again, involvement with previous advocacy activities by key members of the coalition, as well as contributions to the communication and logistical elements of the advocacy events, has fostered very open cooperation from key members of the advocacy organizations in this research effort.

Data Sources

Several kinds of data were used to study the communication practices of advocacy organizations. The triangulation of data-gathering methods provided a check against the weaknesses of specific approaches and allowed for comparison between data types. As Benoit (1988) suggested, "Multiple sources of data contain recurrent themes and such features suggest similarities that cut across sources while features apparent in only some data suggest a source of variation.

Richer explanations of fundamental concepts are the result" (pp. 31–32). First, observations were a key feature of the collection of data for this research project. Observations were recorded from organizational meetings, preparation and execution of public advocacy events, lobbying efforts, attempts to gain mass media access, sessions for the writing and distribution of mail material, and reception of advocate correspondence. Active participation/observation was a vital investigative tool. Through my full participation, it was possible not only to ascertain from others relevant emic knowledge, but I was also able to be a source of some emic knowledge.

Observational Notes

Observations were formulated and recorded at a number of advocacy events. These events were chosen as sources of data because of their importance as instances of a larger process of social activity in which a coalition of groups works together to promote the applicable issues. Many occasions were instances of praxis designed to utilize cooperation among a number of groups to consolidate around an issue and promote a perspective in the public forum. These events were part of a continuing process of activity in a campaign to advocate a policy direction. Data included in this study were gathered from group meetings, related correspondence, and local, state, and national events. These include vigils at the governor's office, publicity and lobbying events at the state capitol, public events in support of national promotional tours of related activists, national rallies, and educational programs.

Field notes accumulated from participant observation from at least three years of activity in each group were important sources of data for this study. Some notes were recorded as events occurred. These events included group meetings as well as public programs. Other notes were constructed based on recall because there was not always adequate time during an event to record thorough notes. A third source of data was notes written after events, utilizing audiotapes of events, when audio taping would not be too intrusive. This increased recall. These three sources of field notes provided a basis for the formulation of interview and focus group questions.

A triangulation of recording methods was utilized in the observatory stage. Field notes were recorded as events took place; the salient features were recorded in handwritten notes. In addition, many events were electronically recorded on audiotape. These tapes provided data for reevaluation of the event at a later point in time, as well as for the development of additional notes. A third strategy used in the observation process immediately after the event was the audio recording of this researcher's reflections of the event during transportation from the event. All of these sources provided key data texts, which were categorically coded and analyzed utilizing the constant comparative method in an effort to develop theory concerning communicative media uses during advocacy campaigns (Glaser and Strauss, 1967).

Interviews

Interviews of individual activists and focus group interviews were data sources. I interviewed over forty advocacy activists; those recognized by other members of the group as leaders, defined as those who spend much time in related activities. The subjects of these formal interviews were chosen because they are key leaders (based on perceptions of others in the groups) of activists throughout the state. These advocates were selected based on their visibility at the center of advocacy activity. These informants were easily recruited due to my participatory role. I also interviewed those in nonleadership roles, people who are involved less frequently and to a lesser degree. Interviewing less active advocates revealed an additional perspective from those who receive such communication rather than send it. These subjects were chosen based on access, convenience, and knowledge of their peripheral involvement over a period of time. I conducted at least ten interviews from each of the three issue groups I studied. Thus, over forty formal interview situations were the source of substantial data. These interviews took between thirty and sixty minutes. The questions asked of interviewees concerned advocate media use and evaluation of different available media. In all instances, I was granted consent to use the interviews and data as well as to inform the participants of their role in the research and their rights as human subjects.

Thus, interviews were key data-text sources. In all of the formal interview situations, written notes were taken during the course of the interviews. The interviews were also recorded on audiotape for future reference, transcription, and development of theoretical notes. Strauss and Corbin (1998) define theoretical notes as "Sensitizing and summarizing memos that contain an analyst's thoughts and ideas about theoretical sampling and other factors" (p. 217). Theoretical sampling guided interview focus as this project proceeded. Theoretical sampling is "sampling on the basis of emerging concepts, with the aim being to explore the dimensional range or varied conditions along which the properties of concepts vary" (p. 215). Notes were developed immediately after the interviews were conducted. I recorded my reaction to the interviews in the development of notes. These notes informed the development of follow-up interview questions. Consistent with theoretical sampling, these follow-up interview situations provided a way to focus on important emerging concepts. Likewise, as theoretical saturation was achieved, this provided areas of further focus. Achievement of theoretical saturation was my goal, or "when no new information seems to emerge during coding, that is, when no new properties, dimensions, conditions, actions/interactions, or consequences are seen in the data" (p. 218). This saturation informed my inquiry in later stages.

Artifacts

An additional source of data was group artifacts such as literature dissemin-ated by the coalition concerning the advocacy of universal single-payer health care. Over 150 printed texts were examined in this research effort. Notes were developed from analysis of this literature. Those notes were important pieces of data in the establishment of subsequent grounded theory. Documents dis-tributed by such organizations were studied. Fliers promoting events and newsletters disseminated to all on groups' mailing lists were studied. As Lofland and Lofland (1995) suggest, many of the matters discussed in their book "apply equally well to analysts of human cultural productions and to researchers of human cultural producers" (p. 18). These artifacts are products designed as communication media. Likewise, questions of motivation and communicative intent were clarified through comparison to other data sources. E-mail was also important in this analysis. I examined two years of e-mail correspondence in these groups, which included over one thousand e-mail messages. I looked at e-mail directed to group members. As a participant/observer, access to such e-mail was not a difficult issue; I usually received them through my e-mail account. Likewise, I received additional artifacts such as newsletters or post-cards in the mail. I also participated in much phone correspondence. Notes were kept on this correspondence as well.

Sample

The goal of this research was not to generate generalizable theory, but to for-mulate theoretical postulates with transferability value. Leininger (1994) defines transferability as "the ability to transfer findings to another similar con-text or situation while still preserving the meaning" (p. 68). The use of three different advocacy groups as sources of analysis enabled the development of theory on these groups. This theory is applicable to other groups in the local community or groups in other communities under similar conditions. Future research would be necessary to establish the transferability to a wider range of social advocacy groups.

Data Analysis

Data analysis was guided by the philosophical assumptions and practical consid-erations offered by grounded theory (Glaser and Strauss, 1967; Strauss and

Corbin, 1998). Rather than analyze data through existing theory, I developed local theory on advocate media use that is grounded in my data and developed through constant comparative analysis of that data. I was guided by previous work in the area of media use, but was limited by previous theoretical discussion. In addition, a review of qualitative research in communication offered by Lindlof (1995) also provided procedural guidance, philosophical justification of procedures, and important discussion of ethical considerations that should guide research. Previous grounded-theory research was also a valuable resource for the development of the research approach utilized in the study of coalition advocacy of a universal single-payer health care system, advocates of abolition of the death penalty, and environmentalists (Benoit, 1997; Strauss and Corbin, 1998). I sorted relevant data from data that were not germane through a constant reconsideration of developing theoretical concepts.

Constant comparative analysis (Charmaz, 1983; Glaser and Strauss, 1967; Strauss and Corbin, 1998) was used to develop a categorical framework of communication media use of local advocacy activists. Several areas of communication have previously been studied utilizing this method, including family communication (Sabourin and Stamp, 1995; Stamp, 1994), dissemination of other types of messages through the mass media (Lange, 1993), leader-member exchange patterns of female business leaders (Fairhurst, 1993), acclaiming and disclaiming discourses (Benoit, 1997), and communication in education contexts (Hart and Williams, 1995; Neuliep, 1991; Tracy and Baratz, 1993).

Analysis of the data-texts developed during the course of this research was conducted using constant comparative method (Glaser and Strauss, 1967). Individual data units were analyzed for characteristics and delineated by theme. They were most often paragraphs from interviews and field notes, although the size of the unit was sometimes larger for artifacts such as advocacy literature or mass media coverage of advocate activity. Individual pieces of data were then categorized according to common characteristics. Each piece of data in a category was compared to other individual pieces of data in order to refine characteristics of each category. Then the categories were compared in an effort to ascertain theoretical relationships between categories. This process was repeated, and theoretical propositions were developed as a result. I repeated these steps with data from all three groups and for the seven media. The process was continually recursive in construction. I refined the theoretical schemata hundreds of times over the course of at least a year.

There are several initial steps involved with this method of data analysis. The initial step for researchers is to examine instances of data and to articulate characteristics of the data. These characteristics are used to identify emerging categories. The researchers use explicit statements about characteristics of data included in particular categories. This constant comparison is used to begin to formulate categories into which individual data can be placed. After analysis of individual units, themes will begin to emerge. Data are then sorted into categories based on similar emerging themes. In this stage, data are compared with other data in a category in order to evaluate whether the data belong in that particular category or another. Strauss and Corbin (1998) call this axial coding, or "The process of relating categories to their subcategories, termed 'axial' because coding occurs around the axis of a category, linking categories at the level of properties and dimensions" (p. 123). Another step in this constant comparison process is the explicit statement of the properties of each category. Contrasting these categories provides another angle from which characteristics of each category can be ascertained, identified, and refined. The perceived similarities and differences of media provided the substance of abstract conceptualizations about these media and the advocates' use of these media that are in the form of lower level theoretical statements.

For instance, all pieces of data from artifacts, interviews, and observational notes were gathered on the use of each medium. As an example, all data on telephone use were isolated. The data were then sorted according to themes that arose from this data. Themes emerged from that data such as cost of the telephone, convenience, instant feedback availability, and the presence of nonverbal cues. Axial coding, or comparing differences and similarities of each data piece, took place throughout this process. These began to reveal the perceived characteristics of the telephone use. Theoretical notes were made about these characteristics. These emerging characteristics were then compared to the emerging features in other media, which further clarified media characteristics and provided the basis for identification of theory about the use of the telephone by activists. A similar process was used to address each of my research questions.

Negative instances were also used to hone this analysis. The goal of analysis was to develop a precise classification scheme of available media, intended audiences, functions of advocate media uses, and factors that influenced advocate media use. The goal of this constant comparative method was the establishment of grounded theory. Grounded theory is analytic abstraction about a phenomenon that arises out of analysis of data. While the resulting theory is very restrained in its transferability, theoretical considerations of advocate use of media are explored. The theory of advocate media use arose out of identification of relationships between categories. Communicative media use plays a critical role in the establishment and maintenance of the local advocacy groups.

References

Alinsky, S. 1971. *Rules for Radicals: A Practical Primer for Realistic Radicals.* New York: Vintage.

Anderson, J. A. 1996. *Communication Theory: Epistemological Foundations.* New York: Guilford.

Bales, R. 1970. *Personality and Interpersonal Behavior.* New York: Holt, Rinehart.

Ballard, C. L., and J. H. Goddeeris. 1999. "Financing Universal Health Care in the United States: A General Equilibrium Analysis of Efficiency and Distributional Effect." *National Tax Journal* 52: 31–51.

Benoit, P. J. 1988. "A Case for Triangulation in Argument Research." *Journal of the American Forensic Association* 25: 31–42.

Benoit, P. J. 1997. *Telling the Success Story: Acclaiming and Disclaiming Discourse.* Albany: State University of New York Press.

Benoit, P. J., and W. L. Benoit. Under review. "Political Campaigning on the Internet: 2000 Presidential Candidate Sites." *Southern Communication Journal.*

Benoit, W. L., J. P. McHale, G. J. Hansen, P. M. Pier, and J. P. McGuire. 2003. *Campaign 2000: A Functional Analysis of Presidential Campaign Discourse.* Lanham, Md.: Rowman & Littlefield.

Berry, J. M. 1993. "Citizen Groups and the Changing Nature of Interest Group Politics in America." *Annals of the American Academy of Political and Social Science* 528: 30–41.

Blumrosen, A. W. 1993. *Modern Law.* Madison: University of Wisconsin Press.

Bowers, J. W., D. J. Ochs, and R. J. Jensen. 1993. *The Rhetoric of Agitation and Control* (2nd ed.). Prospect Heights, Ill.: Waveland Press.

Branscum, D. 1998. "Productivity: Voice Mail vs. Answering Machine." *New York Times* (April 30), available at http://nytimes.qpass.com/qpass-archives/fastWeb?QProd = 19& QIID = 1998arcDOC38 266&NYTID = johnmchale3&Srch = state_id = 1 + view = ! view! + docid = !doc!; pldocdb = 1998arc + dbname = !db! + TemplateName = doc.tmpl (accessed Nov. 10, 2001).

Burgoon, M. 1971. "Amount of Conflicting Information in a Group Discussion and Tolerance for Ambiguity as Predictors of Task Attractiveness." *Speech Monographs* 38: 121–24.

Burstein, P. 1999. "Social Movements and Public Policy." Pp. 3–21 in *How Social Movements Matter*, edited by M. Giugni, D. McAdam, and C. Tilly. Minneapolis: University of Minnesota Press.

Cable News Network. 2000. "Bush Resumes Campaign after Emotional Texas Execution." 2000 (June 23). Available at http://www.cnn.com/2000/ALLPOLITICS/stories/06/23/bush.execution/index.html (accessed July 7, 2000).

Charmaz, K. 1983. "The Grounded Theory Method: An Explication and Interpretation." Pp. 109–26 in *Contemporary Field Research*, edited by R. M. Emerson. Boston: Little, Brown.

Chidi, G. A. 2001. "GAO Cell Phone Safety Report: It's Your Call." *IDG News Service*. Available at idg.net.GAOCellPhoneSafetyReportsIts (accessed November 20, 2001).

Chong, D. 1993. "Coordinating Demands for Social Change." *Annals of the Academy of Political and Social Science* 528: 126–41.

Clark, R. C. 1977. "The Morphogenesis of Subchapter C: An Essay in Statutory Evolution and Reform." *American Journal of Sociology* 9: 755–98.

Costain, A. N., and S. Majstorovic. 1994. "Congress, Social Movements and Public Opinion: Multiple Origins of Women's Rights Legislation." *Political Research Quarterly* 47: 111–39.

Daft, R. L., and R. H. Lengel. 1986. "Organizational Information Requirements, Media Richness, and Structural Design." *Management Science* 32: 554–71.

Daft, R. L., R. H. Lengel, and L. K Trevino. 1987. "Message Equivocality, Media Selection, and Manager Performance: Implications for Informational Systems." *MIS Quarterly* 11: 353–64.

Dalton, R. J. 1993. "Citizens, Protest, and Democracy." *Annals of the American Academy of Political and Social Science* 528: 8–17.

"Death Penalty to Follow Bush." 2000. *New York Times on the Web* (June 22). Available at http://www.nytimes.com/aponline/p/AP-Bush-Death-Penalty.html (accessed September 3, 2000).

DeStephen, R. S. 1988. "Group Interaction Differences between High and Low Consensus Groups." *Western Journal of Speech Communication* 47: 340–63.

Duka, A. 1997. "Transformation of the Local Power Elites: Institutionalization of Social Movements in St. Petersburg." *International Journal of Urban and Regional Research* 21: 430–44.

Fairhurst, G. T. 1993. "The Leader-Member Exchange Patterns of Women Leaders in Industry: A Discourse Analysis." *Communication Monographs* 60: 321–51.

Feldman, M. S., and J. G. March. 1981. "Information in Organizations as Signal and Symbol." *Administrative Science Quarterly* 26: 171–86.

Ferree, M. M. 1992. "The Political Context of Rationality: Rational Choice Theory and Resource Mobilization." Pp. 29–52 in *Frontiers in Social Movement Theory*, edited by A. D. Morris and C. M. Mueller. New Haven, Conn.: Yale University Press.

Flanagan, A. J., and M. J. Metzger. 2001. "Internet Use in the Contemporary Media Environment." *Human Communication Research* 27: 153–81.

Gamson, W. A. 1990. *The Strategy of Social Protest*. Belmont, Calif.: Wadsworth.

Gamson, W. A. 1992. "The Social Psychology of Collective Action." Pp. 53–76 in *Frontiers in Social Movement Theory*, edited by A. D. Morris and C. M. Mueller. New Haven, Conn.: Yale University Press.

Garcelon, M. 1997. "The Estate of Change: The Specialist Rebellion and the Democratic Movement in Moscow, 1989–1991." *Theory and Society* 26: 39–85.

Glaser, B. G., and A. L. Strauss. 1967. *The Discovery of Grounded Theory: Strategies for Qualitative Research.* Chicago: Aldine/Atherton.

Goffman, E. 1974. *Frame Analysis: An Essay on the Organization of Experience.* Boston: Northeastern University Press.

Goldfield, M. 1989. "Worker Insurgency, Radical Organization, and New Deal Labor Legislation." *American Political Science Review* 83: 1257–82.

Gouran, D. S. 1999. "Communication in Groups: The Emergence and Evolution of a Field of Study." Pp. 3–36 in *The Handbook of Group Communication Theory and Research*, edited by L. R. Frey. Thousand Oaks, Calif.: Sage.

Griffin, L. M. 1980. "On Studying Movements." *Central States Speech Journal* 31: 36–39.

Habermas, J. 1973. *Legitimation Crisis.* Boston: Beacon.

Hager, C. 1993. "Citizen Movements and Technological Policymaking in Germany." *Annals of the American Academy of Political and Social Science* 528: 42–55.

Hart, R. D., and D. E. Williams. 1995. "Able-Bodied Instructors and Students with Physical Disabilities: A Relationship Handicapped by Communication." *Communication Education* 44: 140–54.

Hershey, M. R. 1993. "Citizens' Groups and Political Parties in the United States." *Annals of the American Academy of Political and Social Sciences* 528: 142–56.

Hill, T. A. 1976. "An Experimental Study of the Relationship between Opinionated Leadership and Small Group Consensus." *Communication Monographs* 43: 246–57.

Hopper, R. 1992. *Telephone Conversation.* Bloomington: Indiana University Press.

Kirchofer, T. 2001. "Telecom: Cash of Titans?" *Boston Herald* (May 14). Available at www .msnbc.com/local/rtma/m45166.asp (accessed Nov. 2001).

Kitschelt, H. 1993. "Social Movements, Political Parties, and Democratic Theory." *Annals of the Academy of Political and Social Science* 528: 13–29.

Klandermans, B. 1997. *The Social Psychology of Protest.* Cambridge, Mass.: Blackwell.

Klatch, R. 1988. "Coalition and Conflict among Women of the New Right." *Signs: Journal of Women and Culture in Society* 13: 671–94.

Kline, J. A., and J. L. Hullinger. 1973. "Special Report: Redundancy, Self-Orientation, and Group Consensus." *Speech Monographs* 40: 72–74.

Knapp, M. L., and A. L. Vangelisti. 2000. *Interpersonal Communication and Human Relationships.* Boston: Allyn & Bacon.

Knutson, T. J. 1972. "An Experimental Study of the Effects of Orientation Behavior on Small Group Consensus." *Speech Monographs* 39: 159–65.

Knutson, T. J., and W. E. Holdridge. 1975. "Orientation Behavior, Leadership and Consensus: A Possible Functional Relationship." *Speech Monographs* 42: 107–14.

Kriesi, H., and D. Wisler. 1999. "The Impact of Social Movements on Political Institutions: A Comparison of the Introduction of Direct Legislation in Switzerland and the United States." Pp. 42–65 in *How Social Movements Matter*, edited by M. Giugni, D. McAdam, and C. Tilly. Minneapolis: University of Minnesota Press.

Lammers, J. C., and D. H. Krikorian. 1997. "Theoretical Extension and Operationalization of the Bona Fide Group Construct with an Application to Surgical Teams." *Journal of Applied Communication Research* 25: 17–38.

Lange, J. I. 1993. "The Logic of Competing Information Campaigns: Conflict Over Old Growth and the Spotted Owl." *Communication Monographs* 60: 239–57.

Leininger, M. 1994. "Evaluation Criteria and Critique of Qualitative Research Studies." Pp. 95–116 in *Critical Issues in Qualitative Research Methods*, edited by J. M. Morse. Thousand Oaks, Calif.: Sage.

Lindlof, T. R. 1995. *Qualitative Communication Research Methods*. Thousand Oaks, Calif.: Sage.

Lo, C. Y. H. 1990. *Small Property verses Big Government*. Berkeley: University of California Press.

Lofland, J., and L. Lofland. 1995. *Analyzing Social Settings: A Guide to Qualitative Observation and Analysis*. Belmont, Calif.: Wadsworth.

Marr, T. J. 1974. "Conciliation and Verbal Responses as Functions of Orientation and Threat in Group Interaction." *Speech Monographs* 41: 6–18.

McLuhan, M. 1964. *Understanding Media: The Extensions of Man*. New York: McGraw-Hill.

Morris, A. D., and C. M. Mueller. 1992. *Frontiers in Social Movement Theory*. New Haven, Conn..: Yale University Press.

Morris, G. H., and R. Hopper. 1980. "Remediation and Legislation in Everyday Talk: How Communicators Achieve Consensus." *Quarterly Journal of Speech* 66: 266–74.

Nathanson, C.A. 1999. "Social Movements as Catalysts for Policy Change: The Case of Smoking and Guns." *Journal of Health Politics, Policy and Law* 24: 421–88.

NBC News/ *Wall Street Journal*. 2000. (September 7–10). Obtained online via LexisNexis.

Neuliep, J. W. 1991. "An Examination of the Content of High School Teachers' Humor in the Classroom and the Development of an Inductively Derived Taxonomy of Classroom Humor." *Communication Education* 40: 343–55.

Noelle-Neumann, E. 1999. "The Effects of the Mass Media on Opinion Formulation." Pp. 51–76 in *Mass Media, Social Control, and Social Change: A Macrosocial Perspective*, edited by David Demers and K. Viswanath. Ames: Iowa State University Press.

Olson, M. 1971. *The Logic of Collective Action: Public Goods and the Theory of Groups*. Cambridge: Harvard University Press.

Pirsig, R. M. 1974. *Zen and the Art of Motorcycle Maintenance*. New York: Bantam.

Prejean, Helen. 1993. *Dead Man Walking*. New York: Random House.

Putnam, L. 1994. "Revitalizing Small Group Communication: Lessons Learned from a Bona Fide Perspective." *Communication Studies* 45: 97–102.

Putnam, L., and C. Stohl. 1990. "Bona Fide Groups: A Reconceptualization of Groups in Context." *Communication Studies* 41: 97–102.

Rice, R. E. 1987. "Computer Mediated Communication and Organizational Innovation." *Journal of Communication* 37 (4): 65–94.

Rice, R. E., and D. E. Shook. 1990. "Relationships of Job Categories and Organizational Levels to Use of Communication Channels, Including Electronic Mail: A Meta-Analysis and Extension." *Journal on Management Studies* 27: 195–229.

Rochon, T. R., and D. A. Mazmanian. 1993. "Social Movements and the Policy Process." *Annals of the American Academy of Political and Social Science* 528: 75–87.

Rohrschneider, R. 1993. "Impact of Social Movements on European Party Systems." *Annals of the American Academy of Political and Social Sciences* 528: 157–70.

Sabourin, T. C., and G. H. Stamp. 1995. "Communication and the Experience of Dialectical Tensions in Family Life: An Examination of Abusive and Non-Abusive Families." *Communication Monographs* 62: 213–42.

Scenic Digital. 1999. "Vista Voice and Data." Available at http//www.scenic-digital.com (accessed November 15, 2001).

Selnow, G. W. 1998. *Electronic Whistle-Stops: The Impact of the Internet on American Politics.* Westport, Conn.: Greenwood Publishing Group.

Shiloh, E. 2003. "U. Missouri Students Seek a State Moratorium on Death Penalty." February 21. Available at www.pbs.org/weta/was . . . onweek/voices/200302/0221moratori um.html (accessed May 5, 2003).

Sitkin, S. B., K. M. Sutcliffe, and J. R. Barrios-Choplin. 1992. "A Dual-Capacity Model of Communication Media Choice in Organizations." *Human Communication Research* 18: 563–98.

Skocpol, T., and K. Finegold. 1990. "Explaining New Deal Labor Policy." *American Political Science Review* 84: 1297–315.

Spillman, B., J. Bezdek, and R. Spillman. 1979. "Development of an Instrument for the Dynamic Measurement of Consensus." *Communication Monographs* 46: 1–12.

Sproull, L. S., and S. Kiesler. 1986. "Reducing Social Context Cues: The Case of Electronic Mail." *Management Quarterly* 32: 1492–512.

Stamp, G. H. 1994. "The Appropriation of the Parental Role through Communication During the Transition to Parenthood." *Communication Monographs* 61: 89–112.

Stewart, C. J. 1980. "A Functional Approach to the Rhetoric of Social Movements." *Central States Speech Journal* 31: 298–305.

Stewart, C. J., C. A. Smith, and R. E. Denton. 1984. *Persuasion and Social Movements.* Prospect Heights, Ill.: Waveland Press.

Stohl, C., and M. Holmes. 1992. "A Functional Perspective for Bona Fide Groups." Pp. 601–14 in *Communication Yearbook* 16, edited by S. A. Deetz. Newbury Park, Calif.: Sage.

Strauss, A., and J. Corbin. 1998. *Basics of Qualitative Research: Techniques and Procedures for Developing Grounded Theory.* 2nd ed. Thousand Oaks, Calif.: Sage.

Swartz, J. 2001. "New Economy: A Library of Web Pages that Warms the Cockles of the Wired Heart and Beats the Library of Congress for Sheer Volume." *New York Times* (29 October). Available at http://nytimes.qpass.com (accessed Dec. 12, 2001).

Tracy, K., and S. Baratz. 1993. "Intellectual Discussion in the Academy as Situated Discourse." *Communication Monographs* 60: 300–20.

U.S. Census Bureau. 2000. "Statistical Abstract of the U.S." Available at http://www .census.gov/prod/2001pubs/statab/sec18.pdf (accessed May 7, 2001).

Waters, S. 1998. "New Social Movement Politics in France: The Rise of Civic Form of Mobilization." *West European Politics* 21: 170–86.

Webster's New Universal Unabridged Dictionary. 1983. Dorset & Barber.

Zemans, F. K. 1983. "Legal Mobilization: The Neglected Role of the Law in the Political System." *American Political Science Review* 77: 690–703.

Index

Abu-Jamal, Mumia, 51, 61, 66, 68, 76, 89, 96, 103, 111, 115, 119, 142, 181
activists: advice to, 2; civil action, 84–86; communication, importance of, 10, 233; death penalty. *See* death penalty activism; definition, 3; environmental. *See* environmental activism; health care. *See* health care activism; knowledge, 129–31, 161–65, 198; legitimization. *See* legitimizing advocacy efforts; power, 33, 50–52, 73–74, 101–3, 127–28, 157–58, 192–93
Alinsky, S., 10
Amnesty International, 58, 60, 88, 100, 102, 105, 112, 116, 157, 177, 180, 191, 202
Amrine, Joe, x, 1, 143, 147, 156, 162, 230. *See also* unreasonable doubt
Anderson, J. A., 11
anti–death penalty. *See* death penalty activism
arranging logistical detail, 21–22, 34, 35, 40–41, 61–65, 95, 103–4, 129, 160–61, 181, 198–203, 211–12, 222–23
attendance. *See* increasing attendance at events
audiences. *See* intended audience

Benoit, P. J., 175, 235–36
Benoit, W. L., 15, 175

bona fide group perspective, ix, 166–67, 211, 213, 229
building community, 22, 23, 41–42, 65–67, 96–99, 121, 181–82, 212–13, 225

candles, 93, 207
Catholic church, 60, 102
cellular telephone. *See* telephone
characteristics of media uses. *See* media
community. *See* building community
computers, 175–76; arranging logistical detail, 181; building community, 181–82; characteristics of, 186–92; corporate use of, 203; distance, 190–91; educating, 182–84; e-mail, 176–77, 179–203; external factors, 199–202; facilitating mass media coverage, 184–85; faxes, 178, 196; feedback, 186–87; financial resources, 193–98; forms of, 176–78; functions of, 180–85; general technological trends, 201–2; increasing attendance at events, 180–81; influences on, 186–202; intended audience, 178–80; internal group factors, 192–99; knowledge, 198; language variety, 187–88; legitimizing advocate positions, 185; listservs, 197–98; lobbying, 182; logistical resources, 198–203; mul-

About the Author

John P. McHale received a B.S. in political science and an M.S. in communication from Southern Illinois University, Carbondale (1989 and 1990 respectively); a B.A. in history from Columbia College, Columbia, Missouri (1997); an M.A. in political science from University of Missouri, Columbia (2000); and a Ph.D. in communication from the University of Missouri, Columbia (2002). He is an assistant professor in the communication department at Illinois State University in Normal.